THE ROYAL DESCENTS OF

JUDITH IVYE
WIFE OF ANTHONY PRATER

By Thomas Benjamin Hertzel

CLEARFIELD

Printed for Clearfield Company by
Genealogical Publishing Company
Baltimore, Maryland
2015

ISBN 978-0-8063-5726-3

Made in the United States of America

Cover: poem and carvings memorializing Judith Ivye, depicting her husband, Anthony Prater, their six children, and the Prater coat of arms, placed above Judith's tomb in the Church of St. Mary the Virgin, West Kington, Wiltshire, England.

THIS BOOK IS GRATEFULLY DEDICATED TO

MY MOTHER

PATRICIA R. HERTZEL

who inspired its writing, assisted with editing and
proofing, faithfully supported its completion, and
is my personal gateway ancestor to Judith Ivye,
the Middle Ages, and beyond.

*Ivye coat of arms
as recorded in Burke's General Armory*

Arms: Gules, a lion rampant, or (gold).

Crest: A demi-lion, or (gold) supporting a staff raguly, vert (green).

Motto: "Esse quam videri" (To be rather than to appear).

Preface

Considering the enormous amount of information available on the descendants of Judith Ivye, there is remarkably little data regarding her ancestry. This book seeks to rectify that disparity and show that Judith was of noble descent, with ancestors from many of the royal dynasties of England and Europe, as well as several important historical families and individuals.

What we know of Judith herself is limited to very general information. She was born in 1550, and died on February 6, 1578. She was the daughter of Thomas Ivye and his second wife, Elizabeth Malet. She had four full siblings, Richard, Hugh, Mary, and Fortune, as well as five half-siblings from her father's first marriage to Elizabeth de Keynes: Ferdinando, Leonard, George, Margaret, and Prudence.

In 1566, Judith married Anthony Prater, the second son of George Prater and Jane Plott. Judith and Anthony had six children, Thomas, William, Elizabeth, Ferdinando, George, and Thomas, before Judith died after giving birth to her seventh child. Seven years later, Anthony Prater married Judith's sister-in-law, Elizabeth Winter, the widow of Judith's brother Ferdinando. There was no issue from this second marriage.

The family of Judith's father, Thomas Ivye, has been traced back only two more generations. Thomas was the son of Richard Ivye, born ca. 1450 in Sodbury, Gloucestershire, England, and his wife Isabel, the daughter of Michael Canning. Richard Ivye was the son of Thomas Ivye and his wife Elizabeth, the daughter of John Vyell. Beyond this, the Ivye ancestry remains undiscovered.

Judith's mother, however, is a different story. Elizabeth Malet was a member of the prominent Malet family; it is through both her father, Hugh Malet, and her mother, Isabel Michell, that Elizabeth (and therefore her daughter Judith Ivye) descends from many of the noble houses of medieval Europe.

When Judith died in 1578, she was buried in the Ivye section of the church of St. Mary the Virgin in West Kington, Wiltshire. Her husband Anthony Prater wrote a poem for her, had it inscribed in stone, and placed it over her tomb. The inscription no longer is visible, due to new flooring that obscures the tomb. However, sometime in the mid to late 1650s, John Aubrey, an English antiquary, natural philosopher, and writer, visited West Kington, and transcribed the poem for inclusion in his county history book, <u>Aubrey's Collections for Wiltshire</u> (not published until 1821). His transcription of the poem is as follows:

Rest in the lord most loving wife,
Thy daies are spent and gonne,
Thy husband's race and end of life
Shall be God knoweth how soon.
Though death hath doon the worst he can
To part us twayn a space,
Yet time will come to meet again
In heaven that joyfull place.
With bitter teares thy husband spake
These words upon thy tombe,
His hand did write, thes vers did make,
To show in tyme to cum
How faithfull thou hast been to me,
And haddest six children dear,
Within six yeare a marvell to see
All borne one time of yeare;
The seventh also in like manner,
If death had not them lett,
Borne had been as the other wear,
At Midsummer time direct.
Alas how should it chance so bad
To littil babes so young,
To tell in time what losse they had
Bi nature whence they sproung
But God is he who giveth life,
And he that takes away,
Let us therefore avoyd all strife
And geve ourselves to pray.
Thy children's names if men would know,
Which God hath given to thee,
Behold are written here below
In order as they be.
Thomas, William, Elizabeth, Ferdinando, George, Thomas

Anthony Prater also had a memorial plaque engraved with the Prater coat of arms and relief carvings of himself and his six surviving children placed in the wall above Judith's tomb. This plaque is still visible, and includes the following eulogy, also written by Anthony:

> Oh mi dear chilldren marke what I saye,
> Your mothers bonns truli are wrapt her inn clay
> Her soule no doubte to heaven is gone thither
> Wher we most joyfulli shall meet alltogether
> The lord be your guid, the lord be your strength
> And give you his speciall grac to die in him at length
> You gentell readers remember your end
> Be tru unto such whom faythful you find
> Lett this be example and tell hit abroode
> How faithfulli this woman died in the Lorde

Above these verses is written, "Here lieth Judeth Prator, the wife of Anthony Prator, Gentilman, daughter unto Thomas Ivie, Esqr., Who dieth the sixth day of February, Anno Domini 1578".

The church of St. Mary the Virgin in West Kington, Wiltshire.

Rear view of the church of St. Mary the Virgin in West Kington, Wiltshire.

Although she lived only to her 28th year, Judith Ivye has tens of thousands of descendants in the United States today. Her youngest son, Thomas Prater, married Margaret, the daughter of Henry and Alice Quintyne, and they had three children, Alice, Thomas, and Richard. Thomas, the son of Thomas, being from a cadet branch of the Prater family, had little hope of any substantial inheritance, so he emigrated to America in 1622, settling in Elizabeth Cittie (now Newport News), Virginia. It is this younger Thomas who is the ancestor of most of the Prater/Prather descendants of Judith Ivye living in the U.S. today.

Thomas Benjamin Hertzel
2015

Judith Ivye's American Descendants

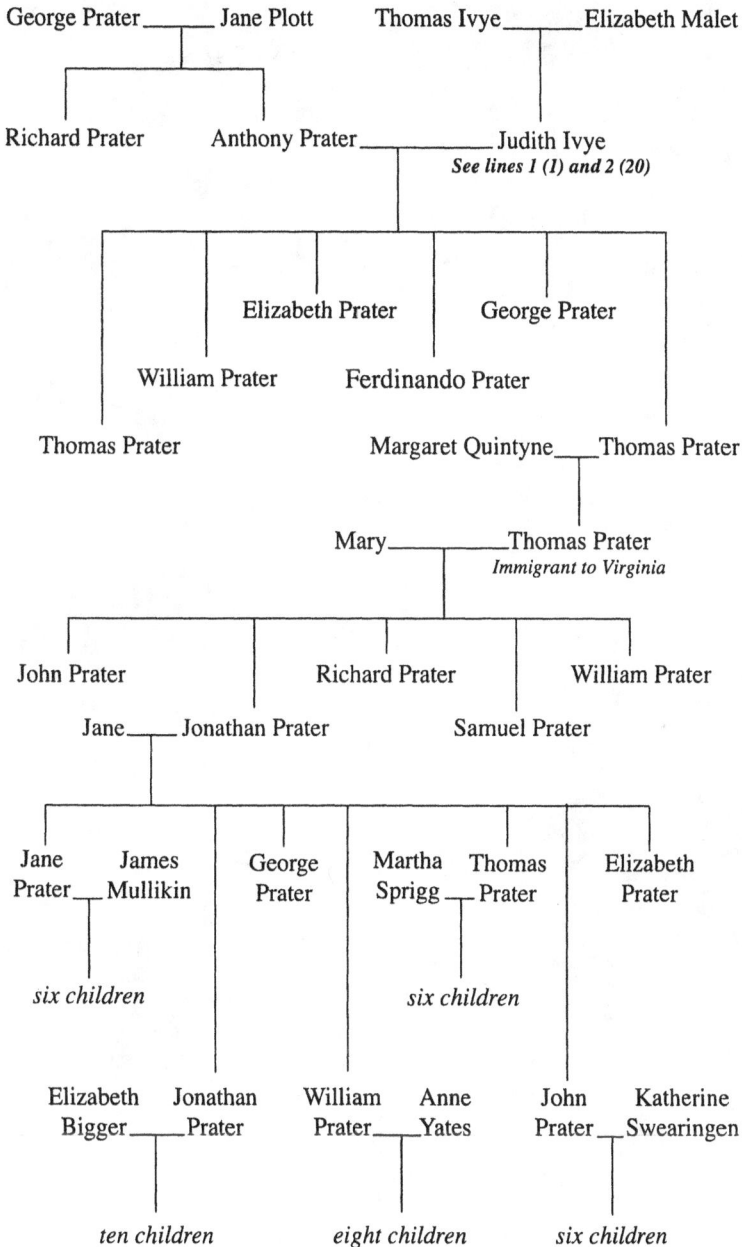

George Prater———Jane Plott   Thomas Ivye———Elizabeth Malet

Richard Prater   Anthony Prater———————Judith Ivye
See lines 1 (1) and 2 (20)

Elizabeth Prater   George Prater

William Prater   Ferdinando Prater

Thomas Prater   Margaret Quintyne———Thomas Prater

Mary————Thomas Prater
Immigrant to Virginia

John Prater   Richard Prater   William Prater

Jane———Jonathan Prater   Samuel Prater

Jane Prater———James Mullikin   George Prater   Martha Sprigg———Thomas Prater   Elizabeth Prater

six children   *six children*

Elizabeth Bigger———Jonathan Prater   William Prater———Anne Yates   John Prater———Katherine Swearingen

ten children   *eight children*   *six children*

Introduction

This book, a compilation of the ancestors of Judith Ivye, represents research to prove her descent from royal and noble families of both England and Europe. Its genealogical structure is generationally organized; every generation is in descending order, each as a separate and distinct paragraph. These paragraphical listings include the ancestor, his or her spouse, the spouse's parents (if known), and the sources from which this information was derived. The lines of descent begin with a specific, well-known ancestor, followed by successive generations down to Judith Ivye. For instance, line 2 begins with William the Conqueror. As the first in the series, he is assigned the position of line 2 (1). His son Henry, as the next generation, becomes line 2 (2). Henry's son Reginald is line 2 (3) and so on until the generations end with Judith herself, at line 2 (20).

To illustrate this, an abreviated example of the generational numbering system is provided below:

LINE 2

1. William the Conqueror, King of England [father of:]
2. Henry I, King of England [father of:]
3. Reginald FitzRoy, Earl of Cornwall [father of:]
4. Maud of Cornwall [mother of:]
5. Maud (Mabel) de Beaumont [mother of:]
6. Mary Vernon [mother of:]
7. Egeline de Courtenay [mother of:]
8. John de Columbiers [father of:]
9. Joan de Columbiers [mother of:]
10. Geoffrey Stawell [father of:]
11. Matthew Stawell [father of:]
12. Margery Stawell [mother of:]
13. Amice Lyffe [mother of:]
14. Hugh Malet [father of:]
15. John Malet [father of:]
16. Thomas Malet [father of:]
17. William Malet [father of:]
18. Hugh Malet [father of:]
19. Elizabeth Malet [mother of:]
20. Judith Ivye

Judith Ivye was descended from William the Conqueror through more than one line. To illustrate this without repeating the entire series, this next descent becomes line 3, picking up at the point where this second descent separates from line 2, in this case, through a second daughter of Reginald FitzRoy, Joan. As Reginald is assigned line 2 (3), line 3 begins at that point and continues with Joan, assigned line 3 (4) in the same generational sequence:

LINE 3 continued from Line 2 (3)

4. Joan of Cornwall [mother of:]
5. Joel Valletort [father of:]
6. Philip Valletort [father of:]
7. John Valletort [father of:]
8. Hugh Valletort [father of:]
9. Juliana Valletort [mother of:]
10. Richard Lyffe [father of:]
11. Amice Lyffe......*See line 2 (13)*

As shown previously, line 2 (13) is also Amice Lyffe. line 3 (11) then merges with line 2 (13) at this point. Going back to line 2 (13), the reader then can continue down from Amice Lyffe through the generations until reaching Judith Ivye. Each and every line of descent will begin either with a prominent historic figure, or a lateral break from a previous generational line. Each line also will end with a redirection to an individual who is listed elsewhere, and then the descent continues from there on to Judith Ivye.

There are 155 separate and distinct lines of descent, including several that tie some of Judith Ivye's Prater/Prather descendants to other historical figures from which Judith herself does not descend.

When an ancestor in any given line of descent marries someone who is also researched and proven to be descended from royalty as well, that spouse's name will be followed by the two numbers that correspond to the line and generation in the book where his or her own lineage is traced. This is done for ease of cross-referencing, as Judith's ancestors often descend from royalty on both the husband's and the wife's side of a family. For instance in the case of Edward "the Elder" (line 8, generation 3), Edward married Æflaeda, the daughter of Æthelhelm,

Ealdorman of Wiltshire. As Æflaeda's family was also of royal lineage, her descent is referenced after her name (line 4, generation 4) as follows:

3. Edward "the Elder", King of England, born ca. 875, died July 17, 924. He married (first) Æflaeda (4–4), died 919. She was the daughter of Æthelhelm, Ealdorman of Wiltshire.

As indicated, Æflaeda's descent can be found at line 4, generation 4, as follows:

4. Ælflaeda, died 919. She married Edward "the Elder" (8–3), King of England, born ca. 875, died July 17, 924. He was the son of Alfred "the Great", King of England, and Æthelswida.

The index uses the same generational system as the rest of the book. Rather than point the reader to a particular page number, the index instead refers the reader to a specific line number, followed by a corresponding generation number. Ancestors of Judith Ivye may occur more than once throughout the book, and so are listed as many times as they occur. Index numbers in **bold** reference individuals who are traced directly to Judith Ivye. Numbers that are not bolded refer to spouses, parents, or in-laws of a person being traced.

References are cited within each line of descent to allow the reader quick access to the sources used for that line. This includes the author, title of the work documented, volume numbers (if any), and relevant page or table numbers. The organizational system employed by each respective author is repeated in this book to simplify cross-referencing. For instance, The Complete Peerage, by George Cokayne is organized alphabetically by title (Cornwall, Devon, Norfolk, etc.), so references to these volumes include a specific title after each volume number, as in *"Cokayne, The Complete Peerage, Volume III (Cornwall), page 429"*. On the other hand, Europäische Stammtafeln uses genealogical tables in each of its volumes. References to these include a table number, rather than a page number: *"Schwennicke, Europäische Stammtafeln, Volume III, table 621"*. Here, the number 621 refers to a specific genealogical table, rather than a page number. It should be noted here that Europäische Stammtafeln has volumes I/1 and I/2, as well as III/1, III/2, and III/3 in addition to the standard Roman numeral volumes.

Contents

Preface i

Introduction vii

Judith Ivye 1

England: The Normans 3

England: The Saxons 9

Wales 17

Ireland 25

France 29

Italy 67

Germania 87

Scandinavia 91

Luxembourg 107

Russia 111

Byzantium 113

Other Historic Figures 115

Descents to Later Prater / Prather Lines 127

Further Research 167

Bibliography 178

Index 186

Judith Ivye

1. **Judith Ivye**, born 1550, died February 6, 1578. She married Anthony Prater, born 1545, died August of 1593. He was the son of George Prater, and Jane Plott. *Brown, Abstracts of Somersetshire Wills, page 47; Prather, Praters in Wiltshire, page 22 (Prather references Wiltshire, the Topographical Collections of John Auberry, F.R.S., A.D. 1659–70, page 89; and Historical Southern Families, Volume 6, by John Bennet Boddie, pages 21–23)*

2. **Thomas Prater**, died 1628. He married Margaret Quintyne. She was the daughter of Henry Quintyne and Alice. *Prather, Praters in Wiltshire, pages 43–44*

3. **Thomas Prater**, born December 26, 1604, died ca. 1666. He married Mary. She may have been the daughter of John Powell. Thomas Prater emigrated to Virginia in 1622 aboard the Marie Providence. His passage was paid by John Powell. Preserved in the State Papers, Department of Her Majesty's Public Record Office, is the Muster Roll of Settlers of Virginia. In these papers concerning Elizabeth Cittie, Virginia, the following is written: "Thomas Prater, servant, age 20, arrived on the Marie Providence in 1622". *Prather, Praters in Wiltshire, page 51.*

Thomas Prater and his wife had the following five children:

4a. **John Prater**, born ca. 1629, died ca. 1640

4b. **Jonathan Prater**, born 1631, died August 21, 1680. He married Jane (possibly MacKay). She may have been the daughter of Robert MacKay. They had seven children: Jane (married James Mullikin), Jonathan (married Elizabeth Bigger), George, William (married Anne Yates), Thomas MacKay (married Martha Sprigg), John (married Katherine Swearingen), and Elizabeth.

4c. **Richard Prater**, born ca. 1632

4d. **Samuel Prater**, born ca. 1633, died ca. 1678

4e. **William Prater**, born ca. 1635

William the Conqueror, Duke of Normandy, King of England
scene from the Bayeux Tapestry

England, The Normans

1. **William the Conqueror, Duke of Normandy, King of England**, born October 14, 1025, died September 9, 1087. He was the son of Robert I, Duke of Normandy, and Herleve. He married Mathilda of Flanders (5–9 and 49–6), born 1031, died November 2, 1083. She was the daughter of Baldwin V, Count of Flanders, and Adele of France, Countess of Contentin. *Moriarty, The Plantagenet Ancestry of King Edward III, pages 13 and 15; Schwennicke, Europäische Stammtafeln, Volume II, tables 79 and 81; Burke, Burke's Peerage (The Royal Lineage), page 28; Douglas, William the Conqueror, page 15, and tables 1, 2, 5, and 6*

2. **Henry I, King of England**, born September, 1068, died December 1, 1135. His mistress was Sybilla Corbet. She was the daughter of Robert Corbet. *Cokayne, The Complete Peerage, Volumes III (Cornwall), page 429, and XI (Appendix D), pages 107–108; Burke, Burke's Peerage (The Royal Lineage), page 28*

3. **Reginald FitzRoy, Earl of Cornwall**, born 1110, died July 1, 1175. He married Maud of Mortain (120–4), died 1162. She was the daughter of William, Count of Mortain, Earl of Cornwall. *Cokayne, The Complete Peerage, Volumes III (Cornwall), page 429, VII (Leicester), page 520, and (Appendix I), page 740, XI (Appendix D), pages 107–108, and XII/2 (Worcester), pages 837–838; Weis, Ancestral Roots of Certain American Colonists, 121 (26) [Note: in both "Cornwall" and "Worcester", Cokayne refers to Maud as Beatrice, while Weis calls her Maud]*

4. **Maud of Cornwall**. She married Robert de Beaumont (38–10 and 107–18), Count of Meulan, died 1207. He was the son of Waleran de Beaumont, Earl of Worcester, and Agnes de Montfort. *Cokayne, The Complete Peerage, Volumes IV (Devon), pages 315–316, VII (Leicester), page 520, and (Appendix I), page 740, and XII/2 (Worcester), pages 837–838; Weis, Ancestral Roots of Certain American Colonists, 50 (26)*

5. **Maud (Mabel) de Beaumont**, died 1204. She married William Vernon, Earl of Devon, born 1155, died September 14, 1217. He was the son of Baldwin de Redvers, Earl of Devon, and Adelise. *Cokayne, The Complete Peerage, Volumes IV (Devon), pages 315–316, and VII (Leicester), page 520, and (Appendix I) (i), page 740*

6. **Mary Vernon**. She married Robert de Courtenay (48–11), Baron Oakhampton, born 1183, died July 27, 1242. He was the son of Renaud de Courtenay and Hawise de Courcy. *Cokayne, The Complete Peerage, Volumes III (Courtenay), page 465, and IV (Devon), pages 317 and 323, and (Appendix H), chart VI; Schwennicke, Europäische Stammtafeln, Volume III, table 629*

7. **Egeline de Courtenay**, born ca. 1210, died ca. 1292. She married Philip de Columbiers, born ca. 1205, died 1262. He was the son of Philip de Columbiers. *Cokayne, The Complete Peerage, Volume III (Columbiers), page 377; Schwennicke, Europäische Stammtafeln, Volume III, table 629; Sanders, English Baronies, page 67*

8. **John de Columbiers**, born 1254, died 1306. He married Alice Penesherst. She was the daughter of Stephen Penesherst and Rohese de Baseville. *Cokayne, The Complete Peerage, Volume III (Columbiers), page 378; Sanders, English Baronies, page 67*

9. **Joan de Columbiers**, born 1275. She married Geoffrey Stawell, died ca. 1325. He was the son of Matthew Stawell. *Cokayne, The Complete Peerage, Volume III (Columbiers), page 379; Brydges, Collins's Peerage of England, pages 269–271; Stawell, A Quantock Family, pages 29–30*

10. **Geoffrey Stawell**, died December 13, 1361. He married Juliana Gastelin. She was the daughter of Walter Gastelin. *Brydges, Collins's Peerage of England, page 271; Stawell, A Quantock Family, pages 30–35*

11. **Matthew Stawell**, born ca. 1340, died 1379. He married Eleanor Merton, died 1357. She was the daughter of Sir Richard Merton and Margaret. *Weaver, The Visitation of Somerset, page 79; Brydges, Collins's Peerage of England, page 271; Stawell, A Quantock Family, pages 35–38 (Note: The Visitations give the husband of Eleanor Merton as Thomas Stawell.)*

12. **Margery Stawell**. She married Richard Lyffe (3–10). He was the son of Godfrey Lyffe and Juliana Valletort. *Weaver, The Visitation of Somerset, page 45; Stawell, A Quantock Family, page 37; Collinson, The History and Antiquities of the County of Somerset, Volume I (Charlinch), page 239*

13. **Amice Lyffe**. She married, as his second wife, Baldwin Malet (102–26), died 1416. He was the son of John Malet and Elizabeth Kingston. *Collinson, The History and Antiquities of the County of Somerset, Volume I (Enmore), page 91; Weaver, The Visitation of Somerset, page 45; Burke, Burke's Peerage (Malet), page 1512; Malet, Notices of an English Branch of the Malet Family, pages 35–36*

14. **Hugh Malet**, died ca. 1466. He married Joan Roynon. She was the daughter of John Roynon and Joan Longland. *Collinson, The History and Antiquities of the County of Somerset, Volume I (Enmore), page 91; Weaver, The Visitation of Somerset, page 45; Burke, Burke's Peerage (Malet), page 1512; Malet, Notices of an English Branch of the Malet Family, pages 38–40; Richardson, Plantagenet Ancestry, page 13*

15. **John Malet**. He married Alice Trivett. She was the daughter of Sir Thomas Trivett. *Weaver, The Visitation of Somerset, page 45 (Note: Collinson, Burke and Malet all omit this generation.)*

16. **Thomas Malet**, died July 9, 1502. He married Joan Wadham. She was the daughter of William Wadham and Margaret Chiselden. *Collinson, The History and Antiquities of the County of Somerset, Volume I (Enmore), page 91; Weaver, The Visitation of Somerset, pages 45–46; Burke, Burke's Peerage (Malet), page 1512; Jackson, Wadham College, pages 4–5; Malet, Notices of an English Branch of the Malet Family, pages 40–41*

17. **William Malet**, born ca. 1471, died September 11, 1511. He married Alice Young, died 1505. She was the daughter of Thomas Young and Alice. *Collinson, The History and Antiquities of the County of Somerset, Volume I (Enmore), page 91; Weaver, The Visitation of Somerset, pages 45–46; Burke, Burke's Peerage (Malet), page 1512; Malet, Notices of an English Branch of the Malet Family, pages 41–43*

18. **Hugh Malet**, died 1541. He married Isabel Michell (28–26). She was the daughter of Thomas Michell and Isabel (or Mary) FitzJames. *Collinson, The History and Antiquities of the County of Somerset, Volume I (Enmore), page 91; Weaver, The Visitation of Somerset, pages 45, 46, and 50; Burke, Burke's Peerage (Malet), page 1512; Malet, Notices of an English Branch of the Malet Family, pages 43–44*

19. **Elizabeth Malet**. She married Thomas Ivye. He was the son of Richard Ivye and Isabel Canning. *Collinson, The History and Antiquities of the County of Somerset, Volume I (Enmore), page 91; Weaver, The Visitation of Somerset, pages 45–46, and 50; Malet, Notices of an English Branch of the Malet Family, page 43; Prather, Praters in Wiltshire, page 22 (Prather references Wiltshire, the Topographical Collections of John Auberry, F.R.S., A.D. 1659–70, page 89; and Historical Southern Families, Volume 6, by John Bennet Boddie, pages 21–23)*

20. **Judith Ivye**, born 1550, died February 6, 1578. She married Anthony Prater, born 1545, died August 1593. He was the son of George Prater and Jane Plott. *Brown, Abstracts of Somersetshire Wills, page 47; Prather, Praters in Wiltshire, page 22 (Prather references Wiltshire, the Topographical Collections of John Auberry, F.R.S., A.D. 1659–70, page 89; and Historical Southern Families, Volume 6, by John Bennet Boddie, pages 21–23)* **See line 1 (1)**

LINE 3 continued from line 2 (3)

4. **Joan of Cornwall**. She married Roger (or possibly Ralph) Valletort. He was the son of Robert (or possibly Reginald) Valletort. *Benson, in Devon and Cornwall Notes and Queries, Volume XX, pages 247-254; Pole, Collections Towards a Description of the County of Devon, page 21*

5. **Joel Valletort**. He married Emma Botreaux. She was the daughter of William Botreaux. *Benson, in Devon and Cornwall Notes and Queries, Volume XX, pages 247-254; Pole, Collections Towards a Description of the County of Devon, pages 21 and 426; Collinson, The History and Antiquities of the County of Somerset, Volume I (Charlinch), page 239*

6. **Philip Valletort**, died before 1253. It is not known whom Philip married. *Benson, in Devon and Cornwall Notes and Queries, Volume XX, pages 247-254; Pole, Collections Towards a Description of the County of Devon, page 426; Collinson, The History and Antiquities of the County of Somerset, Volume I (Charlinch), page 239*

7. **John Valletort**. He married a daughter of Philip de Columbiers and Egeline de Courtenay. *Benson, in Devon and Cornwall Notes and Queries, Volume XX, pages 247-254; Weaver, The Visitation of Somerset, page 45; Pole, Collections Towards a Description of the County of Devon, page 426; Collinson, The History and Antiquities of the County of Somerset, Volume I (Charlinch), page 239*

8. **Hugh Valletort**, dead by 1310. He married Lucy le Bret. She was the daughter of Adam le Bret. *Benson, in Devon and Cornwall Notes and Queries, Volume XX, pages 247-254; Weaver, The Visitation of Somerset, page 45; Pole, Collections Towards a Description of the County of Devon, page 426; Collinson, The History and Antiquities of the County of Somerset, Volume I (Charlinch), page 239*

9. **Juliana Valletort**. She married Godfrey Lyffe. *Benson, in Devon and Cornwall Notes and Queries, Volume XX, pages 247-254; Weaver, The Visitation of Somerset, page 45; Pole, Collections Towards a Description of the County of Devon, page 426; Collinson, The History and Antiquities of the County of Somerset, Volume I (Charlinch), page 239 (Note: Pole identifies the daughter of Hugh Valletort as Lucia, and her husband as Geoffrey Lyffe.)*

10. **Richard Lyffe**. He married Margery Stawell (2–12). She was the daughter of Matthew Stawell and Eleanor Merton. *Weaver, The Visitation of Somerset, page 45; Stawell, A Quantock Family, page 37; Collinson, The History and Antiquities of the County of Somerset, Volume I (Charlinch), page 239*

11. **Amice Lyffe**. She married Baldwin Malet (102–26), died 1416. He was the son of John Malet and Elizabeth Kingston. *Collinson, The History and Antiquities of the County of Somerset, Volume I (Enmore), page 91, and (Charlinch) page 239; Weaver, The Visitation of Somerset, page 45; Malet, Notices of an English Branch of the Malet Family, page 35* **See line 2 (13)**

Æthelwulf, King of Wessex
from the Genealogical Chronicle of the English Kings

England, The Saxons

1. **Æthelwulf, King of Wessex**, died January 13, 858. He was the son of Egbert, King of Wessex, and Raedburga. He married (first), Osburgis, died after 876. She was the daughter of Oslac. *Moriarty, The Plantagenet Ancestry of King Edward III, page 252; Schwennicke, Europäische Stammtafeln, Volume II, table 78*

2. **Æthelred I, King of Wessex**, died 872. *Moriarty, The Plantagenet Ancestry of King Edward III, page 252; Schwennicke, Europäische Stammtafeln, Volume II, table 78*

3. **Æthelhelm, Ealdorman of Wiltshire.** *Moriarty, The Plantagenet Ancestry of King Edward III, page 252; Schwennicke, Europäische Stammtafeln, Volume II, table 78*

4. **Ælflaeda**, died 919. She married Edward "the Elder" (8–3), King of England, born ca. 875, died July 17, 924. He was the son of Alfred "the Great", King of England, and Æthelswida. *Moriarty, The Plantagenet Ancestry of King Edward III, page 252; Schwennicke, Europäische Stammtafeln, Volume II, table 78*

5. **Ædgifu of England**, born ca. 904, died 951. She married Charles III "the Simple" (25–5), King of the Franks, born September 17, 879, died October 27, 929. He was the son of Louis II "the Stammerer", King of the Franks, and Adelaide of Paris. *Moriarty, The Plantagenet Ancestry of King Edward III, page 21; Schwennicke, Europäische Stammtafeln, Volume II, tables 1 and 78; von Redlich, Pedigrees of Some of the Emperor Charlemagne's Descendants, pages 132, 164, and 264 See line 8 (4)*

LINE 5 continued from line 4 (1)

2. **Alfred "the Great", King of Wessex**, born ca 847, died October 26, 899. He married Æthelswida, born, ca. 852, died December 5, 905. She was the daughter of Æthelred, King of Mercia, and Edburga. *Moriarty, The Plantagenet Ancestry of King Edward III, page 252; Schwennicke, Europäische Stammtafeln, Volume II, table 78*

Coin depicting Alfred the Great, King of Wessex

3. **Ælfrida of Wessex,** born ca. 868, died June 7, 929. She married
   Baldwin II (31–5), Count of Flanders, born 865, died January 2,
   918. He was the son of Baldwin I, Count of Flanders, and Judith of
   France, the daughter of Charles II "the Bald", King of the Franks.
   *Moriarty, The Plantagenet Ancestry of King Edward III, pages
   14 and 16; Schwennicke, Europäische Stammtafeln, Volumes I/1,
   table 6, and II, table 78*

4. **Arnold I, Count of Flanders,** born ca. 890, died March 27, 964. He
   married Adela of Vermandois (34–3 and 57–6), born ca. 915, died
   960. She was the daughter of Herbert II, Count of Vermandois, and
   Hildebrante, the daughter of Robert I, King of the Franks. *Moriarty,
   The Plantagenet Ancestry of King Edward III, pages 6 and 14;
   Schwennicke, Europäische Stammtafeln, Volumes II, table 5, and
   III, table 49*

5. **Baldwin III, Count of Flanders,** born ca. 940, died ca. 962. He
   married Mathilda of Saxony, died 1008. She was the daughter of
   Hermann Billung, Duke of Saxony, and Hildegarde of Westerbourg.
   *Moriarty, The Plantagenet Ancestry of King Edward III, pages 14
   and 17; Schwennicke, Europäische Stammtafeln, Volumes I/1, table
   95, I/2, table 202, II, table 5, and VI, table 127*

6. **Arnold II, Count of Flanders**, born ca. 961, died March 30, 987. He married Rosala (Susanna) of Ivrea (72-6 and 85–4), born ca. 952, died 1003. She was the daughter of Berengar II, King of Italy, and Willa of Tuscany. *Moriarty, The Plantagenet Ancestry of King Edward III, pages 14 and 18; Schwennicke, Europäische Stammtafeln, Volume II, table 5*

7. **Baldwin IV, Count of Flanders**, born 980, died May 30, 1035. He married Ogiva of Luxembourg (114–3), died February 21, 1030. She was the daughter of Frederick I, Count of Luxembourg, and (possibly) Ermentrude of Gleiberg. *Moriarty, The Plantagenet Ancestry of King Edward III, pages 14, 22, and 24; Schwennicke, Europäische Stammtafeln, Volumes II, table 5, and VI, table 128; Douglas, William the Conqueror, page 77*

8. **Baldwin V, Count of Flanders**, born ca. 1012, died September 1, 1067. He married Adele of France (49–5), Countess of Contentin, died January 8, 1079, widow of Richard III, Duke of Normandy. She was the daughter of Robert II, King of the Franks, and Constance of Provence. *Moriarty, The Plantagenet Ancestry of King Edward III, pages 13 and 15; Schwennicke, Europäische Stammtafeln, Volume II, tables 5, 11, and 79; Roberts, The Royal Descents of 600 Immigrants, page 534; Weis, Ancestral Roots of Certain American Colonists, 128 (21–22)*

9. **Mathilda of Flanders**, born ca. 1031, died 1083. She married William the Conqueror (2–1), King of England, born October 14, 1025, died September 9, 1087. He was the son of Robert I, Duke of Normandy, and Herleve. *Moriarty, The Plantagenet Ancestry of King Edward III, pages 13 and 15; Schwennicke, Europäische Stammtafeln, Volume II, tables 5, 79, and 81; Burke, Burke's Peerage (The Royal Lineage), page 28; Weir, Britain's Royal Families, pages 39–45*

10. **Henry I, King of England**, born September, 1068, died December 1, 1135. His mistress was Sybilla Corbet. She was the daughter of Robert Corbet. *Cokayne, The Complete Peerage, Volumes III (Cornwall), page 429, and XI (Appendix D), pages 107–108; Schwennicke, Europäische Stammtafeln, Volume II, table 81; Burke, Burke's Peerage (The Royal Lineage), page 28; Weir, Britain's Royal Families, pages 46–50* **See line 2 (2)**

7. **Eudes, Count of Cambrai.** He married Odele of Bois Ferrand. She was the daughter of Thebaud, Seigneur de Bois Ferrand. *Moriarty, The Plantagenet Ancestry of King Edward III, pages 240 and 277; Stuart, Royalty for Commoners, 184 (34) and 254 (36)*

8. **Engelbert, Count of Brienne.** *Moriarty, The Plantagenet Ancestry of King Edward III, page 277; Stuart, Royalty for Commoners, 254 (36)*

9. **Engeltrude of Brienne.** She married Milo III, Count of Tonnerre, died 987. He was the son of Gui I, Count of Tonnerre, and Adela of Salins. *Moriarty, The Plantagenet Ancestry of King Edward III, page 65; Stuart, Royalty for Commoners, 254 (36)*

10. **Gui II, Count of Tonnerre**, born ca. 920, dead by 993. He married Adela. *Moriarty, The Plantagenet Ancestry of King Edward III, page 240; Stuart, Royalty for Commoners, 254 (35)*

11. **Milo IV, Count of Tonnerre**, died 998. He married Ermengarde of Bar-sur-Seine, died after 1035. She was the daughter of Renaud, Count of Bar-sur-Seine. *Moriarty, The Plantagenet Ancestry of King Edward III, pages 134, 135, and 240; Stuart, Royalty for Commoners, 254 (34)*

12. **Renaud, Count of Tonnerre**, died July 16, 1039. He married Helvise. *Moriarty, The Plantagenet Ancestry of King Edward III, page 240; Schwennicke, Europäische Stammtafeln, Volume III, table 730; Stuart, Royalty for Commoners, 254 (33)*

13. **Ermengarde, Countess of Tonnerre**, died 1085. She married William I (48–6), Count of Nevers, born ca. 1030, died June 20, 1100. He was the son of Renaud I, Count of Nevers, and Aelis of France, Countess of Auxerre. *Moriarty, The Plantagenet Ancestry of King Edward III, page 240; Schwennicke, Europäische Stammtafeln, Volume III, tables 716 and 730; Stuart, Royalty for Commoners, 254 (33)*

14. **Renaud II, Count of Nevers**, died August 5, 1089. He married Ida. She was the daughter of Artald, Count of Lyon and Forez. *Moriarty,*

The Plantagenet Ancestry of King Edward III, pages 64 and 66; Schwennicke, Europäische Stammtafeln, Volume III, tables 716 and 717 See line 48 (7)

LINE 7 continued from line 5 (4)

5. **Hildegarde of Flanders,** died 990. She married Dietrich II (Dirk II), Count of Holland, born 924, died 988. He was the son of Dietrich I (Dirk I), Count of Holland, and Gerberge. *Moriarty, The Plantagenet Ancestry of King Edward III, pages 14, 55, and 163; Schwennicke, Europäische Stammtafeln, Volume II, table 2*

6. **Arnulf, Count of Holland,** born ca. 951, died 993. He married Liutgarde of Luxembourg (115–2), died 1005. She was the daughter of Siegfried, Count of Luxembourg, and Hedwig. *Moriarty, The Plantagenet Ancestry of King Edward III, pages 22 and 55; Schwennicke, Europäische Stammtafeln, Volumes I, table 158, and II, table 2*

7. **Adele of Holland (Ada of Ghent),** born ca. 985. She married Baudouin II, (32–9) Count of Boulogne, born 976, died 1033. He was the son of Arnulf II, Count of Boulogne. *Schwennicke, Europäische Stammtafeln, Volume II, table 2; Turton, The Plantagenet Ancestry, page 105; Tanner, Families, Friends and Allies, pages 290 and 299*

8. **Eustace I, Count of Boulogne,** died ca. 1049. He married Matilda (Maud) of Louvain (28–9). She was the daughter of Lambert I, Count of Louvain, and Gerberge of Lorraine. *Cokayne, The Complete Peerage, Volume I (Aumale), page 352; Moriarty, The Plantagenet Ancestry of King Edward III, pages 125 and 165; Schwennicke, Europäische Stammtafeln, Volumes I, table 95, I/2, table 236, and III, table 621*

9. **Lambert, Count of Lens,** died 1054. He married Adelaide of Normandy (119–2), Countess of Aumale. She was the daughter of Robert I, Duke of Normandy, and Herleve (parents of William the Conqueror). *Cokayne, The Complete Peerage, Volumes I (Aumale), pages 351–352, and XII/1 (Tony), pages 760–762 and (Appendix K), pages 30–34; Moriarty, The Plantagenet Ancestry of King Edward III, pages 165 and 184; Schwennicke, Europäische Stammtafeln, Volumes II, table 79, and III, table 621 See line 28 (10)*

3. **Edward "the Elder", King of England**, born ca. 875, died July 17, 924. He married (first) Æflaeda (4–4), died 919. She was the daughter of Æthelhelm, Ealdorman of Wiltshire. *Moriarty, The Plantagenet Ancestry of King Edward III, page 252; Schwennicke, Europäische Stammtafeln, Volume II, table 78; Weis, Ancestral Roots of Certain American Colonists, 1 (15) and 45 (16)*

4. **Ædgifu (Ogiva) of England**, born ca. 904, died 951. She married Charles III "the Simple" (25–5), King of the Franks, born September 17, 879, died October 27, 929. He was the son of Louis II "the Stammerer", King of the Franks, and Adelaide of Paris. *Moriarty, The Plantagenet Ancestry of King Edward III, pages 21 and 35; Schwennicke, Europäische Stammtafeln, Volume II, tables 1 and 78; von Redlich, Pedigrees of Some of the Emperor Charlemagne's Descendants, pages 132, 164, and 264; Weis, Ancestral Roots of Certain American Colonists, 50 (20) and 148 (17)*

5. **Louis IV, "the Transmarine" King of the Franks**, born September 10, 920, died September 10, 954. He married Gerberge of Saxony (90–2 and 92–2), born 913, died May 5, 984. She was the daughter of Heinrich "the Fowler", King of the Saxons, and St. Mathilda. *Moriarty, The Plantagenet Ancestry of King Edward III, pages 25 and 35; Schwennicke, Europäische Stammtafeln, Volumes I/1, table 6, and II, tables 1 and 3; von Redlich, Pedigrees of Some of the Emperor Charlemagne's Descendants, pages 132, 164, and 264; Weis, Ancestral Roots of Certain American Colonists, 148 (18)* *See line 25 (6)*

Edward the Elder, King of England
from a 13th century genealogical scroll

Hywel Dda ap Cadell, King of South Wales
from a 14th-century Welsh manuscript

Wales

1. **Brochwel Ysgythrog, King of Powys,** died 617. He was the son of Cynan ap Cadell Deyrnllwg. He married St. Arddun verch Pabo (136–2). She was the daughter of St. Pabo Post Prydain. *Griffith, Pedigrees of Anglesey and Carnarvonshire Families, page 309: Williams, A Biographical Dictionary of Eminent Welshmen, pages 19 and 47*

2. **Cynan Garwyn ap Brochwel, King of Powys.** *Griffith, Pedigrees of Anglesey and Carnarvonshire Families, page 309; Lloyd, A History of Wales, page 181*

3. **Selyf ap Cynan, King of Powys.** *Griffith, Pedigrees of Anglesey and Carnarvonshire Families, page 309; Lloyd, A History of Wales, pages 180–181*

4. **Mael Mynan ap Selyf.** *Griffith, Pedigrees of Anglesey and Carnarvonshire Families, page 309*

5. **Beli ap Mynan.** *Griffith, Pedigrees of Anglesey and Carnarvonshire Families, page 309*

6. **Gwallawg ap Beli.** He married Sanan verch Noe. She was the daughter of Noe ap Arthur. *Griffith, Pedigrees of Anglesey and Carnarvonshire Families, page 309; Lloyd, A History of Wales, page 244*

7. **Eliseg ap Gwallawg.** *Griffith, Pedigrees of Anglesey and Carnarvonshire Families, page 309; Lloyd, A History of Wales, page 244*

8. **Brochwel ap Eliseg, King of Powys.** *Griffith, Pedigrees of Anglesey and Carnarvonshire Families, page 309*

9. **Cadell ap Brochwel, King of Powys.** *Griffith, Pedigrees of Anglesey and Carnarvonshire Families, page 309; Lloyd, A History of Wales, page 244*

10. **Nesta verch Cadell.** She married Gwriad ap Elidwr, King of the Isle of Man. He was the son of Elidwr ap Handaer. *Griffith, Pedigrees of Anglesey and Carnarvonshire Families, page 309; Williams, A Biographical Dictionary of Eminent Welshmen, page 329*

11. **Merfyn Frych ap Gwriad, King of Powys, the Isle of Man, and Gwynedd,** died 843. He married Essylt Vodrwyog verch Conan. She was the daughter of Conan Tindaethwy ap Rhodri, King of North Wales. *Griffith, Pedigrees of Anglesey and Carnarvonshire Families, page 309; Williams, A Biographical Dictionary of Eminent Welshmen, page 329*

12. **Rhodri Mawr ap Merfyn, King of Powys and Gwynedd,** died 878. He married Angharad verch Meyric (13–3). She was the daughter of Meyric ap Dyfnwal, King of Greater Ceredigion. *Griffith, Pedigrees of Anglesey and Carnarvonshire Families, page 309; Nicholas, Annals and Antiquities of the Counties and County Families of Wales, page 847; Maund, The Welsh Kings, page 52; Williams, A Biographical Dictionary of Eminent Welshmen, page 438*

13. **Cadell ap Rhodri, King of Gwynedd,** died 909. *Griffith, Pedigrees of Anglesey and Carnarvonshire Families, page 309; Nicholas, Annals and Antiquities of the Counties and County Families of Wales, pages 143, 228, and 847; Maund, The Welsh Kings, pages 52 and 70; Lloyd, A History of Wales, page 332; Williams, A Biographical Dictionary of Eminent Welshmen, page 53; Meyrick, Heraldic Visitations of Wales, page xvii*

14. **Hywel Dda ap Cadell, King of South Wales,** born ca. 880, died 949. He married Elen verch Llywarch (12–3). She was the daughter of Llywarch ap Hyfaidd, King of South Wales. *Griffith, Pedigrees of Anglesey and Carnarvonshire Families, page 301; Nicholas, Annals and Antiquities of the Counties and County Families of Wales, pages 231 and 847; Maund, The Welsh Kings, pages 47–50; Lloyd, A History of Wales, pages 333–343; Williams, A Biographical Dictionary of Eminent Welshmen, pages 231–233*

15. **Owain ap Hywel Dda, King of Deheubarth,** died 988. He married Angharad verch Llewellyn (11–15). She was the daughter of Llewellyn ap Merfyn. *Nicholas, Annals and Antiquities of the Counties and County Families of Wales, page 231; Maund, The*

Welsh Kings, pages 51–53; Lloyd, A History of Wales, page 344;
Williams, A Biographical Dictionary of Eminent Welshmen, page
328; Meyrick, Heraldic Visitations of Wales, page xvii

16. **Maredudd ap Owain, King of Gwynedd,** died 999. *Griffith,*
    Pedigrees of Anglesey and Carnarvonshire Families, page 309;
    Maund, The Welsh Kings, page 52; Lloyd, A History of Wales, page
    345; Williams, A Biographical Dictionary of Eminent Welshmen,
    page 328; Weis, Ancestral Roots of Certain American Colonists,
    176 (1); Meyrick, Heraldic Visitations of Wales, page xvii

17. **Angharad verch Maredudd.** She married Llewellyn ap Seisyll (10–
    16), Prince of North Wales, King of Gwynedd and Deheubarth, died
    1023. He was the son of Seisyll ap Ednywain, and Trawst (Prawst)
    verch Eliseg. *Griffith, Pedigrees of Anglesey and Carnarvonshire*
    Families, page 309; Nicholas, Annals and Antiquities of the
    Counties and County Families of Wales, page 231; Maund, The
    Welsh Kings, page 52; Williams, A Biographical Dictionary of
    Eminent Welshmen, pages 301 and 328; Weis, Ancestral Roots of
    Certain American Colonists, 176 (1)

18. **Gruffydd ap Llewellyn, Prince of North Wales, King of**
    Gwynedd, Powys and Deheubarth, died August 5, 1063. He
    married Ældgyth (Edith) of Mercia (122–3). She was the daughter
    of Ælfgar, Earl of Mercia, and Ælfgifu. *Griffith, Pedigrees of*
    Anglesey and Carnarvonshire Families, page 301; Maund, The
    Welsh Kings, page 52; Williams, A Biographical Dictionary of
    Eminent Welshmen, page 186; Weis, Ancestral Roots of Certain
    American Colonists, 176 (2), and 176A (3–4)

19. **Nesta of North Wales**, born ca. 1055. She married Osborn
    FitzRichard, sheriff of Hereford. He was the son of Richard
    FitzScrob. *Maund, The Welsh Kings, page 68; Weis, Ancestral*
    Roots of Certain American Colonists, 176 (3) and 177 (2)

20. **Nesta.** She married Bernard de Neufmarche, Lord of Brecon, died
    1093. He was the son of Geoffrey de Neufmarche and Ada de
    Hugleville. *Cokayne, The Complete Peerage, Volume VI (Hereford),*
    page 453; Sanders, English Baronies, page 6; Maund, The Welsh
    Kings, page 68; Weis, Ancestral Roots of Certain American
    Colonists, 177 (3)

21. **Sibyl de Neufmarche**. She married Miles of Gloucester (FitzWalter) de Pitres, Earl of Hereford, died December 24, 1143. He was the son of Walter FitzRoger and Bertha. *Cokayne, The Complete Peerage, Volumes I (Abergavenny), page 20, and VI (Hereford), pages 451–454; Sanders, English Baronies, page 7*

22. **Bertha of Gloucester**. She married William de Braose, Lord of Braose and Bramber. He was the son of Philip de Braose and Aenor de Toteneis. *Cokayne, The Complete Peerage, Volumes I (Abergavenny), pages 21–22, and VI (Hereford), page 452; Sanders, English Baronies, page 7*

23. **William de Braose, Lord of Braose, Bramber, Brecon and Over-Gwent**, died August 9, 1211. He married Maud de St. Valeri (46–13), died 1210. She was the daughter of Bernard de St. Valeri and Maud. *Cokayne, The Complete Peerage, Volumes I (Abergavenny), page 22, and VI (Hereford), pages 456–457; Sanders, English Baronies, pages 7 and 89*

24. **Reginald de Braose**, died May 2, 1227. He married Grace de Briwere. She was the daughter of William de Briwere and Beatrice de Vaux. *Cokayne, The Complete Peerage, Volume I (Abergavenny), page 22; Sanders, English Baronies, pages 7 and 90*

25. **William de Braose, Baron Braose**, died May 2, 1230. He married Eve Marshall (16–9), died before 1246. She was the daughter of William Marshall, Earl of Pembroke, and Isabel de Clare, Countess of Pembroke. *Cokayne, The Complete Peerage, Volumes I (Abergavenny), page 22, and X (Pembroke), page 364; Sanders, English Baronies, pages 7 and 90*

26. **Eve de Braose**, died 1255. She married William de Cantelou (76–13), Baron Abergavenny, died September 25, 1254. He was the son of William de Cantelou and Milicent de Gournay. *Cokayne, The Complete Peerage, Volumes I (Abergavenny), pages 22–23, and XII/2 (Tregoz), pages 19–20; Sanders, English Baronies, pages 7–8, and 90*

27. **Milicent de Cantelou**, born 1250, died January 7, 1299. She married Eudes la Zouche (44–14), died May, 1279. He was the

son of Roger la Zouche and Margaret. *Cokayne, The Complete Peerage, Volumes I (Abergavenny), page 23, II (Berkeley), page 129, and XII/2 (Zouche), page 938; Sanders, English Baronies, page 90; Weis, Ancestral Roots of Certain American Colonists, 39 (29) and 66 (30)* **See line 76 (14)**

LINE 10 continued from line 9 (12)

13. **Anarawd ap Rhodri, King of North Wales,** died 916. *Griffith, Pedigrees of Anglesey and Carnarvonshire Families, page 309; Maund, The Welsh Kings, page 52; Lloyd, A History of Wales, pages 326 and 332; Williams, A Biographical Dictionary of Eminent Welshmen, page 16*

14. **Eliseg ap Anarawd,** a son. *Griffith, Pedigrees of Anglesey and Carnarvonshire Families, page 309; Williams, A Biographical Dictionary of Eminent Welshmen, page 47*

15. **Trawst (Prawst) verch Eliseg.** She married Seisyll ap Ednywain. *Griffith, Pedigrees of Anglesey and Carnarvonshire Families, page 309; Lloyd, A History of Wales, page 347; Williams, A Biographical Dictionary of Eminent Welshmen, page 301*

16. **Llewellyn ap Seisyll, Prince of North Wales, King of Gwynedd and Deheubarth,** died 1023. He married Angharad verch Maredudd (9–17). She was the daughter of Maredudd ap Owain, King of Gwynedd. *Griffith, Pedigrees of Anglesey and Carnarvonshire Families, page 309; Lloyd, A History of Wales, page 347; Williams, A Biographical Dictionary of Eminent Welshmen, pages 301 and 328; Weis, Ancestral Roots of Certain American Colonists, 176 (1)*

17. **Gruffydd ap Llewellyn, Prince of North Wales, King of Gwynedd, Powys and Deheubarth,** died August 5, 1063. He married Ældgyth (Edith) of Mercia. (122–3). She was the daughter of Ælfgar, Earl of Mercia, and Ælfgifu. *Griffith, Pedigrees of Anglesey and Carnarvonshire Families, page 301; Maund, The Welsh Kings, page 52; Williams, A Biographical Dictionary of Eminent Welshmen, page 186; Weis, Ancestral Roots of Certain American Colonists, 176 (2), and 176A (3–4)* **See line 9 (18)**

21

13. **Merfyn ap Rhodri, King of Powys**, died 904. *Griffith, Pedigrees of Anglesey and Carnarvonshire Families, page 309; Lloyd, A History of Wales, page 326; Williams, A Biographical Dictionary of Eminent Welshmen, page 329*

14. **Llewellyn ap Merfyn**, a son. *Griffith, Pedigrees of Anglesey and Carnarvonshire Families, page 309*

15. **Angharad verch Llewellyn**. She married Owain ap Hywel Dda (9–15), died 988. He was the son of Hywel Dda ap Cadell, King of South Wales, and Elen verch Llywarch. *Griffith, Pedigrees of Anglesey and Carnarvonshire Families, page 309; Nicholas, Annals and Antiquities of the Counties and County Families of Wales, page 231; Williams, A Biographical Dictionary of Eminent Welshmen, page 328*

16. **Maredudd ap Owain, King of Gwynedd,** died 999. *Griffith, Pedigrees of Anglesey and Carnarvonshire Families, page 309; Maund, The Welsh Kings, page 52; Lloyd, A History of Wales, page 345; Williams, A Biographical Dictionary of Eminent Welshmen, page 328; Weis, Ancestral Roots of Certain American Colonists, 176 (1)* **See line 9 (16)**

LINE 12

1. **Hyfaidd ap Bledri, King of South Wales**. He was the son of Bledri and Tangwystyl verch Owain. *Williams, Smyth and Kirby, A Biographical Dictionary of Dark Age Britain, page xxxviii, table XVII; Ashley, The Mammoth Book of British Kings and Queens, pages 139 and 194*

2. **Llywarch ap Hyfaidd, King of South Wales**, died 904. *Maund, The Welsh Kings, page 57, Lloyd, A History of Wales, page 333; Ashley, The Mammoth Book of British Kings and Queens, pages 139 and 194*

3. **Elen verch Llywarch**. She married Hywel Dda ap Cadell (9–14), King of South Wales, died 949. He was the son of Cadell ap Rhodri, King of Gwynedd. *Griffith, Pedigrees of Anglesey and*

Carnarvonshire Families, pages 301 and 309; Nicholas, Annals and Antiquities of the Counties and County Families of Wales, page 231; Maund, The Welsh Kings, page 47; Lloyd, A History of Wales, page 333; Williams, A Biographical Dictionary of Eminent Welshmen, pages 231–233

4. **Owain ap Hywel Dda, King of Deheubarth,** died 988. He married Angharad verch Llewellyn (11–15). She was the daughter of Llewellyn ap Merfyn. *Nicholas, Annals and Antiquities of the Counties and County Families of Wales, page 231; Maund, The Welsh Kings, pages 51–53; Lloyd, A History of Wales, page 344; Williams, A Biographical Dictionary of Eminent Welshmen, page 328 See line 9 (15)*

LINE 13

1. **Dyfnwal ap Arthen, Prince of North Wales.** *Griffith, Pedigrees of Anglesey and Carnarvonshire Families, page 309; Meyrick, Heraldic Visitations of Wales, page xvii*

2. **Meyric ap Dyfnwal, King of Greater Ceredigion.** *Griffith, Pedigrees of Anglesey and Carnarvonshire Families, page 309; Meyrick, Heraldic Visitations of Wales, page xvii*

3. **Angharad verch Meyric.** She married Rhodri Mawr ap Merfyn (9–12), King of Gwynedd, died 878. He was the son of Merfyn Frych ap Gwriad, King of Powys, the Isle of Man, and Gwynedd, and Essylit Vodrwyog verch Conan. *Griffith, Pedigrees of Anglesey and Carnarvonshire Families, page 309; Nicholas, Annals and Antiquities of the Counties and County Families of Wales, page 847; Maund, The Welsh Kings, page 52; Williams, A Biographical Dictionary of Eminent Welshmen, page 438; Meyrick, Heraldic Visitations of Wales, page xvii*

4. **Cadell ap Rhodri, King of Gwynedd,** died 909. *Griffith, Pedigrees of Anglesey and Carnarvonshire Families, page 309; Nicholas, Annals and Antiquities of the Counties and County Families of Wales, page 847; Maund, The Welsh Kings, page 52; Lloyd, A History of Wales, page 332; Williams, A Biographical Dictionary of Eminent Welshmen, page 53; Meyrick, Heraldic Visitations of Wales, page xvii See line 9 (13)*

LINE 14 continued from line 13 (3)

4. **Anarawd ap Rhodri, King of North Wales,** died 916. *Griffith, Pedigrees of Anglesey and Carnarvonshire Families, page 309; Maund, The Welsh Kings, page 52; Lloyd, A History of Wales, pages 326 and 332; Williams, A Biographical Dictionary of Eminent Welshmen, page 16* **See line 10 (13)**

LINE 15 continued from line 13 (3)

4. **Merfyn ap Rhodri, King of Powys,** died 904. *Griffith, Pedigrees of Anglesey and Carnarvonshire Families, page 309; Lloyd, A History of Wales, page 326; Williams, A Biographical Dictionary of Eminent Welshmen, page 329* **See line 11 (13)**

Coin depicting Brian Boru, High King of Ireland

Ireland

1. **Brian Boru, King of the Dalcassians, King of Munster, and High King of Ireland**, born ca. 941, died 1014. He married Gormflaith of Naas, died 1030. She was the daughter of Murchad, King of Leinster. *Weis, Ancestral Roots of Certain American Colonists, 175 (1); MacManus, The Story of the Irish Race, pages 275–282; Worsaã, An Account of the Danes and Norwegians in England, Scotland, and Ireland, page 320*

2. **Donnchad, King of Munster**, died 1064. *Weis, Ancestral Roots of Certain American Colonists, 175 (2); Jones, The History of Gruffydd ap Cynan, page 109; Worsaã, An Account of the Danes and Norwegians in England, Scotland, and Ireland, page 320; Cosgrove, A New History of Ireland, page 254*

3. **Darbforgaill**, died 1080. She married Diarmait MacMael nam Bo, King of Hy Kinsale and Leinster, died February 1072. *Weis, Ancestral Roots of Certain American Colonists, 175 (3)*

4. **Murchada**, died December 8, 1070. He married Sadb. She was the daughter of MacBricc. *Weis, Ancestral Roots of Certain American Colonists, 175 (4)*

5. **Donnchad Mac Murchada, King of Dublin**, died 1115. He married Orlaith. *Weis, Ancestral Roots of Certain American Colonists, 175 (5)*

6. **Diarmait Mac Murchada, King of Leinster**, born 1100, died January 1, 1171. He married Mor Ní Tuathail. She was the daughter of Muirchertach Ua Tuathail. *Weis, Ancestral Roots of Certain American Colonists, 175 (6); Cosgrove, A New History of Ireland, page 23*

7. **Aoife (Eva) of Leinster**, born ca. 1145, died 1187. She married Richard "Strongbow" de Clare (50–10), Earl of Pembroke, born ca. 1130, died April 20, 1176. He was the son of Gilbert de Clare, Earl of Pembroke, and Isabel de Beaumont. *Cokayne, The Complete Peerage, Volume X (Pembroke), pages 352–357; Schwennicke, Europäische Stammtafeln, Volume III, table 156*

Seal of Richard "Strongbow" de Clare, Earl of Pembroke

8. **Isabel de Clare, Countess of Pembroke**, born October 9, 1176, died 1220. She married William Marshall, Earl of Pembroke, born 1146, died May 14, 1219. He was the son of John Marshall and Sibyl Devereaux. *Cokayne, The Complete Peerage, Volume X (Pembroke), pages 358–362; Schwennicke, Europäische Stammtafeln, Volume III, table 156*

9. **Eve Marshall**, died before 1246. She married William de Braose (9–25), Baron Braose, born 1204, died May 2, 1230. He was the son of Reginald de Braose and Grace de Briwere. *Cokayne, The Complete Peerage, Volumes I (Abergavenny), page 22, and X (Pembroke), page 364; Sanders, English Baronies, pages 7 and 90*

10. **Eve de Braose**, died 1255. She married William de Cantelou (76–13), Baron Abergavenny, died September 25, 1254. He was the son of William de Cantelou and Milicent de Gournay. *Cokayne, The Complete Peerage, Volumes I (Abergavenny), pages 22–23, and XII/2 (Tregoz), pages 19–20 See line 9 (26)*

William Marshall, Earl of Pembroke
from the Historia Major of Matthew Paris

Charlemagne, King of the Franks
painting by Albrecht Dürer

France

1. **Charlemagne, King of the Franks**, born April 2, 747, died January 28, 814. He was the son of Pepin "the Short" (54–2), King of the Franks, and Bertrada of Laon (124–10). His mistress was Himiltrude. *Moriarty, The Plantagenet Ancestry of King Edward III, pages 5, 7, and 220; Schwennicke, Europäische Stammtafeln, Volumes I, table 2, and I/1, table 4*

2. **Aupais**. She married Bégue (55–4), Count of Paris, died 816. He was the son of Girard, Count of Paris, and Rotrude. *Moriarty, The Plantagenet Ancestry of King Edward III, pages 22–23 (Note: some references give Aupais' parents as Louis I and Ermengarde, making her the granddaughter, not daughter, of Charlemagne.)*

3. **Leutaud, Count of Paris**. He may have married Grimhild (Grimeut). *Moriarty, The Plantagenet Ancestry of King Edward III, page 23*

4. **Engeltrude**. She married Eudes (129–10), Count of Orleans, died 834. He was the son of Hadrian, Count of Orleans, and Waldrada. *Moriarty, The Plantagenet Ancestry of King Edward III, pages 9, 23, and 233*

5. **Ermentrude of Orleans**, born September 27, 823, died October 6, 869. She married Charles II "the Bald" (25–3 and 33–3), King of the Franks, born June 13, 823, died October 6, 877. He was the son of Louis I, "the Pious", King of the Franks, and Judith of Bavaria. *Moriarty, The Plantagenet Ancestry of King Edward III, pages 16, 23, and 233; Schwennicke, Europäische Stammtafeln, Volumes I, table 2, I/1, table 4, and II, table 1*

6. **Louis II, "the Stammerer", King of the Franks**, born 844, died April 10, 879. He married Adelaide of Paris, died after 901. She was the daughter of Adelhard, Count of Paris. *Moriarty, The Plantagenet Ancestry of King Edward III, pages 16 and 21; Schwennicke, Europäische Stammtafeln, Volumes I/1, table 6, and II, table 1* **See line 25 (4)**

LINE 18 continued from line 17 (5)

6. **Judith of France**, born ca. 846. She married Baldwin I, Count of Flanders, died 879. *Moriarty, The Plantagenet Ancestry of King Edward III, pages 14 and 16; Schwennicke, Europäische Stammtafeln, Volume II, tables 1 and 5* **See line 31 (4)**

LINE 19

1. **Charlemagne, King of the Franks**, born April 2, 747, died January 28, 814. He married Hildegarde, born 758, died April 30, 783. She was the daughter of Gerold, Count of Anglachau, and Emma of Alemania. *Moriarty, The Plantagenet Ancestry of King Edward III, pages 5, 7, and 220; Schwennicke, Europäische Stammtafeln, Volumes I, table 2, and I/1, table 4*

2. **Pepin, King of Italy**, born 777, died July 8, 810. *Moriarty, The Plantagenet Ancestry of King Edward III, pages 5 and 220; Schwennicke, Europäische Stammtafeln, Volumes I, table 2, I/1, table 4, and III, table 49* **See line 57 (1)**

LINE 20 continued from line 19 (1)

2. **Louis I, "the Pious", King of the Franks**, born August, 778, died June 20, 840. He married (first), Ermengarde, died October 3, 818. She was the daughter of Ingerman, Count of Hasbaye. *Moriarty, The Plantagenet Ancestry of King Edward III, pages 5, 16, 20, and 21; Schwennicke, Europäische Stammtafeln, Volumes I, table 2, and I/1, table 4*

3. **Lothair I, King of Italy**, died September 29, 855. He married Ermengarde, died March 20, 851. She was the daughter of Hugh II, Count of Tours. *Moriarty, The Plantagenet Ancestry of King Edward III, pages 16, 20, 21, and 259; Schwennicke, Europäische Stammtafeln, Volumes I, table 2, and I/1, table 4* **See line 64 (1)**

LINE 21 continued from line 20 (2)

3. **Matilda (Rotrude) of France**. She married Gerhard I, Count of Auvergne, died June 25, 841. *Moriarty, The Plantagenet Ancestry*

of King Edward III, pages 16 and 26; Schwennicke, Europäische Stammtafeln, Volumes I/1, table 4 and II, table 76

4. **Ranulph I, Count of Poitou,** died July 5, 866. He married Blichilde. She was the daughter of Rorick, Count of Maine, and Blichilde. *Moriarty, The Plantagenet Ancestry of King Edward III, pages 26 and 27; Schwennicke, Europäische Stammtafeln, Volume II, table 76*

5. **Ranulph II, Count of Poitou,** born ca. 855, died August 5, 890. His mistress was Ermengarde (Ada). *Moriarty, The Plantagenet Ancestry of King Edward III, page 26; Schwennicke, Europäische Stammtafeln, Volume II, table 76*

6. **Ebles, Count of Poitou,** died 932. He married Aremburge. *Moriarty, The Plantagenet Ancestry of King Edward III, page 27; Schwennicke, Europäische Stammtafeln, Volume II, 7 table 6*

7. **William I, Count of Poitou, Duc d'Aquitaine,** born ca. 900, died April 3, 963. He married Gerloc (Adele) (97–11), died ca. 970. She was the daughter of Rollo "the Viking", Duke of Normandy, and Poppa de Bayeux. *Moriarty, The Plantagenet Ancestry of King Edward III, pages 11 and 27; Schwennicke, Europäische Stammtafeln, Volume II, tables 76 and 79*

8. **Adelaide of Poitou,** born ca. 945, died June 15, 1006. She married Hugh Capet (47–3), King of the Franks, born 939, died October 24, 996. He was the son of Hugh "the Great", Count of Paris, and Hedwig of Saxony. *Moriarty, The Plantagenet Ancestry of King Edward III, pages 24 and 27; Schwennicke, Europäische Stammtafeln, Volume II, tables 11 and 76*

9. **Robert II, "the Pious" King of the Franks,** born March 27, 972, died July 20, 1031. He married Constance of Provence (65–8), born ca. 986, died July 25, 1032. She was the daughter of William I, Count of Provence, and Adelaide of Anjou. *Moriarty, The Plantagenet Ancestry of King Edward III, pages 24 and 28; Schwennicke, Europäische Stammtafeln, Volume II, 1 tables 1 and 187; von Redlich, Pedigrees of Some of the Emperor Charlemagne's Descendants, page 63* **See line 47 (4)**

9. **Hedwig (Edith) Capet**, died 1013. She married Reginar IV (81–6), Count of Hainaut, died 1013. He was the son of Reginar III, Count of Hainaut, and Adele. *Moriarty, The Plantagenet Ancestry of King Edward III, pages 24 and 50; Schwennicke, Europäische Stammtafeln, Volumes I, table 95, and II, table 11* **See line 50 (4)**

LINE 23 continued from Line 19 (1)

2. **Louis I, "the Pious", King of the Franks**, born August, 778, died June 20, 840. He married (second), Judith of Bavaria, died April 19, 843. She was the daughter of Welf I, Duke of Bavaria. *Moriarty, The Plantagenet Ancestry of King Edward III, pages 16 and 17; Schwennicke, Europäische Stammtafeln, Volumes I, table 2, I/1, table 4, and III, table 736; von Redlich, Pedigrees of Some of the Emperor Charlemagne's Descendants, page 63*

3. **Gisele**, born 820, died July 1, 874. She married Eberhard, Marquis of Friuli, died ca. 864. He was the son of Hunroch, Marquis of Friuli, and Engeltrude. *Moriarty, The Plantagenet Ancestry of King Edward III, page 16; Schwennicke, Europäische Stammtafeln, Volumes I/1, table 4, and II, table 188A; Weis, Ancestral Roots of Certain American Colonists, 250 (15); von Redlich, Pedigrees of Some of the Emperor Charlemagne's Descendants, page 63*

4. **Berengar I, King of Italy**, born 850, died April 7, 924. He married Bertila of Spoleto, died December 915. She was the daughter of Suppo, Marquis of Spoleto, Count of Turin, and Berta. *Moriarty, The Plantagenet Ancestry of King Edward III, pages 18 and 19; Schwennicke, Europäische Stammtafeln, Volumes I/1, table 4, and II, table 188A* **See line 83 (1)**

Line 24 continued from line 23 (3)

4. **Helwise (Heiliwich) of Friuli**, died after 895. She married Hucbold, Count of Ostrevant, dead by 895. *Moriarty, The Plantagenet Ancestry of King Edward III, pages 18 and 228; Schwennicke, Europäische Stammtafeln, Volume III, table 657; Weis, Ancestral Roots of Certain American Colonists, 250 (16)*

5. **Raoul I, Count of Ostrevant and Amiens,** died 926. He married Eldegarde. She was perhaps the daughter (or niece) of Ermenfroi, Count of Amiens. *Moriarty, The Plantagenet Ancestry of King Edward III, pages 135 and 228; Schwennicke, Europäische Stammtafeln, Volume III, table 657; Weis, Ancestral Roots of Certain American Colonists, 250 (17)*

6. **Gautier I (Walter I), Count of Valois, the Vexin and Amiens,** died 992 or 998. He married Adele. She was probably the daughter of Fulk II, Count of Anjou, and Gerberge. *Moriarty, The Plantagenet Ancestry of King Edward III, pages 135 and 229; Schwennicke, Europäische Stammtafeln, Volume III, table 657; Weis, Ancestral Roots of Certain American Colonists, 250 (18) (Note: Schwennicke makes Gautier the son of another Raoul, Count of Valois, and grandson of Raoul I. Weis says this is in error.)*

7. **Gautier II (Walter II), Count of Valois, the Vexin and Amiens,** died 1017 or 1024. He married Adele. *Moriarty, The Plantagenet Ancestry of King Edward III, pages 135 and 229; Schwennicke, Europäische Stammtafeln, Volume III, table 657*

8. **Raoul II, Seigneur de Crépy and Valois,** died 1040. He married Adelaide of Breteuil. She was the daughter of Hildouin, Count of Chartres, and Emeline. *Moriarty, The Plantagenet Ancestry of King Edward III, pages 135–136; Schwennicke, Europäische Stammtafeln, Volume III, table 657*

9. **Raoul III, Seigneur de Crépy and Valois,** died September 9, 1074. He married Adela of Bar-sur-Aube. She was said to be the daughter of Nocher III, Count Bar-sur-Aube. *Moriarty, The Plantagenet Ancestry of King Edward III, pages 135 and 137; Schwennicke, Europäische Stammtafeln, Volume III, table 657*

10. **Adela of Valois.** She married Herbert IV, (37–6) Count of Vermandois, born ca. 1032, died ca. 1080. He was the son of Eudes (Odo), Count of Vermandois, and Parvie. *Moriarty, The Plantagenet Ancestry of King Edward III, pages 134 and 136; Schwennicke, Europäische Stammtafeln, Volume III, tables 49 and 657; von Redlich, Pedigrees of Some of the Emperor Charlemagne's Descendants, page 120*

11. **Adelaide, Countess of Vermandois**, died September 28, 1124. She married Hugh Magnus (47–6), Duke of France and Burgundy, Marquis of Orleans, Count of Amiens, Chaumont, Paris, Valois and Vermandois, died October 10, 1101. He was the son of Henri I, King of the Franks, and Anna of Kiev. *Moriarty, The Plantagenet Ancestry of King Edward III, pages 51, 134, and 136; Schwennicke, Europäische Stammtafeln, Volumes II, 1 table 1, and III, tables 49 and 55 See line 37 (7)*

LINE 25 continued from line 23 (2)

3. **Charles II, "the Bald", King of the Franks**, born June 13, 823, died October 6, 877. He married (first) Ermentrude of Orleans (17–5), born September 27, 823, died October 6, 869. She was the daughter of Eudes, Count of Orleans, and Engeltrude. *Moriarty, The Plantagenet Ancestry of King Edward III, pages 16, 23, and 233; Schwennicke, Europäische Stammtafeln, Volumes I, table 2, I/1, table 4, and II, table 1*

4. **Louis II, "the Stammerer", King of the Franks**, born 844, died April 10, 879. He married Adelaide of Paris, died after 901. She was the daughter of Adelhard, Count of Paris. *Moriarty, The Plantagenet Ancestry of King Edward III, pages 16 and 21; Schwennicke, Europäische Stammtafeln, Volumes I/1, table 6, and II, table 1*

5. **Charles III, "the Simple", King of the Franks**, born September 17, 879, died October 7, 929. He married Ædgifu of England (8–4), died 951. She was the daughter of Edward "the Elder", King of England, and Ælflaeda. *Moriarty, The Plantagenet Ancestry of King Edward III, pages 21 and 31; Schwennicke, Europäische Stammtafeln, Volumes I/1, table 6, and II, tables 1 and 78; von Redlich, Pedigrees of Some of the Emperor Charlemagne's Descendants, pages 132, 164, and 264*

6 **Louis IV, "the Transmarine" King of the Franks**, born September 10, 920, died September 10, 954. He married Gerberge of Saxony (90–2 and 92–2), born 913, died May 5, 984. She was the daughter of Heinrich "the Fowler", King of the Saxons, and St. Mathilda. *Moriarty, The Plantagenet Ancestry of King Edward III, pages 25 and 35; Schwennicke, Europäische Stammtafeln, Volumes I/1,*

table 6, and II, tables 1 and 3; von Redlich, Pedigrees of Some of the Emperor Charlemagne's Descendants, pages 132, 164, and 264

7. **Matilda of France**, born 943, died November 26, 981. She married Conrad I, "the Peaceful" King of Burgundy (68–6), born 925, died October 19, 993. He was the son of Rudolph II, King of Burgundy, and Bertha of Swabia. *Moriarty, The Plantagenet Ancestry of King Edward III, pages 33, 34, and 35; Schwennicke, Europäische Stammtafeln, Volumes I, table 57, I/1, table 6, II, table 1, and III, table 736; von Redlich, Pedigrees of Some of the Emperor Charlemagne's Descendants, page 264*

8. **Bertha of Burgundy**, born 964, died January 16, 1016. She married (first) Eudes I (36–4), Count of Blois, born 950, died March 12, 995. He was the son of Thebaud I, Count of Blois, and Luitgarde of Vermandois. *Moriarty, The Plantagenet Ancestry of King Edward III, pages 34 and 117; Schwennicke, Europäische Stammtafeln, Volumes I, table 57, II, table 46, and III, table 736*

9. **Eudes II, Count of Blois**, born ca. 990, died November 15, 1037. He married Ermengarde d'Auvergne (64–9), died March 10, 1040. She was the daughter of Robert I, Count d'Auvergne, and Ermengarde of Provence. *Moriarty, The Plantagenet Ancestry of King Edward III, pages 117 and 118; Schwennicke, Europäische Stammtafeln, Volumes II, table 46, and III, table 732 See line 36 (5)*

LINE 26 continued from line 25 (7)

8. **Gerberge of Burgundy**, born 965. She married Hermann II (62–7), Duke of Swabia, died May 4, 1003. He was the son of Konrad, Duke of Swabia, and Jutta (Judith). *Moriarty, The Plantagenet Ancestry of King Edward III, pages 34, 94, and 205; Schwennicke, Europäische Stammtafeln, Volume I, tables 11 and 57*

9. **Mathilda of Swabia**. She married Friedrich II (53–5), Duke of Upper Lorraine, Count of Bar, died 1026. He was the son of Dietrich I, Duke of Upper Lorraine, Count of Bar, and Richilde. *Moriarty, The Plantagenet Ancestry of King Edward III, pages 94 and 160; Schwennicke, Europäische Stammtafeln, Volumes I/2, table 202, and VI, table 127*

10. **Sophia, Countess Bar-le-Duc**, died January 21, 1093. She married Louis, Count of Montbéliard, died 1073. He was the son of Richwin, Count of Scarpone, and Hildegarde. *Moriarty, The Plantagenet Ancestry of King Edward III, page 160; Schwennicke, Europäische Stammtafeln, Volumes I, table 4, I/2, tables 202 and 226, and VI, tables 127 and 146 See line 53 (6)*

LINE 27 continued from line 25 (6)

7. **Charles, Duke of Lower Lorraine**, born 951, died June 22, 991 or 994. He married Adelaide. *Moriarty, The Plantagenet Ancestry of King Edward III, pages 35 and 125; Schwennicke, Europäische Stammtafeln, Volumes I/1, table 6, and II, table 1; Weis, Ancestral Roots of Certain American Colonists, 148 (19)*

8. **Ermentrude (Adelheid) of Lorraine**. She married Albert I, Count of Namur. He was the son of Robert I, Count of Lomme, and Ermengarde. *Moriarty, The Plantagenet Ancestry of King Edward III, pages 125 and 128; Schwennicke, Europäische Stammtafeln, Volumes I/1, table 6, and VII, table 68 [Note: in table 6 Schwennicke refers to her as Adelheid; in table 68, he calls her Ermengarde.]*

9. **Hedwig of Namur**, died 1080. She married Gerhard IV, Duke of Upper Lorraine, Count of Alsace, died 1070. He was the son of Gerhard III, Count of Alsace, and Gisele. *Moriarty, The Plantagenet Ancestry of King Edward III, pages 128 and 130; Schwennicke, Europäische Stammtafeln, Volumes VI, table 128, and VII, table 68*

10. **Gerhard, Count of Vaudemont**, born 1057, died 1118. He married Heilwig of Egisheim. She was the daughter of Gerhard III, Count of Egisheim, and Richarde. *Moriarty, The Plantagenet Ancestry of King Edward III, pages 130, 194, and 195; Schwennicke, Europäische Stammtafeln, Volumes VI, table 128, and VII, table 68*

11. **Gisele of Vaudemont**, died before 1127. She married Renaud I, Count of Bar and Mousson, died 1149 or 1150. He was the son of Thierry I (Dietrich), Count of Montbéliard, and Ermentrude of Burgundy. *Moriarty, The Plantagenet Ancestry of King Edward III, pages 193 and 194; Schwennicke, Europäische Stammtafeln, Volumes I/2, table 226, and VI, tables 144 and 146*

12. **Clemence of Bar-le-Duc, Countess Dammartin**. She married Renaud II (51–8), Count of Clermont, died ca. 1162. He was the son of Hugh, Count of Clermont in Beauvaisis, and Marguerite de Roucy. *Moriarty, The Plantagenet Ancestry of King Edward III, page 194; Schwennicke, Europäische Stammtafeln, Volumes I/2, table 227, and III, table 653 See line 84 (10)*

LINE 28 continued from line 27 (7)

8. **Gerberge of Lorraine**. She married Lambert I (82–6), Count of Louvain, born ca. 950, died September 12, 1015. He was the son of Reginar III, Count of Hainaut, and Adele. *Moriarty, The Plantagenet Ancestry of King Edward III, page 125; Schwennicke, Europäische Stammtafeln, Volumes I/2, table 236, and II, table 1; von Redlich, Pedigrees of Some of the Emperor Charlemagne's Descendants, page 164*

9. **Matilda (Maud) of Louvain**. She married Eustace I (7–8), Count of Boulogne, died 1049. He was the son of Baudouin II, Count of Boulogne, and Adele of Holland. *Cokayne, The Complete Peerage, Volume I (Aumale), page 352; Moriarty, The Plantagenet Ancestry of King Edward III, pages 125 and 165; Schwennicke, Europäische Stammtafeln, Volumes I, table 95, I/2, table 236, and III, table 621*

10. **Lambert, Count of Lens**, died 1054. He married Adelaide of Normandy (42–8), Countess of Aumale. She was the daughter of Robert I, Duke of Normandy, and Herleve (parents of William the Conqueror). *Cokayne, The Complete Peerage, Volumes I (Aumale), pages 351–352, and XII/1 (Tony), pages 760–762 and (Appendix K), pages 30–34; Moriarty, The Plantagenet Ancestry of King Edward III, pages 165 and 184*

11. **Judith of Lens**. She married Waltheof II, Earl of Huntingdon, Northampton and Northumberland, died May 31, 1075. He was the son of Sigurd, Earl of Northumberland, and Ælflaeda. *Cokayne, The Complete Peerage, Volumes VI (Huntingdon), pages 638–639, and XII/1 (Tony), pages 760–762; Moriarty, The Plantagenet Ancestry of King Edward III, pages 183 and 184; Schwennicke, Europäische Stammtafeln, Volume III, table 621; Douglas, William the Conqueror, tables 2 and 6*

12. **Alice of Northumberland**. She married Ralph de Toeni, died ca. 1126. He was the son of Ralph de Toeni and Isabel de Montfort. *Cokayne, The Complete Peerage, Volumes VI (Huntingdon), page 639, and XII/1 (Tony), pages 760–762; Schwennicke, Europäische Stammtafeln, Volume III, table 705*

13. **Godelbreda de Toeni**. She married Robert de Newburgh (52–9), born ca. 1100, died August 30, 1149. He was the son of Henry de Newburgh, Earl of Warwick, and Marguerite of Perche. *Cokayne, The Complete Peerage, Volumes XII/1 (Tony), page 762, and XII/2 (Warwick), page 360 (g); Schwennicke, Europäische Stammtafeln, Volume III, tables 704 and 705; Bartlett, Newberry Genealogy, pages 6–7*

14. **Roger de Newburgh**, born ca. 1135, died ca. 1192. He married Matilda de Glastonia. She was the daughter of Robert de Glastonia and Alice. *Schwennicke, Europäische Stammtafeln, Volume III, table 704; Sanders, English Baronies, page 72; Bartlett, Newberry Genealogy, page 7*

15. **Robert de Newburgh**, born ca. 1175, died ca. 1230. *Schwennicke, Europäische Stammtafeln, Volume III, table 704; Sanders, English Baronies, page 72; Bartlett, Newberry Genealogy, pages 7–8*

16. **Sir Robert de Newburgh**, born ca. 1200, died 1246. He married Lucy. *Cokayne, The Complete Peerage, Volume XII (Appendix A), pages 3–6; Bartlett, Newberry Genealogy, pages 8–9 (Note: Sanders skips this generation.)*

17. **Henry de Newburgh**, born ca. 1223. He married Matilda. *Cokayne, The Complete Peerage, Volume XII (Appendix A), pages 3–6; Sanders, English Baronies, page 72–73; Bartlett, Newberry Genealogy, page 9; Urmston, Records of the Anglo-Norman House of Glanville, page 72*

18. **John de Newburgh**, born ca. 1250, died ca. 1309. He married Margery. *Sanders, English Baronies, page 73; Bartlett, Newberry Genealogy, page 9; Urmston, Records of the Anglo-Norman House of Glanville, page 72*

19. Robert de Newburgh, born ca. 1280, died 1338. He married Margaret. *Sanders, English Baronies, page 73; Bartlett, Newberry Genealogy, pages 9–10; Urmston, Records of the Anglo-Norman House of Glanville, page 72*

20. Sir Thomas de Newburgh, born ca. 1315, died ca. 1365. He married Hawise, died November 1381. *Bartlett, Newberry Genealogy, page 10; Urmston, Records of the Anglo-Norman House of Glanville, page 72*

21. John de Newburgh, born ca. 1340, died June 4, 1381. He married Margaret Poyntz (43–20). She was the daughter of Nicholas Poyntz, Baron Poyntz, and Eleanor Erleigh. *Cokayne, The Complete Peerage, Volume X (Poyntz), page 676; Banks, Baronia Anglica Concentrata, Volume I, page 374; Bartlett, Newberry Genealogy, page 10; MacLean, Historical and Genealogical Memoir of the Family of Poyntz, pages 27–29*

22. John de Newburgh, born ca. 1370, died ca. 1440. He married Joan de la Mare, died 1426. She was the daughter of John de la Mare. *Banks, Baronia Anglica Concentrata, Volume I, page 374; Bartlett, Newberry Genealogy, page 11; Weis, Ancestral Roots of Certain American Colonists, 253 (34)*

23. Alice de Newburgh. She married John FitzJames, born 1413, died 1476. He was the son of John FitzJames and Isabel. *Wedgwood, History of Parliament, page 332; Bartlett, Newberry Genealogy, page 11*

24. John FitzJames, born 1443, died 1510. He married Elizabeth Bluett. She was the daughter of William Bluett. *Wedgwood, History of Parliament, page 332; Weaver, The Visitation of Somerset, page 106*

25. Isabel (or Mary) FitzJames, born ca. 1476. She married Thomas Michell, died 1503. He was the son of Walter Michell and Agnes. *Weaver, The Visitation of Somerset, page 10; Burke, Burke's Peerage (Malet), page 1512; Malet, Notices of an English Branch of the Malet Family, page 43*

26. Isabel Michell. She married Hugh Malet (2–18), died 1541. He was the son of William Malet and Alice Young. *Weaver, The Visitation of Somerset, pages 45–46; Burke, Burke's Peerage (Malet), page 1512; Malet, Notices of an English Branch of the Malet Family, pages 43–44*

27. Elizabeth Malet. She married Thomas Ivye. He was the son of Richard Ivye and Isabel Canning. *Weaver, The Visitation of Somerset, pages 45, 46, and 50; Malet, Notices of an English Branch of the Malet Family, page 43; Prather, Praters in Wiltshire, page 22 (Prather references Wiltshire, the Topographical Collections of John Auberry, F.R.S., A.D. 1659–70, page 89; and Historical Southern Families, Volume 6, by John Bennet Boddie, pages 21–23) See line 2 (19)*

LINE 29 continued from line 25 (4)

5. Ermentrude of France, a daughter born ca. 870. It is not known whom Ermentrude married. *Moriarty, The Plantagenet Ancestry of King Edward III, page 21; Schwennicke, Europäische Stammtafeln, Volumes I/1, table 6, and II, table 1*

6. Kunegunde, born about 890. She married (first) Wigeric, Count d'Ardennes, died ca 919. *Moriarty, The Plantagenet Ancestry of King Edward III, page 126; Schwennicke, Europäische Stammtafeln, Volumes I/2, table 202, II, table 1, and VI, table 127*

7. Friedrich I, Count of Bar, Duke of Upper Lorraine, died 978. He married Beatrice (53–3). She was the daughter of Hugh "the Great", Count of Paris, and Hedwig of Saxony. *Moriarty, The Plantagenet Ancestry of King Edward III, pages 126 and 160; Schwennicke, Europäische Stammtafeln, Volumes I/2, table 202, II, table 11, and VI, table 127*

8. Dietrich I, Count of Bar, Duke of Upper Lorraine, died ca. 1030. He married Richilde. She was the daughter of Folmer I, Count of Metz. *Moriarty, The Plantagenet Ancestry of King Edward III, pages 160 and 190; Schwennicke, Europäische Stammtafeln, Volumes I/2, table 202, and VI, table 127 See line 53 (4)*

LINE 30 continued from Line 29 (5)

6. **Kunegunde**, born about 890. She married (first) Wigeric, Count d'Ardennes. She married (second) Richwin, Count of Verdun, died 923. *Moriarty, The Plantagenet Ancestry of King Edward III, page 21; Schwennicke, Europäische Stammtafeln, Volumes I/2, table 202, and VI, table 127*

7. **Siegfried, Count of Luxembourg**, died October 28, 998. He married Hedwig, died December 13, 992. She may have been the daughter of Eberhard, Count in the Nordgau. *Moriarty, The Plantagenet Ancestry of King Edward III, pages 21 and 22; Schwennicke, Europäische Stammtafeln, Volumes I/2, table 203, and VI, tables 127 and 128; Weis, Ancestral Roots of Certain American Colonists, 143 (18–19) (Note: Schwennicke makes Siegfried the son of Wigeric, but Weis says he more probably was the son of Richwin.) See line 114 (1)*

LINE 31 continued from line 25 (3)

4. **Judith of France**, born ca. 846. She married Baldwin I, Count of Flanders, died 879. *Moriarty, The Plantagenet Ancestry of King Edward III, pages 14 and 16; Schwennicke, Europäische Stammtafeln, Volume II, tables 1 and 5*

5. **Baldwin II, Count of Flanders**, born 865, died January 2, 918. He married Ælfrida of Wessex, (5–3), died June 7, 929. She was the daughter of Alfred the Great, King of Wessex, and Æthelswida. *Moriarty, The Plantagenet Ancestry of King Edward III, pages 14 and 16; Schwennicke, Europäische Stammtafeln, Volume II, tables 5 and 78*

6. **Arnold I, Count of Flanders**, born ca. 890, died March 27, 964. He married Adela of Vermandois (34–3), born ca. 915, died 960. She was the daughter of Herbert II, Count of Vermandois, and Hildebrante, the daughter of Robert I, King of the Franks. *Moriarty, The Plantagenet Ancestry of King Edward III, pages 6 and 14; Schwennicke, Europäische Stammtafeln, Volumes II, table 5, and III, table 49 See line 5 (4)*

6. **Adalulf, Count of Boulogne**, died November 13, 933. It is not known whom Adalulf married. *Schwennicke, Europäische Stammtafeln, Volume II, table 5; Mickel, Les Enfances Godefroi, page 63; Bridgeford, The Hidden History in the Bayeux Tapestry, page xii*

7. **Arnulf I, Count of Boulogne**, died 972. It is not known whom Arnulf married. *Schwennicke, Europäische Stammtafeln, Volume II, table 5; Mickel, Les Enfances Godefroi, page 63; Bridgeford, The Hidden History in the Bayeux Tapestry, page xii; Chibnall, Proceedings of the Battle Conference, table 1*

8. **Arnulf II, Count of Boulogne**, died 990. It is not known whom Arnulf married. *Bridgeford, The Hidden History in the Bayeux Tapestry, page xii; Chibnall, Proceedings of the Battle Conference, table 1*

9. **Baudouin II, Count of Boulogne**, died 1033. He married Adele of Holland (7–7 & 115–3). She was the daughter of Arnulf, Count of Holland, and Liutgarde of Luxembourg. *Mickel, Les Enfances Godefroi, pages 63–64; Bridgeford, The Hidden History in the Bayeux Tapestry, page xii; Chibnall, Proceedings of the Battle Conference, table 1*

10. **Eustace I, Count of Boulogne**, died ca. 1049. He married Matilda (Maud) of Louvain (28–9). She was the daughter of Lambert I, Count of Louvain, and Gerberge of Lorraine. *Cokayne, The Complete Peerage, Volume I (Aumale), page 352; Moriarty, The Plantagenet Ancestry of King Edward III, pages 125 and 165; Schwennicke, Europäische Stammtafeln, Volumes I, table 95, I/2, table 236, and III, table 621* **See line 7 (8)**

3. **Charles II, "the Bald", King of the Franks** married (second) Richilde (Richaut) of Metz (87–5). She was the daughter of Bouvin, Count of Metz. *Moriarty, The Plantagenet Ancestry of King Edward III, pages 16, 37, 51, and 234; Schwennicke, Europäische Stammtafeln, Volumes I/1, table 4, and II, tables 1 and 189*

Charles II, "the Bald", King of the Franks
from the Psalter of Charles the Bald

4. Richilde (Rothilde) of France, died ca. 928. She married (as her second husband) Roger, Count of Maine, died before October 31, 900. *Moriarty, The Plantagenet Ancestry of King Edward III, page 37; Schwennicke, Europäische Stammtafeln, Volumes I/1, table 6, and II, table 1; Weis, Ancestral Roots of Certain American Colonists, 49 (17)*

5. Richilde. She married Thebaud, Count of Chartres, died 904. *Moriarty, The Plantagenet Ancestry of King Edward III, pages 36 and 37; Schwennicke, Europäische Stammtafeln, Volume II, table 46; Weis, Ancestral Roots of Certain American Colonists, 49 (18)*

6. **Thebaud I, Count of Blois**, died January 16, 975. He married Luitgarde of Vermandois (36–3), died after 978, the widow of William "Longsword", Duke of Normandy. She was the daughter of Herbert II, Count of Vermandois, and Hildebrante of France. *Moriarty, The Plantagenet Ancestry of King Edward III, page 36; Schwennicke, Europäische Stammtafeln, Volume II, tables 46 and 79; Weis, Ancestral Roots of Certain American Colonists, 49 (19), and 136 (19)*

7. **Eudes I, Count of Blois**, died March 12, 995/996. He married Bertha of Burgundy (25–8), born ca. 964, died after 1010. She was the daughter of Conrad I, King of Burgundy, and Matilda of France. *Moriarty, The Plantagenet Ancestry of King Edward III, pages 36 and 117; Schwennicke, Europäische Stammtafeln, Volumes I, table 57, and II, tables 11 and 46* **See line 36 (4)**

LINE 34

1. **Robert I, Count of Paris, King of the Franks**, born 866, died June 15, 923. He was the son of Robert "the Strong", Count of Paris, and Adelaide of Alsace. He married (first) Aelis. *Moriarty, The Plantagenet Ancestry of King Edward III, page 9; Schwennicke, Europäische Stammtafeln, Volumes II, table 10, and III, table 49*

2. **Hildebrante of France**. She married Herbert II (57–5), Count of Vermandois and Troyes, born ca. 885, died ca. 943. He was the son of Herbert I, Count of Vermandois, Seigneur de Senlis, Peronne and St. Quentin, and Bertha of Morvois. *Moriarty, The Plantagenet Ancestry of King Edward III, pages 6 and 9; Schwennicke, Europäische Stammtafeln, Volumes II, table 10 and III, table 49*

3. **Adela of Vermandois**, born ca. 915, died 960. She married Arnold I (5–4), Count of Flanders, died March 27, 964. He was the son of Baldwin II, Count of Flanders, and Ælfrida of Wessex. *Moriarty, The Plantagenet Ancestry of King Edward III, pages 6 and 14; Schwennicke, Europäische Stammtafeln, Volumes II, table 5 and III, table 49*

4. **Baldwin III, Count of Flanders**, born ca. 940, died ca. 962. He married Mathilda of Saxony, died 1008. She was the daughter of Hermann Billung, Duke of Saxony, and Hildegarde of Westerbourg.

Moriarty, The Plantagenet Ancestry of King Edward III, pages 14 and 17; Schwennicke, Europäische Stammtafeln, Volumes I/1, table 95, I/2, table 202, II, table 5, and VI, 127 **See line 5 (5)**

LINE 35 continued from line 34 (3)

4. **Hildegarde of Flanders**, born ca. 936, died 990. She married Dietrich II (Dirk II), Count of Holland, born 924, died 988. He was the son of Dietrich I (Dirk I), Count of Holland, and Gerberge. *Moriarty, The Plantagenet Ancestry of King Edward III, pages 14, 55, and 163; Schwennicke, Europäische Stammtafeln, Volume II, table 2* **See line 7 (5)**

LINE 36 continued from line 34 (2)

3. **Luitgarde of Vermandois**, died 978. She married Thebaud I, (33–6), Count of Blois, died January 16, 975. He was the son of Thebaud, Count of Chartres, and Richilde. *Moriarty, The Plantagenet Ancestry of King Edward III, pages 6 and 36; Schwennicke, Europäische Stammtafeln, Volumes II, table 46, and III, table 49*

4. **Eudes I, Count of Blois**, died March 12, 995 or 996. He married Bertha of Burgundy (25–8), born ca. 964, died after 1010. She was the daughter of Conrad I, King of Burgundy, and Matilda of France. *Moriarty, The Plantagenet Ancestry of King Edward III, pages 36 and 117; Schwennicke, Europäische Stammtafeln, Volumes I, table 57, and II, tables 11 and 46*

5. **Eudes II, Count of Blois**, born ca. 990, died November 15, 1037. He married Ermengarde d'Auvergne (64–9), died March 10, 1040. She was the daughter of Robert I, Count d'Auvergne, and Ermengarde of Provence. *Moriarty, The Plantagenet Ancestry of King Edward III, pages 117 and 118; Schwennicke, Europäische Stammtafeln, Volumes II, table 46, and III, table 732*

6. **Bertha of Blois**, born ca. 1012, died June 1084. She married Alan III (40–7), Duke of Brittany, born ca. 997, died October 1, 1040. He was the son of Geoffrey, Duke of Brittany, and Hawise of Normandy. *Cokayne, The Complete Peerage, Volume X (Richmond), page 780; Schwennicke, Europäische Stammtafeln, Volume II, tables 46 and 75* **See line 64 (10)**

3. **Albert I, Count of Vermandois**, born ca. 920, died 987 or 988. He married Gerberge of Lorraine (91–3), born ca. 935. She was the daughter of Giselbert, Duke of Lorraine, and Gerberge of Saxony. *Moriarty, The Plantagenet Ancestry of King Edward III, pages 6, 39, and 134; Schwennicke, Europäische Stammtafeln, Volumes I, table 95, and III, table 49*

4. **Herbert III, Count of Vermandois**, born ca. 955, died 993. He married Ermengarde of Bar. She was the daughter of Renaud, Count of Bar-sur-Seine. *Moriarty, The Plantagenet Ancestry of King Edward III, pages 134–135; Schwennicke, Europäische Stammtafeln, Volume III, table 49; von Redlich, Pedigrees of Some of the Emperor Charlemagne's Descendants, page 120*

5. **Eudes (Odo), Count of Vermandois**, born before 993, died May 25, 1045. He married Parvie. *Moriarty, The Plantagenet Ancestry of King Edward III, page 134; Schwennicke, Europäische Stammtafeln, Volume III, table 49; von Redlich, Pedigrees of Some of the Emperor Charlemagne's Descendants, page 120*

6. **Herbert IV, Count of Vermandois**, born ca. 1032, died ca. 1080. He married Adela of Valois. She was the daughter of Raoul III, Seigneur de Crépy and Valois, and Adela of Bar-sur-Aube. *Moriarty, The Plantagenet Ancestry of King Edward III, pages 134 and 136; Schwennicke, Europäische Stammtafeln, Volume III, tables 49 and 657*

7. **Adelaide, Countess of Vermandois**, died September 28, 1124. She married Hugh Magnus (47–6), Duke of France and Burgundy, Marquis of Orleans, Count of Amiens, Chaumont, Paris, Valois and Vermandois, died October 10, 1101. He was the son of Henri I, King of the Franks, and Anna of Kiev. *Moriarty, The Plantagenet Ancestry of King Edward III, pages 51, 134, and 136; Schwennicke, Europäische Stammtafeln, Volumes II, table 11, and III, tables 49 and 55*

8. **Isabel of Vermandois**, born 1081, died February 13, 1131. She married Robert de Beaumont, Count of Meulan, Earl of Leicester, born ca. 1046, died June 5, 1118. He was the son of Roger de Beaumont

and Aveline, Countess of Meulan. *Cokayne, The Complete Peerage, Volumes VII (Leicester), pages 520 and 523–526, and XII/1 (Appendix J), pages 26–29; Moriarty, The Plantagenet Ancestry of King Edward III, pages 134 and 184*

9. **Isabel de Beaumont**, born ca. 1102. She married Gilbert de Clare (50–9 and 99–17), Earl of Pembroke, born 1100, died January 6, 1147. He was the son of Gilbert FitzRichard de Clare, Earl of Clare, and Adelaide de Clermont. *Cokayne, The Complete Peerage, Volumes III (Clare), page 243 (d), VII (Leicester), page 520, and X (Pembroke), page 351; Schwennicke, Europäische Stammtafeln, Volume III, tables 156 and 700*

10. **Richard "Strongbow" de Clare, Earl of Pembroke**, born 1130, died April 5, 1176. He married Aoife (Eva) of Leinster (16–7), born 1145, died 1187. She was the daughter of Diarmait Mac Murchada, King of Leinster, and Mor Ní Tuathail. *Cokayne, The Complete Peerage, Volumes III (Clare), page 243 (d), and X (Pembroke), pages 352–357; Schwennicke, Europäische Stammtafeln, Volume III, table 156* **See line 50 (10)**

LINE 38 continued from line 37 (8)

9. **Waleran de Beaumont, Count of Meulan, Earl of Leicester, Earl of Worcester**, born 1104, died April, 1166. He married Agnes de Montfort (107–17), died December 15, 1181. She was the daughter of Amauri de Montfort, Count of Evreux, and Agnes de Garlande. *Cokayne, The Complete Peerage, Volumes III (Appendix D), page 714, VII (Leicester), pages 520 and 527, and (Appendix I), pages 737–738, XII/1 (Appendix J), pages 26–29, and XII/2 (Worcester), pages 829–837; Schwennicke, Europäische Stammtafeln, Volume III, tables 642 and 700*

10. **Robert de Beaumont, Count of Meulan**, died 1207. He married Maud of Cornwall (2–4). She was the daughter of Reginald FitzRoy, Earl of Cornwall, (the illegitimate son of Henry I, King of England), and Maud de Mortain. *Cokayne, The Complete Peerage, Volumes VII (Leicester), page 520, and (Appendix I), pages 739–740, and XII/1 (Appendix J), page 29; Schwennicke, Europäische Stammtafeln, Volume III, table 700* **See line 107 (18)**

3. **Robert I, Count of Troyes and Meaux**, died August 967. He married Adelaide of Burgundy. She was the daughter of Giselbert, Count of Burgundy, and Ermengarde. *Moriarty, The Plantagenet Ancestry of King Edward III, pages 6 and 10; Schwennicke, Europäische Stammtafeln, Volume III, tables 49 and 116*

4. **Adelaide of Troyes**, born 950, died 975 or 978. She married Geoffrey I, Count of Anjou, died July 21, 987. He was the son of Fulk II, Count of Anjou, and Gerberge. *Moriarty, The Plantagenet Ancestry of King Edward III, pages 4 and 6; Schwennicke, Europäische Stammtafeln, Volume III, tables 49 and 116*

5. **Fulk III, Count of Anjou**, died June 21, 1040. He married Hildegarde of Lorraine, died April 1, 1040. *Moriarty, The Plantagenet Ancestry of King Edward III, page 4; Schwennicke, Europäische Stammtafeln, Volume III, table 116*

6. **Ermengarde of Anjou**, died March 21, 1076. She married Aubri-Geoffrey (77–8), Count of Gastinois, died April 1, 1046. He was the son of Geoffrey III, Count of Gastinois, and Beatrix of Mâcon. *Moriarty, The Plantagenet Ancestry of King Edward III, pages 2 and 4; Schwennicke, Europäische Stammtafeln, Volumes II, table 82, and III, table 116*

7. **Fulk IV, Count of Anjou**, born 1043, died April 14, 1109. He married Hildegarde de Beaugency. She was the daughter of Lancelin II, Seigneur de Beaugency, and Alberge. *Moriarty, The Plantagenet Ancestry of King Edward III, page 2; Schwennicke, Europäische Stammtafeln, Volumes II, table 82, and XIII, table 45*

8. **Ermengarde of Anjou**, died June 1, 1147. She married Alan IV (40–9), Duke of Brittany, died 1119. He was the son of Hoël II, Duke of Brittany, and Hawise. *Cokayne, The Complete Peerage, Volumes X (Richmond), page 780, and XI (Appendix D), page 114; Schwennicke, Europäische Stammtafeln, Volume II, tables 75 and 82*

9. **Hawise of Brittany**, born ca. 1110. She married Geoffrey la Zouche, Vicomte Porhoët, died 1141. He was the son of Eudes I,

Vicomte Porhoët. *Cokayne, The Complete Peerage, Volume XII/2 (Zouche), page 930; Schwennicke, Europäische Stammtafeln, Volume X, table 13*

10. **Alan la Zouche, Duke of Brittany,** died 1190. He married Alice de Belmeis (44–12), born 1138, died ca. 1198. She was the daughter of Philip de Belmeis and Maud de Meschin. *Cokayne, The Complete Peerage, Volume XII/2 (Zouche), pages 930–931; Schwennicke, Europäische Stammtafeln, Volume X, table 13; Weis, Ancestral Roots of Certain American Colonists, 39 (27)*

11. **Roger la Zouche,** born 1175, died 1238. He married Margaret, living 1220. *Cokayne, The Complete Peerage, Volume XII/2 (Zouche), pages 931–932; Schwennicke, Europäische Stammtafeln, Volume X, table 13; Weis, Ancestral Roots of Certain American Colonists, 39 (28)* **See line 44 (13)**

LINE 40 continued from line 39 (4)

5. **Ermengarde of Anjou.** She married Conan I, Count of Rennes, Duke of Brittany, died June 27, 992. He was the son of Jubel Berenger, Count of Rennes, and Gerberge. *Moriarty, The Plantagenet Ancestry of King Edward III, pages 4 and 14; Schwennicke, Europäische Stammtafeln, Volumes II, table 75, and III, table 116; Roberts, The Royal Descents of 600 Immigrants, page 562; Turton, The Plantagenet Ancestry, pages 6 and 188*

6. **Geoffrey, Duke of Brittany,** died November 20, 1008. He married Hawise of Normandy (108–13), died February 21, 1034. She was the daughter of Richard I, Duke of Normandy. *Cokayne, The Complete Peerage, Volume X (Richmond), page 780; Schwennicke, Europäische Stammtafeln, Volume II, tables 75 and 79; Douglas, William the Conqueror, table 9; Turton, The Plantagenet Ancestry, page 188*

7. **Alan III, Duke of Brittany,** died October 1, 1040. He married Bertha of Blois (64–10), died 1085. She was the daughter of Eudes II, Count of Blois, and Ermengarde d'Auvergne. *Cokayne, The Complete Peerage, Volume X (Richmond), page 780; Schwennicke, Europäische Stammtafeln, Volume II, tables 46 and 75; Douglas, William the Conqueror, table 9*

8. **Hawise of Brittany**, died 1072. She married Hoël II, Count of Cornouaille, Léon and Nantes, Duke of Brittany, died April 13, 1084. He was the son of Alain Cagniart, Count of Cornouaille, and Judith of Nantes. *Cokayne, The Complete Peerage, Volume X (Richmond), page 780; Schwennicke, Europäische Stammtafeln, Volume II, table 75*

9. **Alan IV, Duke of Brittany**, died October 13, 1119. He married Ermengarde of Anjou (39–8), died June 1, 1147. She was the daughter of Fulk IV, Count of Anjou, and Hildegarde of Beaugency. *Cokayne, The Complete Peerage, Volumes X (Richmond), page 780, and XI (Appendix D), page 114; Schwennicke, Europäische Stammtafeln, Volume II, table 75*

10. **Hawise of Brittany**, born ca. 1110. She married Geoffrey la Zouche, Vicomte Porhoët, died 1141. He was the son of Eudes I, Vicomte Porhoët. *Cokayne, The Complete Peerage, Volume XII/2 (Zouche), page 930; Schwennicke, Europäische Stammtafeln, Volume X, table 13 See line 39 (9)*

LINE 41 continued from line 40 (5)

6. **Judith of Brittany**, born 982, died June 16, 1017. She married Richard II (103–13), Duke of Normandy, died August 28, 1026. He was the son of Richard I, Duke of Normandy, and Gunnora de Crepon. *Moriarty, The Plantagenet Ancestry of King Edward III, pages 13–14; Schwennicke, Europäische Stammtafeln, Volume II, tables 75 and 79*

7. **Robert I, Duke of Normandy**, died July 22, 1035. His mistress was Herleve. She was the daughter of Fulbert. *Cokayne, The Complete Peerage, Volume I (Aumale), page 351; Moriarty, The Plantagenet Ancestry of King Edward III, page 13; Schwennicke, Europäische Stammtafeln, Volume II, table 79*

8. **William the Conqueror, King of England**, born October 14, 1025, died September 9, 1087. He married (Edith) Mathilda (5–9), born 1031, died November 2, 1083. She was the daughter of Baldwin V, Count of Flanders, and Adele of France, Countess of Contentin. *Cokayne, The Complete Peerage, Volumes I (Aumale), page 351,*

and XII/1 (Appendix K), pages 30–34; Moriarty, The Plantagenet Ancestry of King Edward III, pages 13 and 15; Schwennicke, Europäische Stammtafeln, Volume II, tables 79 and 81; Douglas, William the Conqueror, page 15, and tables 1, 2, 5, and 6 See line 2 (1)

LINE 42 continued from line 41 (7)

8. **Adelaide of Normandy, Countess of Aumale**, born 1030, died before 1090. She was the sister of William the Conqueror. She married Lambert (28–10), Count of Lens, died 1054. He was the son of Eustace I, Count of Boulogne, and Matilda of Louvain. *Cokayne, The Complete Peerage, Volumes I (Aumale), pages 351–352, and XII/1 (Appendix K), pages 30–34; Moriarty, The Plantagenet Ancestry of King Edward III, pages 13, 165, and 184; Schwennicke, Europäische Stammtafeln, Volume II, table 79; Douglas, William the Conqueror, tables 2 and 6; Planché, The Conqueror and his Companions, Volume I, pages 118 and 122*

9. **Judith of Lens**. She married Waltheof II, Earl of Huntingdon, Northampton and Northumberland, died May 31, 1075. He was the son of Sigurd, Earl of Northumberland, and Ælflaeda. *Cokayne, The Complete Peerage, Volumes VI (Huntingdon), pages 638–639, and XII/1 (Tony), pages 760–762; Moriarty, The Plantagenet Ancestry of King Edward III, pages 183 and 184; Schwennicke, Europäische Stammtafeln, Volume III, table 621; Douglas, William the Conqueror, tables 2 and 6* See line 28 (11)

LINE 43 continued from line 41 (6)

7. **Richard III, Duke of Normandy**, died August 6, 1028. His mistress is unknown. *Schwennicke, Europäische Stammtafeln, Volume II, table 79; Douglas, William the Conqueror, table 1; Weis, Ancestral Roots of Certain American Colonists, 132A (23)*

8. **Alice of Normandy**. She married Ranulph I, Vicomte of the Bessin. He was the son of Anschitil, Vicomte of the Bessin. *Schwennicke, Europäische Stammtafeln, Volume II, table 79; Weis, Ancestral Roots of Certain American Colonists, 132A (24) [Note: E.S. does not name Alice]*

51

9. **Ranulph II, Vicomte de Bayeux**. He married Marguerite d'Avranches (109–16). She was the daughter of Richard le Goz, Vicomte d'Avranches, and Emma. *Cokayne, The Complete Peerage, Volume III (Chester), pages 164–166; Schwennicke, Europäische Stammtafeln, Volume III, table 694B*

10. **Ranulph le Meschin, Vicomte de Bayeux, Earl of Chester**, died ca. 1129. He married Lucy. *Cokayne, The Complete Peerage, Volumes III (Chester), page 166, and VII (Appendix J), pages 743–746; Sanders, English Baronies, pages 32–33; Farrer, Early Yorkshire Charters, Volume II, page 195*

11. **Adeliz**. She married Robert de Condet, Lord of Thorngate Castle, died ca. 1141. He was the son of Osbert de Condet, Lord of Wickhambreux, and Adelaide. *Cokayne, The Complete Peerage, Volume I (Clare), page 243: Sanders, English Baronies, pages 34–35 and 62–63; Weis, Ancestral Roots of Certain American Colonists, 132D (27), and 246B (25)*

12. **Isabel de Condet**. She married Hugh Bardolf, Lord of Waddington, Riseholm and Scothern, died ca. 1176. *Cokayne, The Complete Peerage, Volume X (Poyntz), page 671; Weis, Ancestral Roots of Certain American Colonists, 132D (28)*

13. **Juliana Bardolf**. She married Nicholas Poyntz, Lord of Tockington, died ca. 1223. He was the son of Pons FitzSimon. *Cokayne, The Complete Peerage, Volume X (Poyntz), pages 670–672; Weis, Ancestral Roots of Certain American Colonists, 132D (29); MacLean, Historical and Genealogical Memoir of the Family of Poyntz, page 28*

14. **Sir Hugh Poyntz**, died 1220. He married Hawise Malet (123–2). She was the daughter of William Malet, Baron of Curry Malet and a Magna Charta Surety, and Alice Basset. *Cokayne, The Complete Peerage, Volume X (Poyntz), page 672; Sanders, English Baronies, pages 38–39; Malet, Notices of an English Branch of the Malet Family, pages 77–79; Collinson, The History and Antiquities of the County of Somerset, Volume I (Curry-Mallett), page 32; MacLean, Historical and Genealogical Memoir of the Family of Poyntz, page 29*

15. **Nicholas Poyntz**, born ca. 1220, died 1273. He married Elizabeth Dyall. She was the daughter of Timothy Dyall. *Cokayne, The Complete Peerage, Volume X (Poyntz), page 673; Metcalfe, The Visitation of Essex, page 268; Sanders, English Baronies, page 39; MacLean, Historical and Genealogical Memoir of the Family of Poyntz, page 29*

16. **Hugh Poyntz, Baron Poyntz**, born August 25, 1252, died 1307. He married (possibly) Margaret de Paveley. She may have been the daughter of William Paveley. *Cokayne, The Complete Peerage, Volume X (Poyntz), pages 673–674; Sanders, English Baronies, page 39; MacLean, Historical and Genealogical Memoir of the Family of Poyntz, page 29*

17. **Nicholas Poyntz, Baron Poyntz**, born ca. 1278, died ca. 1311. He married Elizabeth la Zouche (44–15 and 76-15), died ca. 1320. She was the daughter of Eudes la Zouche and Milicent de Cantelou. *Cokayne, The Complete Peerage, Volume X (Poyntz), pages 674–675; Sanders, English Baronies, page 39; MacLean, Historical and Genealogical Memoir of the Family of Poyntz, page 29*

18. **Hugh Poyntz, Baron Poyntz**, died 1337. He married Margaret, probably the daughter of Sir William Paveley. *Cokayne, The Complete Peerage, Volume X (Poyntz), pages 675–676; MacLean, Historical and Genealogical Memoir of the Family of Poyntz, page 29 (Note: MacLean calls Margaret the daughter of Walter Paynell.)*

19. **Nicholas Poyntz, Baron Poyntz**, died 1376. He married Eleanor Erleigh. She was the daughter of Sir John Erleigh. *Cokayne, The Complete Peerage, Volume X (Poyntz), pages 675–676; Banks, Baronia Anglica Concentrata, Volume I, page 373; Stawell, A Quantock Family, page 280; MacLean, Historical and Genealogical Memoir of the Family of Poyntz, page 29*

20. **Margaret Poyntz**. She married John de Newburgh (28–21), born 1340, died 1381. He was the son of Thomas de Newburgh and Hawise. *Cokayne, The Complete Peerage, Volume X (Poyntz), page 676; Banks, Baronia Anglica Concentrata, Volume I, page 373; MacLean, Historical and Genealogical Memoir of the Family of Poyntz, page 29; Bartlett, Newberry Genealogy, page 10*

21. **John de Newburgh,** born ca. 1370, died ca. 1440. He married Joan de la Mare, died 1426. She was the daughter of John de la Mare. *Banks, Baronia Anglica Concentrata, Volume I, page 374; Bartlett, Newberry Genealogy, page 11; Weis, Ancestral Roots of Certain American Colonists, 253 (34)* **See line 28 (22)**

LINE 44 continued from line 43 (9)

10. **William le Meschin, Lord of Skipton-in-Craven.** He married Cecily de Romilly. She was the daughter of Robert de Romilly. *Cokayne, The Complete Peerage, Volume IX (Mortimer), pages 270–272; Farrer, Early Yorkshire Charters, Volumes II, page 195, and III, page 470*

11. **Maud de Meschin.** She married Philip de Belmeis. He was the son of Walter de Belmeis. *Cokayne, The Complete Peerage, Volumes IX (Mortimer), pages 270–272, and XII/2 (Zouche), pages 930–931; Bridgeman, Collections for a History of Staffordshire, Volume 12, Addenda and Corrigenda, page 18*

12. **Alice de Belmeis.** She married Alan la Zouche (39–10), died 1190. He was the son of Geoffrey la Zouche and Hawise of Brittany. *Cokayne, The Complete Peerage, Volumes IX (Mortimer), page 271, and XII/2 (Zouche), pages 930–931; Schwennicke, Europäische Stammtafeln, Volume X, table 13; Bridgeman, Collections for a History of Staffordshire, Volume 12, Addenda and Corrigenda, page 18*

13. **Roger la Zouche,** born 1175, died 1238. He married Margaret, living 1220. *Cokayne, The Complete Peerage, Volume XII/2 (Zouche), pages 931–932; Schwennicke, Europäische Stammtafeln, Volume X, table 13; Bridgeman, Collections for a History of Staffordshire, Volume 12, Addenda and Corrigenda, page 18*

14. **Eudes la Zouche,** died May, 1279. He married Milicent de Cantelou (9–27 and 76–14), died January 7, 1299. She was the daughter of William de Cantelou, Baron Abergavenny, and Eve de Braose. *Cokayne, The Complete Peerage, Volumes I (Abergavenny), pages 22–23 (a), X (Poyntz), page 674, and XII/2 (Zouche), page 937; Schwennicke, Europäische Stammtafeln, Volume X, table 13*

15. **Elizabeth la Zouche.** She married Nicholas Poyntz (43–17), Baron Poyntz, died 1311. He was the son of Hugh Poyntz, Baron Poyntz, and (possibly) Margaret de Paveley. *Cokayne, The Complete Peerage, Volume X (Poyntz), page 674; MacLean, Historical and Genealogical Memoir of the Family of Poyntz, page 29*

16. **Hugh Poyntz, Baron Poyntz,** died 1337. He married Margaret, probably the daughter of Sir William Paveley. *Cokayne, The Complete Peerage, Volume X (Poyntz), pages 675–676; MacLean, Historical and Genealogical Memoir of the Family of Poyntz, page 29 (Note: MacLean calls Margaret the daughter of Walter Paynell.) See line 43 (18)*

LINE 45 continued from line 41 (6)

7. **Adelaide (Judith) of Normandy.** She married Renaud I (84–6), Count of Burgundy, died September of 1057. He was the son of Otto William, Count of Burgundy, and Ermentrude de Roucy. *Moriarty, The Plantagenet Ancestry of King Edward III, pages 13, 37, and 62; Schwennicke, Europäische Stammtafeln, Volume II, tables 59 and 79; Douglas, William the Conqueror, table 5*

8. **William I, Count of Burgundy,** died November 12, 1087. He married Etienne (Stephanie). *Moriarty, The Plantagenet Ancestry of King Edward III, page 62; Schwennicke, Europäische Stammtafeln, Volume II, table 59 See line 84 (7)*

LINE 46 continued from line 41 (6)

7. **Papia of Normandy.** She married Gilbert de St. Valeri. *Schwennicke, Europäische Stammtafeln, Volume II, table 79; Aungier, History and Antiquities of Syon Monastery, pages 193–194; Crispin, The Falaise Roll, page 9; Planché, The Conqueror and his Companions, Volume II, page 208*

8. **Bernard de St. Valeri.** It is not known whom Bernard married. *Aungier, History and Antiquities of Syon Monastery, pages 193–194; Crispin, The Falaise Roll, page 9; Forester, The Ecclesiastical History of England and Normandy, page 266; Planché, The Conqueror and his Companions, Volume II, page 208*

9. **Walter de St. Valeri**. He married a daughter of Milo, Lord of Monthery and Bray, Vicomte de Troyes. *Aungier, History and Antiquities of Syon Monastery, pages 193–194; Crispin, The Falaise Roll, page 9; Forester, The Ecclesiastical History of England and Normandy, page 266; Planché, The Conqueror and his Companions, Volume II, page 208*

10. **Bernard de St. Valeri**. It is not known whom Bernard married. *Aungier, History and Antiquities of Syon Monastery, pages 193–194; Planché, The Conqueror and his Companions, Volume II, page 210*

11. **Renaud de St. Vallery**. It is not known whom Renaud married. *Sanders, English Baronies, pages 9–10; Aungier, History and Antiquities of Syon Monastery, pages 193–194*

12. **Bernard de St. Valeri**. He married Maud. *Sanders, English Baronies, pages 9, 10, and 108; Aungier, History and Antiquities of Syon Monastery, page 194*

13. **Maud de St. Valeri**, died 1210. She married William de Braose, (9–23), Lord of Braose, Bramber, Brecon and Over-Gwent, died August 9, 1211. He was the son of William de Braose, Lord of Braose and Bramber, and Bertha of Gloucester. *Cokayne, The Complete Peerage, Volumes I (Abergavenny), page 22, and VI (Hereford), pages 456–457; Sanders, English Baronies, pages 7, 89, and 108*

14. **Reginald de Braose**, died May 2, 1227. He married Grace de Briwere. She was the daughter of William de Briwere and Beatrice de Vaux. *Cokayne, The Complete Peerage, Volume I (Abergavenny), page 22; Sanders, English Baronies, pages 7 and 90 See line 9 (24)*

LINE 47 continued from Line 34 (1)

1. **Robert I, King of the Franks**, born 866, died June 15, 923 He married (second) Beatrice of Vermandois (61–5), died 931. She was the daughter of Herbert I, Count of Vermandois, and Bertha of Morvois. *Moriarty, The Plantagenet Ancestry of King Edward III, page 9; Schwennicke, Europäische Stammtafeln, Volumes II, table 10, and III, table 49*

2. **Hugh "the Great", Count of Paris, Orleans, the Vexin, and Le Mans, Duke of France,** born ca. 895, died June 16, 956. He married Hedwig of Saxony (94–2), born 921, died May 10, 965. She was the daughter of Heinrich "the Fowler", King of the Saxons, and St. Mathilda. *Moriarty, The Plantagenet Ancestry of King Edward III, pages 9, 24, and 25; Schwennicke, Europäische Stammtafeln, Volumes I, table 3, and II, tables 10 and 11*

3. **Hugh Capet, King of the Franks,** born 941, died October 24, 996. He married Adelaide of Poitou (21–8 and 97–12), born 945, died June 15, 1006. She was the daughter of William I, Count of Poitou, Duc d'Aquitaine, and Gerloc (Adele) of Normandy. *Moriarty, The Plantagenet Ancestry of King Edward III, pages 24 and 27; Schwennicke, Europäische Stammtafeln, Volume II, tables 11 and 76*

4. **Robert II, "the Pious" King of the Franks,** born March 27, 972, died July 20, 1031. He married Constance of Provence (65–8), born ca. 986, died July 25, 1032. She was the daughter of William I, Count of Provence, and Adelaide of Anjou. *Moriarty, The Plantagenet Ancestry of King Edward III, pages 24 and 28; Schwennicke, Europäische Stammtafeln, Volume II, tables 11 and 187; von Redlich, Pedigrees of Some of the Emperor Charlemagne's Descendants, page 63*

5. **Henri I, King of the Franks,** born May 17, 1008, died August 4, 1060. He married Anna of Kiev (96–9 and 116–6), born 1036, died after 1075. She was the daughter of Yaroslav I, Grand Prince of Kiev, and Ingegarde of Sweden. *Moriarty, The Plantagenet Ancestry of King Edward III, pages 24 and 51; Schwennicke, Europäische Stammtafeln, Volume II, tables 11 and 128*

6. **Hugh Magnus, Duke of France and Burgundy, Marquis of Orleans, Count of Amiens, Chaumont, Paris, Valois, and Vermandois,** born 1057, died October 18, 1101. He married Adelaide, (37–7), Countess of Vermandois, born 1050, died September 28, 1124. She was the daughter of Herbert IV, Count of Vermandois, and Adela of Valois. *Moriarty, The Plantagenet Ancestry of King Edward III, pages 51, 134, and 135; Schwennicke, Europäische Stammtafeln, Volumes II, table 11, and III, tables 49 and 55*

7. **Isabel of Vermandois**, born 1081, died February 13, 1131. She married Robert de Beaumont, Count of Meulan, Earl of Leicester, born ca. 1046, died June 5, 1118. He was the son of Roger de Beaumont and Aveline, Countess of Meulan. *Cokayne, The Complete Peerage, Volumes VII (Leicester), pages 520 and 523–526, and XIII/1 (Appendix J), pages 26–29; Moriarty, The Plantagenet Ancestry of King Edward III, pages 134 and 184; Schwennicke, Europäische Stammtafeln, Volume III, tables 55 and 700 See line 37 (8)*

LINE 48 continued from line 47 (4)

5. **Aelis (Adelaide) of France, Countess of Auxerre**, born ca. 1003, died ca. 1063. She married Renaud I (83–7), Count of Nevers, died May 29, 1040. He was the son of Landry III, Count of Nevers, and Matilda of Burgundy. *Moriarty, The Plantagenet Ancestry of King Edward III, pages 24 and 64; Schwennicke, Europäische Stammtafeln, Volumes II, table 11, and III, table 716 (Note: Moriarty makes Aelis a sister, not a daughter, of King Robert II.)*

6. **William I, Count of Nevers**, born ca. 1030, died June 20, 1100. He married Ermengarde (6–13), Countess of Tonnerre, died 1085. She was the daughter of Renaud, Count of Tonnerre, and Helvise. *Moriarty, The Plantagenet Ancestry of King Edward III, pages 64 and 65; Schwennicke, Europäische Stammtafeln, Volume III, tables 716 and 730*

7. **Renaud II, Count of Nevers**, died August 5, 1089. He married Ida. She was the daughter of Artald, Count of Lyon and Forez. *Moriarty, The Plantagenet Ancestry of King Edward III, pages 64 and 66; Schwennicke, Europäische Stammtafeln, Volume III, tables 716 and 717*

8. **Ermengarde of Nevers**. She married Miles de Courtenay, born ca. 1075, died ca. 1127. He was the son of Joceline de Courtenay and Isabel de Montlhéry. *Moriarty, The Plantagenet Ancestry of King Edward III, pages 63 and 64; Schwennicke, Europäische Stammtafeln, Volume III, tables 629 and 716*

9. **Renaud de Courtenay**, died 1161. He married (possibly Helvis) du Donjon. *Cokayne, The Complete Peerage, Volumes III (Courtenay), page 465 (c), IV (Devon), page 317, and XI (Appendix*

D), pages 108–109; Moriarty, The Plantagenet Ancestry of King Edward III, page 63; Schwennicke, Europäische Stammtafeln, Volume III, table 629

10. **Renaud de Courtenay**, born ca. 1150, died September 27, 1194. He married Hawise de Courcy (100–19), died July 31, 1219. She was the daughter of William de Courcy and Maud d'Avranches. *Cokayne, The Complete Peerage, Volumes III (Courtenay), page 465 (c); and IV (Devon), pages 317–318; Schwennicke, Europäische Stammtafeln, Volume III, table 629*

11. **Robert de Courtenay, Baron Oakhampton**, born 1183, died July 26, 1242. He married Mary Vernon (2–6). She was the daughter of William Vernon, Earl of Devon, and Maud de Beaumont. *Cokayne, The Complete Peerage, Volumes III (Courtenay), page 465, and IV (Devon) pages 317 and 323, and (Appendix H), chart VI; Schwennicke, Europäische Stammtafeln, Volume III, table 629*

12. **Egeline de Courtenay**, died ca. 1292. She married Philip de Columbiers, born ca. 1205, died 1262. He was the son of Philip de Columbiers. *Cokayne, The Complete Peerage, Volume III (Columbiers), page 377; Schwennicke, Europäische Stammtafeln, Volume III, table 629; Sanders, English Baronies, page 67* **See line 2 (7)**

LINE 49 continued from line 47 (4)

5. **Adele of France, Countess of Contentin**, died January 8, 1079. She married Baldwin V (5–8), Count of Flanders, born ca. 1012, died September 1, 1067. He was the son of Baldwin IV, Count of Flanders, and Ogiva of Luxembourg. *Moriarty, The Plantagenet Ancestry of King Edward III, pages 15 and 24; Schwennicke, Europäische Stammtafeln, Volume II, tables 5, 11, and 79*

6. **Mathilda of Flanders**, born ca. 1031, died 1083. She married William the Conqueror (2–1), Duke of Normandy, King of England, born October 14, 1025, died September 9, 1087. He was the son of Robert I, Duke of Normandy, and Herleve. *Moriarty, The Plantagenet Ancestry of King Edward III, pages 13 and 15; Schwennicke, Europäische Stammtafeln, Volume II, tables 5, 79, and 81; Burke, Burke's Peerage (The Royal Lineage), page 28* **See line 5 (9)**

4. **Hedwig (Edith) Capet**, died 1013. She married Reginar IV (81–6), Count of Hainaut, died 1013. He was the son of Reginar III, Count of Hainaut, and Adele. *Moriarty, The Plantagenet Ancestry of King Edward III, pages 24 and 50; Schwennicke, Europäische Stammtafeln, Volumes I, table 95, and II, table 11*

5. **Beatrix of Hainaut**. She married Ebles I (75–7), Count of Rheims and Roucy, Archbishop of Rheims, died 1033. He was the son of Giselbert, Count of Roucy. *Moriarty, The Plantagenet Ancestry of King Edward III, page 50; Schwennicke, Europäische Stammtafeln, Volumes I, table 95, and III, table 675A*

6. **Adele (Alix) de Roucy**, died 1062. She married Hildouin III, Count of Montdidier and Roucy, died ca. 1063. He was the son of Hildouin II, Count of Montdidier. *Moriarty, The Plantagenet Ancestry of King Edward III, pages 49–50; Schwennicke, Europäische Stammtafeln, Volumes III, table 675A, and VII, table 42*

7. **Marguerite de Roucy**. She married Hugh, Count of Clermont in Beauvaisis, died 1101. He was the son of Renaud. *Cokayne, The Complete Peerage, Volume III (Clare), page 243; Schwennicke, Europäische Stammtafeln, Volume III, tables 653 and 677; Weis, Ancestral Roots of Certain American Colonists, 246 (22–23); Turton, The Plantagenet Ancestry, page 176*

8. **Adelaide de Clermont**. She married Gilbert FitzRichard de Clare (99–16), Earl of Clare, born before 1066, died 1114 or 1117. He was the son of Richard FitzGilbert de Clare, Lord of Clare, and Rohese de Giffard. *Cokayne, The Complete Peerage, Volumes III (Clare), pages 242–243, and X (Pembroke), page 348; Schwennicke, Europäische Stammtafeln, Volume III, tables 156 and 653*

9. **Gilbert de Clare, Earl of Pembroke**, born ca. 1100, died January 6, 1147 or 1148. He married Isabel de Beaumont (37–9), born ca. 1102. She was the daughter of Robert de Beaumont, Count of Meulan, Earl of Leicester, and Isabel of Vermandois. *Cokayne, The Complete Peerage, Volumes VII (Leicester), page 526 (c), and X (Pembroke), pages 348–352; Schwennicke, Europäische Stammtafeln, Volume III, tables 156 and 700*

10. **Richard "Strongbow" de Clare, Earl of Pembroke**, born 1130, died April 5, 1176. He married Aoife (Eva) of Leinster (16–7), born 1145, died 1187. She was the daughter of Diarmait Mac Murchada, King of Leinster, and Mor Ní Tuathail. *Cokayne, The Complete Peerage, Volume X (Pembroke), pages 352–357; Schwennicke, Europäische Stammtafeln, Volume III, table 156*

11. **Isabel de Clare, Countess of Pembroke**, born October 9, 1176, died 1220. She married William Marshall, Earl of Pembroke, born 1146, died May 14, 1219. He was the son of John Marshall and Sibyl Devereaux. *Cokayne, The Complete Peerage, Volume X (Pembroke), pages 358–362; Schwennicke, Europäische Stammtafeln, Volume III, table 156* **See line 16 (8)**

LINE 51 continued from line 50 (7)

8. **Renaud II, Count of Clermont**, died ca. 1162. He married Clemence of Bar-le-Duc (84–10), Countess Dammartin. She was the daughter of Renaud I, Count of Bar and Mousson, and Gisele of Vaudemont. *Moriarty, The Plantagenet Ancestry of King Edward III, page 194; Schwennicke, Europäische Stammtafeln, Volumes I/2, table 227, and III, table 653*

9. **Maud de Clermont**, died after October 1200. She married Alberic II, Count of Dammartin, died September 19, 1200. He was the son of Alberic I, Count of Dammartin. *Schwennicke, Europäische Stammtafeln, Volume III, tables 649 and 653; Weis, Ancestral Roots of Certain American Colonists, 144 (25–26) (Note: Moriarty makes Maud the daughter of Clemence's first husband, Lancelin I, Count of Dammartin, but Weis says Lancelin died d.s.p. Schwennicke agrees that Maud was the daughter of Clemence's second husband.)*

10. **Juliana Dammartin**. She married Hugh de Gournay (76–11), died 1238. He was the son of Hugh de Gournay and Melesinde de Couci. *Weis, Ancestral Roots of Certain American Colonists, 152 (27)*

11. **Milicent de Gournay**, born ca. 1185, died 1260. She married William de Cantelou, born 1180, died 1251. He was the son of William de Cantelou and Sibyl. *Cokayne, The Complete Peerage, Volume XII/2 (Tregoz), pages 18–20; Weis, Ancestral Roots of Certain American Colonists, 255A (29)* **See line 76 (12)**

7. **Beatrice of Montdidier**. She married Geoffrey II, Count of Perche, died 1100. He was the son of Rotrou II, Vicomte of Chateaudun, and Adeline of Domfront. *Cokayne, The Complete Peerage, Volume XI (Appendix D), page 112; Schwennicke, Europäische Stammtafeln, Volume III, tables 677 and 689*

8. **Marguerite of Perche**. She married Henry de Newburgh, Earl of Warwick, born ca. 1046, died June 20, 1119. He was the son of Roger de Beaumont, Seigneur de Beaumont Pont-Audemar, and Aveline, Countess Meulan. *Cokayne, The Complete Peerage, Volume XII/2 (Warwick), pages 357–360; Schwennicke, Europäische Stammtafeln, Volume III, tables 689, 700, and 704; Weis, Ancestral Roots of Certain American Colonists, 151 (24)*

9. **Robert de Newburgh**, died August 30 1149. He married Godelbreda de Toeni (28–13). She was the daughter of Ralph de Toeni and Alice of Northumberland. *Cokayne, The Complete Peerage, Volume XII/2 (Warwick), page 360; Schwennicke, Europäische Stammtafeln, Volume III, tables 704 and 705; Bartlett, Newberry Genealogy, pages 6–7*

10. **Roger de Newburgh**, born ca. 1135, died ca. 1192. He married Matilda de Glastonia. She was the daughter of Robert de Glastonia and Alice. *Schwennicke, Europäische Stammtafeln, Volume III, table 704; Sanders, English Baronies, page 72; Bartlett, Newberry Genealogy, page 7* **See line 28 (14)**

LINE 53 continuation from Line 47 (2)

3. **Beatrice**, died after 987. She married Friedrich I (29–7), Duke of Upper Lorraine, Count of Bar, died 978. He was the son of Wigeric, Count d'Ardennes, and Kunegunde. *Moriarty, The Plantagenet Ancestry of King Edward III, pages 24 and 160; Schwennicke, Europäische Stammtafeln, Volumes I/2, table 202, II, table 11, and VI, table 127*

4. **Dietrich I, Count of Bar, Duke of Upper Lorraine**, died ca. 1030. He married Richilde. She was the daughter of Folmer I, Count of

Metz. *Moriarty, The Plantagenet Ancestry of King Edward III, pages 160 and 190; Schwennicke, Europäische Stammtafeln, Volumes I/2, table 202, and VI, table 127*

5. **Friedrich II, Count of Bar, Duke of Upper Lorraine**, born ca. 995, died 1026. He married Mathilda of Swabia (26–9). She was the daughter of Hermann II, Duke of Swabia, and Gerberge of Burgundy. *Moriarty, The Plantagenet Ancestry of King Edward III, pages 94 and 160; Schwennicke, Europäische Stammtafeln, Volumes I, table 11, I/2, table 202, and VI, table 127*

6. **Sophia, Countess Bar-le-Duc**, died January 21, 1093. She married Louis, Count of Montbéliard, died 1073. He was the son of Richwin, Count of Scarpone, and Hildegarde. *Moriarty, The Plantagenet Ancestry of King Edward III, page 160; Schwennicke, Europäische Stammtafeln, Volumes I, table 4, I/2, tables 202 and 226, and VI, tables 127 and 146*

7. **Thierry I, Count of Montbéliard**, died 1105. He married Ermentrude of Burgundy (84–8), died after 1105. She was the daughter of William I, Count of Burgundy, and Etienne. *Moriarty, The Plantagenet Ancestry of King Edward III, pages 62 and 193; Schwennicke, Europäische Stammtafeln, Volumes I/2, table 226, and VI, table 146*

8. **Renaud I, Count Bar, Count of Mousson**, died 1150. He married Gisele of Vaudemont. She was the daughter of Gerard, Count of Vaudemont, and Heilwig of Egisheim. *Moriarty, The Plantagenet Ancestry of King Edward III, pages 193 and 194; Schwennicke, Europäische Stammtafeln, Volumes I/2, table 226, and VI, table 146 See line 84 (9)*

LINE 54

1. **Charles Martel, Mayor of the Palace in Austrasia**, born 689, died 741. He was the son of Pepin II, Mayor of the Palace, and Aupais. He married Rotrou, died 724. She was the daughter of St. Liutwin. *Moriarty, The Plantagenet Ancestry of King Edward III, page 9; Schwennicke, Europäische Stammtafeln, Volume I, table 2; Weis, Ancestral Roots of Certain American Colonists, 190 (11)*

Charles Martel, Mayor of the Palace
from the collection of the British Library

2. **Pepin "the Short", King of the Franks,** born 714, died 768. He
   married Bertrada of Laon (124–10), died 783. She was the daughter
   of Heribert, Count of Laon. *Moriarty, The Plantagenet Ancestry*
   of King Edward III, pages 5 and 8; Schwennicke, Europäische
   Stammtafeln, Volume I, table 2

3. **Charlemagne, King of the Franks,** born April 2, 747, died January
   28, 814. *Moriarty, The Plantagenet Ancestry of King Edward III,*
   pages 5, 7, and 220; Schwennicke, Europäische Stammtafeln,
   Volumes I, table 2, and I/1, table 4 **See lines 17 (1)** *for descents*
   from Himiltrude, **and 19 (1)** *for descents from Hildegarde*

LINE 55 continued from line 54 (1)

2. **Carloman, Mayor of the Palace of Austrasia,** born ca. 720, died
   754 or 755. *Moriarty, The Plantagenet Ancestry of King Edward*
   III, pages 5 and 7; Schwennicke, Europäische Stammtafeln,
   Volume I, table 2; Weis, Ancestral Roots of Certain American
   Colonists, 191 (11–12)

3. **Rotrude,** died 775. She married Girard, Count of Paris, died ca.
   755. *Moriarty, The Plantagenet Ancestry of King Edward III, page*
   22; Weis, Ancestral Roots of Certain American Colonists, 191 (13)

4. Bégue, Count of Paris, died 816. He married Aupais (17–2). She was the daughter of Charlemagne, King of the Franks, and Himiltrude. *Moriarty, The Plantagenet Ancestry of King Edward III, pages 22–23; Weis, Ancestral Roots of Certain American Colonists, 191 (14) (Note: some references give Aupais' parents as Louis I and Ermengarde, making her the granddaughter, not daughter, of Charlemagne.)*

5. Leutaud, Count of Paris. He may have married Grimhild (Grimeut). *Moriarty, The Plantagenet Ancestry of King Edward III, page 23* **See line 17 (3)**

LINE 56 continued from line 54 (1)

2. Duke Bernard, died ca. 784. *Moriarty, The Plantagenet Ancestry of King Edward III, page 220; Europäische Stammtafeln, Volume I/1, table 3; Weis, Ancestral Roots of Certain American Colonists, 50 (14)*

3. (A daughter, possibly named **Ingeltrude).** She was a mistress to Pepin (57–1), King of Italy, died July 8, 810. He was the son of Charlemagne, King of the Franks, and Hildegarde. *Moriarty, The Plantagenet Ancestry of King Edward III, pages 5 and 220; Schwennicke, Europäische Stammtafeln, Volumes I, table 2, I/1, table 4, and III, table 49; Weis, Ancestral Roots of Certain American Colonists, 50 (14)*

4. Bernard, King of Italy, born 797, died April 17, 818. He married Cunigunde, died ca. 835. *Moriarty, The Plantagenet Ancestry of King Edward III, pages 5 and 220; Schwennicke, Europäische Stammtafeln, Volumes I, table 2, I/1, table 4, and III, table 49* **See line 57 (2)**

Lothair I, King of Italy
from the collection of Paris Bibliotheque Nationale de France

Italy

1. **Pepin, King of Italy**, born 777, died July 8, 810. He was the son of Charlemagne, King of the Franks (19–1), and Hildegarde. His mistress was a granddaughter (56–3) of Charles Martel. *Moriarty, The Plantagenet Ancestry of King Edward III, pages 5 and 220; Schwennicke, Europäische Stammtafeln, Volumes I, table 2, I/1, table 4, and III, table 49*

2. **Bernard, King of Italy**, born 797, died April 17, 818. He married Cunigunde, died ca. 835. *Moriarty, The Plantagenet Ancestry of King Edward III, pages 5 and 220; Schwennicke, Europäische Stammtafeln, Volumes I, table 2, I/1, table 4, and III, table 49*

3. **Pepin, Count of Senlis**, died after 834. *Moriarty, The Plantagenet Ancestry of King Edward III, page 5; Schwennicke, Europäische Stammtafeln, Volumes I/1, table 4, and III, table 49; von Redlich, Pedigrees of Some of the Emperor Charlemagne's Descendants, page 120*

4. **Herbert I, Count of Vermandois**, born ca. 840, died ca. 902. He married Bertha of Morvois. She was the daughter of Guerri I, Count of Morvois, and Eve de Roussillon. *Moriarty, The Plantagenet Ancestry of King Edward III, page 6; Schwennicke, Europäische Stammtafeln, Volume III, table 49*

5. **Herbert II, Count of Vermandois**, born ca. 885, died ca. 943. He married Hildebrante of France (34–2). She was the daughter of Robert I, King of the Franks, and Aelis. *Moriarty, The Plantagenet Ancestry of King Edward III, pages 6 and 9; Schwennicke, Europäische Stammtafeln, Volume III, table 49*

6. **Adela of Vermandois**, born ca. 915, died 960. She married Arnold I, (5–4), Count of Flanders, died March 27, 964. He was the son of Baldwin II, Count of Flanders, and Ælfrida of Wessex. *Moriarty, The Plantagenet Ancestry of King Edward III, pages 6 and 14; Schwennicke, Europäische Stammtafeln, Volumes II, table 5, and III, table 49 See line 34 (3)*

LINE 58 continued from line 57 (5)

6. **Albert I, Count of Vermandois**, born ca. 920, died 987 or 988. He married Gerberge of Lorraine (91–3), born ca. 938. She was the daughter of Giselbert, Duke of Lorraine, and Gerberge of Saxony. *Moriarty, The Plantagenet Ancestry of King Edward III, pages 6, 39, and 134; Schwennicke, Europäische Stammtafeln, Volumes I, table 95, and III, table 49 See line 37 (3)*

LINE 59 continued from line 57 (5)

6. **Luitgarde of Vermandois**, died 978. She married Thebaud I, (33–6), Count of Blois, died January 16, 975. He was the son of Thebaud, Count of Chartres, and Richilde. *Moriarty, The Plantagenet Ancestry of King Edward III, pages 6 and 36; Schwennicke, Europäische Stammtafeln, Volumes II, table 46, and III, table 49 See line 36 (3)*

LINE 60 continued from line 57 (5)

6. **Robert I, Count of Troyes and Meaux**, born ca. 920, died August 967. He married Adelaide of Burgundy. She was the daughter of Giselbert, Count of Burgundy, and Ermengarde. *Moriarty, The Plantagenet Ancestry of King Edward III, pages 6 and 10; Schwennicke, Europäische Stammtafeln, Volume III, tables 49 and 116 See line 39 (3)*

LINE 61 continued from line 57 (4)

5. **Beatrice of Vermandois**, died 931. She married Robert I (34–1 and 47–1), King of the Franks, died June 15, 923. He was the son of Robert "the Strong", Count of Paris, and Adelaide of Alsace. *Moriarty, The Plantagenet Ancestry of King Edward III, page 9; Schwennicke, Europäische Stammtafeln, Volumes II, table 10, and III, table 49*

6. **Hugh "the Great", Count of Paris, Orleans, the Vexin, and Le Mans, Duke of France**, born ca. 895, died June 16, 956. He married Hedwig of Saxony (94–2), born 921, died May 10, 965. She was the daughter of Heinrich "the Fowler", King of the Saxons, and St. Mathilda. *Moriarty, The Plantagenet Ancestry of King Edward III,*

pages 9 and 24; Schwennicke, *Europäische Stammtafeln, Volume II, tables 10 and 11* **See line 47 (2)**

LINE 62 continued from line 57 (4)

5. **(Unknown) daughter of Vermandois.** She married Odo (Eudes) Count in the Wetterau, died 949. He was the son of Gebhard, Count in the Wetterau, Duke of Lorraine. *Moriarty, The Plantagenet Ancestry of King Edward III, pages 6 and 23; Schwennicke, Europäische Stammtafeln, Volume III, table 49*

6. **Konrad, Duke of Swabia,** died 997. He married Jutta (Judith). *Moriarty, The Plantagenet Ancestry of King Edward III, pages 23 and 94; Schwennicke, Europäische Stammtafeln, Volume I, table 11*

7. **Hermann II, Duke of Swabia,** died 1003. He married Gerberge of Burgundy (26–8). She was the daughter of Conrad I, King of Burgundy, and Matilda of France. *Moriarty, The Plantagenet Ancestry of King Edward III, page 94; Schwennicke, Europäische Stammtafeln, Volume I, tables 11 and 57*

8. **Mathilda of Swabia.** She married Friedrich II (53–5), Count of Bar, Duke of Upper Lorraine, died 1026. He was the son of Dietrich I, Count of Bar, Duke of Upper Lorraine, and Richilde. *Moriarty, The Plantagenet Ancestry of King Edward III, pages 94 and 160; Schwennicke, Europäische Stammtafeln, Volumes I/2, table 202, and VI, table 127* **See line 26 (9)**

LINE 63 continued from Line 62 (5)

6. **Herbert, Count of Gleiburg,** died 992. He married Ermentrude. She was the daughter of Megingoz, Count of Avalgau, and Gerberge of Alsace. *Moriarty, The Plantagenet Ancestry of King Edward III, pages 23 and 206; Schwennicke, Europäische Stammtafeln, Volume I, table 11*

7. **(Daughter) possibly Ermentrude.** She married Frederick I, (114–2) Count of Luxembourg, died 1019. He was the son of Siegfried I, Count of Luxembourg, and Hedwig. *Moriarty, The Plantagenet Ancestry of King Edward III, pages 22 and 24; Schwennicke, Europäische Stammtafeln, Volumes I/2, table 203, and VI, table 128*

8. **Ogiva of Luxembourg**, born ca. 995, died February 21, 1030. She married Baldwin IV (85–5), Count of Flanders, born 980, died May 30, 1035. He was the son of Arnold II, Count of Flanders, and Rosala of Ivrea. *Moriarty, The Plantagenet Ancestry of King Edward III, pages 22 and 248; Schwennicke, Europäische Stammtafeln, Volumes I/2, table 203, II, table 5, and VI, table 128; von Redlich, Pedigrees of Some of the Emperor Charlemagne's Descendants, page 189* **See line 114 (3)**

LINE 64

1. **Lothair I, King of Italy**, died September 29, 855. He was the son of Louis I "the Pious", King of the Franks, and Ermengarde. He married Ermengarde, died March 20, 851. She was the daughter of Hugh II, Count of Tours. *Moriarty, The Plantagenet Ancestry of King Edward III, pages 16, 20, 21, and 259; Schwennicke, Europäische Stammtafeln, Volumes I, table 2, and I/1, table 4; von Redlich, Pedigrees of Some of the Emperor Charlemagne's Descendants, page 183*

2. **Louis II, Emperor of the West**, born ca. 823, died August 12, 875. He married Engelberge, died ca. 900. She was the daughter of Gui I, Duke of Spoleto. *Moriarty, The Plantagenet Ancestry of King Edward III, pages 20 and 259; Schwennicke, Europäische Stammtafeln, Volumes I, table 2, and I/1, table 4*

3. **Ermengarde**, born ca. 855, died 897. She married Boso, (88–5), King of Provence, King of Burgundy, Count of Vienne, died 887. He was the son of Bouvin, Count of Metz, and Richilde of Arles. *Moriarty, The Plantagenet Ancestry of King Edward III, pages 20, 51, and 259; Schwennicke, Europäische Stammtafeln, Volumes I/1, table 4, and II, table 189*

4. **Louis III, "the Blind", Emperor of the West, King of Italy and Provence**, born ca. 883, died June 5, 928. He married Anna of Byzantium (117–3), born ca. 887, died ca. 914. She was the daughter of Leo VI, Emperor of Byzantium, and Zoe Tzautzina. *Schwennicke, Europäische Stammtafeln, Volume II, table 189; Weis, Ancestral Roots of Certain American Colonists, 141A (17), and 141B (18); Norwich, A Short History of Byzantium, page 161, and chart V (xxvi)*

5. **Charles Constantine, Count of Vienne**, died 962. He married Teutberga of Troyes (73–5), died ca. 960. She was the daughter of Garnier, Count of Troyes, Vicomte of Sens, and Teutberga of Arles. *Schwennicke, Europäische Stammtafeln, Volume II, tables 189 and 789; Weis, Ancestral Roots of Certain American Colonists, 141A (18); Norwich, A Short History of Byzantium, page 161, and chart V (xxvi)*

6. **Constance of Provence**, died ca. 965. She married Boso II, Comtes de Provence, Avignon, and Arles, died ca. 966. He was the son of Rotbald I, Comtes de Provence. *Moriarty, The Plantagenet Ancestry of King Edward III, page 27; Schwennicke, Europäische Stammtafeln, Volume II, table 187 (Note: Moriarty identifies Constance only as a kinswoman of Charles Constantine.)*

7. **William I, Count of Arles, Count of Provence**, born 950, died ca. 993. He married Adelaide of Anjou, died 1026. She was the daughter of Fulk II, Count of Anjou. *Moriarty, The Plantagenet Ancestry of King Edward III, pages 4, 27, and 28; Schwennicke, Europäische Stammtafeln, Volumes II, table 187, and III, table 116*

8. **Ermengarde of Provence**. She married Robert I, Count d'Auvergne, died 1032. He was the son of William IV, Count d'Auvergne, and Humberga. *Moriarty, The Plantagenet Ancestry of King Edward III, pages 28 and 118; Schwennicke, Europäische Stammtafeln, Volumes II, tables 46 and 187, and III, table 732*

9. **Ermengarde d'Auvergne**, died March 10, 1040. She married Eudes II, (25–9 and 36–5), Count of Blois, born 990, died November 15, 1037. He was the son of Eudes I, Count of Blois, and Bertha of Burgundy. *Moriarty, The Plantagenet Ancestry of King Edward III, pages 117 and 118; Schwennicke, Europäische Stammtafeln, Volumes II, table 46, and III, table 732*

10. **Bertha of Blois**, born ca. 1012, died June 1084. She married Alan III (40–7), Duke of Brittany, born ca. 997, died October 1, 1040. He was the son of Geoffrey, Duke of Brittany, and Hawise of Normandy. *Cokayne, The Complete Peerage, Volume X (Richmond), page 780; Schwennicke, Europäische Stammtafeln, Volume II, tables 46 and 75; Douglas, William the Conqueror, table 9*

11. **Hawise of Brittany**, died 1072. She married Hoël II, Count of Cornouaille, Léon and Nantes, Duke of Brittany, died April 13, 1084. He was the son of Alain Cagniart, Count of Cornouaille, and Judith of Nantes. *Cokayne, The Complete Peerage Volume X (Richmond), page 780; Schwennicke, Europäische Stammtafeln, Volume II, table 75* **See line 40 (8)**

LINE 65 continued from line 64 (7)

8. **Constance of Provence**, born ca. 986, died July 25, 1032. She married Robert II (21–9 and 47–4), King of the Franks, born March 27, 972, died July 20, 1031. He was the son of Hugh Capet, King of the Franks, and Adelaide of Poitou. *Moriarty, The Plantagenet Ancestry of King Edward III, pages 24 and 28; Schwennicke, Europäische Stammtafeln, Volume II, tables 11 and 187*

9. **Henri I, King of the Franks**, born May 17, 1008, died August 4, 1060. He married Anna of Kiev (96–9 and 116–6), born 1036, died after 1075. She was the daughter of Yaroslav I, Grand Prince of Kiev, and Ingegarde of Sweden. *Moriarty, The Plantagenet Ancestry of King Edward III, pages 24 and 51;. Schwennicke, Europäische Stammtafeln, Volume II, tables 11 and 128* **See line 47 (5)**

LINE 66 continued from line 65 (8)

9. **Aelis of France, Countess of Auxerre**, born ca. 1003, died ca. 1063. She married Renaud I (83–7), Count of Nevers, died May 29, 1040. He was the son of Landry III, Count of Nevers, and Matilda of Burgundy. *Moriarty, The Plantagenet Ancestry of King Edward III, pages 24 and 64; Schwennicke, Europäische Stammtafeln, Volumes II, table 11, and III, table 716 (Note: Moriarty makes Adele a sister, not a daughter, of King Robert II.)* **See line 48 (5)**

LINE 67 continued from line 65 (8)

9. **Adele of France, Countess of Contentin**, died January 8, 1079. She married Baldwin V (5–8), Count of Flanders, born 1012, died September 1, 1067. He was the son of Baldwin IV, Count of Flanders, and Ogiva of Luxembourg. *Moriarty, The Plantagenet Ancestry*

of King Edward III, pages 15 and 24; Schwennicke, Europäische Stammtafeln, Volume II, tables 5, 11, and 79 **See line 49 (5)**

LINE 68 continued from line 64 (3)

4. **Willa of Vienna**. She married Rudolph I, King of Burgundy, born 847, died October 25, 912. He was the son of Conrad II, Duke of Burgundy, and Waldrata. *Moriarty, The Plantagenet Ancestry of King Edward III, page 51; Schwennicke, Europäische Stammtafeln, Volumes I, table 57, and III, table 736*

5. **Rudolph II, King of Burgundy**, died July 11, 937. He married Bertha of Swabia, died January 2, 966. She was the daughter of Burchard, Duke of Swabia, and Reginlinde of Nullenburg. *Moriarty, The Plantagenet Ancestry of King Edward III, pages 33 and 35; Schwennicke, Europäische Stammtafeln, Volumes I, table 57, and III, table 736*

6. **Conrad I "the Peaceful" King of Burgundy**, born ca. 925, died October 19, 993. He married Matilda of France (25–7), born ca. 933, died 981. She was the daughter of Louis IV, King of the Franks, and Gerberge of Saxony. *Moriarty, The Plantagenet Ancestry of King Edward III, pages 34 and 35; Schwennicke, Europäische Stammtafeln, Volumes I, table 57, and III, table 736*

7. **Bertha of Burgundy**, born 964, died January 16, 1016. She married (first) Eudes I (36–4), Count of Blois, born 950, died March 12, 995. He was the son of Thebaud I, Count of Blois, and Luitgarde of Vermandois. *Moriarty, The Plantagenet Ancestry of King Edward III, pages 34 and 117; Schwennicke, Europäische Stammtafeln, Volumes I, table 57, II, table 46, and III, table 736* **See line 25 (8)**

LINE 69 continued from line 68 (6)

7. **Gerberge of Burgundy**, born 965. She married Hermann II (62–7), Duke of Swabia, died May 4, 1003. He was the son of Konrad, Duke of Swabia, and Jutta (Judith). *Moriarty, The Plantagenet Ancestry of King Edward III, pages 34, 94, and 205; Schwennicke, Europäische Stammtafeln, Volume I, tables 11 and 57* **See line 26 (8)**

73

5. **Willa of Tuscany**. She married Boso, (71–4) Count of Arles, Marquis of Tuscany, born 885, died 936. He was the son of Thebaud, Count of Arles, and Bertha of Lorraine. *Moriarty, The Plantagenet Ancestry of King Edward III, page 19; Schwennicke, Europäische Stammtafeln, Volume II, tables 59 and 186; Weis, Ancestral Roots of Certain American Colonists, 145 (18)*

6. **Willa of Tuscany**. She married Berengar II (83–3), King of Italy, died August 6, 966. He was the son of Adalbert I, Marquis of Ivrea in Turin, and Gisele. *Moriarty, The Plantagenet Ancestry of King Edward III, pages 18 and 20; Schwennicke, Europäische Stammtafeln, Volume II, tables 59 and 186* **See line 71 (5)**

LINE 71 continued from line 64 (1)

2. **Lothair II, King of Lorraine**, born 827, died August 8, 869. He married Waldrada, died 868. *Moriarty, The Plantagenet Ancestry of King Edward III, page 20; Schwennicke, Europäische Stammtafeln, Volumes I, table 2, I/1, table 4, and II, table 186*

3. **Bertha of Lorraine**, born ca. 863, died March 3, 925. She married Thebaud, Count of Arles, dead by 895. He was the son of Herbert, Marquis of Burgundy. *Moriarty, The Plantagenet Ancestry of King Edward III, pages 19 and 20; Schwennicke, Europäische Stammtafeln, Volumes I/1, table 4, and II, table 186*

4. **Boso, Count of Arles, Marquis of Tuscany**, born 885, died 936. He married Willa of Tuscany (70–5). She was the daughter of Rudolph I, King of Burgundy, and Willa of Vienne. *Moriarty, The Plantagenet Ancestry of King Edward III, pages 19 and 20; Schwennicke, Europäische Stammtafeln, Volume II, table 186*

5. **Willa of Tuscany**. She married Berengar II (83–3), King of Italy, died August 6, 966. He was the son of Adalbert I, Marquis of Ivrea in Turin, and Gisele. *Moriarty, The Plantagenet Ancestry of King Edward III, pages 18 and 20; Schwennicke, Europäische Stammtafeln, Volume II, tables 59 and 186*

6. **Adalbert, King of Italy**, born ca. 936, died ca. 971. He married Gerberge of Mâcon, died 986 or 991. She may have been the daughter of Lietaud, Count of Mâcon, and Ermengarde, or of Lambert I, Count of Mâcon, and Aelis. *Moriarty, The Plantagenet Ancestry of King Edward III, pages 1, 18, and 37; Schwennicke, Europäische Stammtafeln, Volume II, table 59; Turton, The Plantagenet Ancestry, page 42 See line 83 (4)*

LINE 72 continued from line 71 (5)

6. **Rosala (Susanna) of Ivrea**, died 1003. She married (first) Arnold II (5–6), Count of Flanders, died March 30, 987. He was the son of Baldwin III, Count of Flanders, and Mathilda of Saxony. *Moriarty, The Plantagenet Ancestry of King Edward III, pages 14 and 18; Schwennicke, Europäische Stammtafeln, Volume II, tables 5 and 59 See line 85 (4)*

LINE 73 continued from line 71 (3)

4. **Teutberga of Arles**. She married Garnier, Vicomte of Sens, and Count of Troyes, born ca. 868, died December 6, 925. He was the son of Richard. *Moriarty, The Plantagenet Ancestry of King Edward III, pages 19, 59, and 257; Schwennicke, Europäische Stammtafeln, Volume II, table 186*

5. **Teutberga of Troyes**. She married Charles Constantine (64–5 and 117–4), Count of Vienne, died 962. He was the son of Louis III, King of Provence and Italy, Emperor of the West, and Anna of Byzantium. *Schwennicke, Europäische Stammtafeln, Volume II, table 189; Weis, Ancestral Roots of Certain American Colonists, 141A (17–18)*

6. **Constance of Provence**, died ca. 965. She married Boso II, Comtes de Provence, Avignon, and Arles, died ca. 966. He was the son of Rotbald I, Comtes de Provence. *Moriarty, The Plantagenet Ancestry of King Edward III, page 27; Schwennicke, Europäische Stammtafeln, Volume II, table 187 (Note: Moriarty identifies Constance only as a kinswoman of Charles Constantine.) See line 64 (6)*

3. **Gisele of Lorraine**, died 907. She married Godefrid, King of Haithabu. He was the son of Harald Klak, King of Jutland. *Europäische Stammtafeln, Volume II, table 104; Stuart, Royalty for Commoners, 217 (38)*

4. **Reginhilde of Friesland**. She married Dietrich, Count of Ringelheim, died 917. He may have been the son of Reginhert, Count of Ringelheim, and Mathilda. *Moriarty, The Plantagenet Ancestry of King Edward III, page 26; Europäische Stammtafeln, Volume II, table 104; Stuart, Royalty for Commoners, 65 (41) and 338 (36). (Note: Moriarty does not identify the name of Dietrich's father.)*

5. **St. Mathilda (Mechtilda)**, born ca. 890, died March 14, 968. She married Heinrich "the Fowler" (90–1), Duke of Saxony, King of the Saxons, born 876, died July 2, 936. He was the son of Otto "the Illustrious", Duke of Saxony, and Hedwig, the daughter of Arnulf, Emperor of Germany. *Moriarty, The Plantagenet Ancestry of King Edward III, pages 25 and 26; Schwennicke, Europäische Stammtafeln, Volume I, table 3; Engelbert, The Lives of the Saints, pages 101–102 See line 111 (9)*

2. **Ermengarde of Lorraine**. She married Giselbert, Count of Darnau. He was the son of Giselbert, Count in the Massgau. *Moriarty, The Plantagenet Ancestry of King Edward III, pages 20 and 39; Schwennicke, Europäische Stammtafeln, Volumes I, table 95, and I/1, table 4*

3. **Reginar I, Count of Hainaut, Duke of Lorraine**, born ca. 850, died after 915. He married Alberade. *Moriarty, The Plantagenet Ancestry of King Edward III, page 39; Schwennicke, Europäische Stammtafeln, Volumes I, table 95, and I/2, table 236*

4. **Giselbert, Duke of Lorraine**, died October 2, 939. He married Gerberge of Saxony (90–2), died May 5, 984. She was the daughter of Heinrich "the Fowler", King of the Saxons, and St. Mathilda. *Moriarty, The Plantagenet Ancestry of King Edward III, pages 25*

and 39; Schwennicke, Europäische Stammtafeln, Volumes I, tables 3 and 95, and I/2, table 236

5. **Alberade of Lorraine.** She married Renaud, Count of Rheims and Roucy, died March 15, 973. *Moriarty, The Plantagenet Ancestry of King Edward III, pages 38 and 39; Schwennicke, Europäische Stammtafeln, Volumes I, table 95, I/2, table 236, and III, table 675A*

6. **Giselbert, Count of Roucy,** died 990. *Moriarty, The Plantagenet Ancestry of King Edward III, pages 39 and 50; Schwennicke, Europäische Stammtafeln, Volume III, table 675A*

7. **Ebles I, Count of Rheims and Roucy,** died May 11, 1033. He married Beatrix of Hainaut (50–5). She was the daughter of Reginar IV, Count of Hainaut, and Hedwig (Edith) Capet. *Moriarty, The Plantagenet Ancestry of King Edward III, page 50; Schwennicke, Europäische Stammtafeln, Volumes I/2, table 236, and III, table 675A*

8. **Adele (Alix) de Roucy,** died 1062. She married Hildouin III, Count of Montdidier and Roucy, died ca. 1063. He was the son of Hildouin II, Count of Montdidier. *Moriarty, The Plantagenet Ancestry of King Edward III, pages 49 and 50; Schwennicke, Europäische Stammtafeln, Volumes III, table 675A, and VII, table 42 See line 50 (6)*

LINE 76 continued from Line 75 (6)

7. **Létard de Roucy, Seigneur de Marle.** He married Matilda. *Moriarty, The Plantagenet Ancestry of King Edward III, page 50; Schwennicke, Europäische Stammtafeln, Volume III, table 675A*

8. **Ada de Roucy.** She married Enguerrand de Couci, died 1116. He was the son of Dreux, Seigneur de Boves, and Adela. *Moriarty, The Plantagenet Ancestry of King Edward III, pages 50 and 196; Schwennicke, Europäische Stammtafeln, Volume III, table 675A*

9. **Thomas de Couci,** died 1130. He married Melesinde de Creci. She was said to be the daughter of Gui II, Count d'Rochefort. *Moriarty, The Plantagenet Ancestry of King Edward III, page 196; Schwennicke, Europäische Stammtafeln, Volume VII, table 80*

10. **Melesinde de Couci**. She married Hugh de Gournay, died 1180. He was the son of Gerard de Gournay and Edith of Warenne. *Schwennicke, Europäische Stammtafeln, Volume VII, table 80; Turton, The Plantagenet Ancestry, page 90 (Note: Schwennicke does not show Melesinde's name, only that she married Hugh de Gournay.)*

11. **Hugh de Gournay**, died 1238. He married Juliana Dammartin (51–10), born ca. 1170. She was the daughter of Alberic II, Count of Dammartin, and Maud de Clermont. *Weis, Ancestral Roots of Certain American Colonists, 152 (27), and 255A (29); Turton, The Plantagenet Ancestry, page 90*

12. **Milicent de Gournay**, born ca. 1185, died 1260. She married William de Cantelou, born 1180, died 1251. He was the son of William de Cantelou and Sibyl. *Cokayne, The Complete Peerage, Volume XII/2 (Tregoz), pages 18–20; Weis, Ancestral Roots of Certain American Colonists, 255A (29)*

13. **William de Cantelou, Baron Abergavenny**, died September 25, 1254. He married Eve de Braose (9–26), born 1220, died July 1255. She was the daughter of William de Braose, Baron Braose, and Eve Marshall. *Cokayne, The Complete Peerage, Volumes I (Abergavenny), page 22, and XII/2 (Zouche), page 938*

14. **Milicent de Cantelou**, born 1250, died January 7, 1299. She married Eudes la Zouche (44–14), died May, 1279. He was the son of Roger la Zouche and Margaret. *Cokayne, The Complete Peerage, Volumes I (Abergavenny), page 23 (a), II (Berkeley), page 129, and XII/2 (Zouche), page 938; Schwennicke, Europäische Stammtafeln, Volume X, table 13; Sanders, English Baronies, page 90*

15. **Elizabeth la Zouche**. She married Nicholas Poyntz (43–17), Baron Poyntz, died 1311. He was the son of Hugh Poyntz, Baron Poyntz, and Margaret (possibly Paveley). *Cokayne, The Complete Peerage, Volume X (Poyntz), pages 674–675; Sanders, English Baronies, page 39; MacLean, Historical and Genealogical Memoir of the Family of Poyntz, page 29* **See line 44 (15)**

6. **Ermentrude de Roucy**. She married (first) Aubri II, Count of Mâcon, died 985. He was the son of Lietaud, Count of Mâcon, and (possibly) Ermengarde. *Moriarty, The Plantagenet Ancestry of King Edward III, pages 1 and 39; Schwennicke, Europäische Stammtafeln, Volume III, table 675A*

7. **Beatrix de Mâcon**. She married Geoffrey III, Count of Gastinois and Château-Landon. He was the son of Aubri, Count of Gastinois. *Moriarty, The Plantagenet Ancestry of King Edward III, page 1; Norgate, England under the Angevin Kings, Volume I, page 250; Weis, Ancestral Roots of Certain American Colonists, 118 (22)*

8. **Aubri-Geoffrey, Count of Gastinois**, died April 11, 1046. He married Ermengarde of Anjou (39–6), died March 21, 1076. She was the daughter of Fulk III, Count of Anjou, and Hildegarde of Lorraine. *Moriarty, The Plantagenet Ancestry of King Edward III, pages 2 and 4; Schwennicke, Europäische Stammtafeln, Volumes II, table 82, and III/1, table 116; Norgate, England under the Angevin Kings, Volume I, page 250; Weis, Ancestral Roots of Certain American Colonists, 118 (22)*

9. **Fulk IV, Count of Anjou**, born 1043, died April 14, 1109. He married Hildegarde of Beaugency. She was the daughter of Lancelin II, Seigneur de Beaugency, and Alberge. *Moriarty, The Plantagenet Ancestry of King Edward III, page 2; Schwennicke, Europäische Stammtafeln, Volumes II, table 82, and XIII, table 45; Norgate, England under the Angevin Kings, Volume I, page 250* **See line 39 (7)**

LINE 78 continued from line 75 (5)

6. **Ermentrude de Roucy**. She married (second) Otto William (83–5), Count of Mâcon and Burgundy, died October 23, 1026. He was the son of Adalbert, King of Italy, and Gerberge of Mâcon. *Moriarty, The Plantagenet Ancestry of King Edward III, pages 37–39; Schwennicke, Europäische Stammtafeln, Volumes II, table 59, and III, table 675A*

7. **Matilda of Burgundy**, died 1005. She married Landry III, Count of Nevers and Auxerre, died 1028. He was the son of Bodo, Seigneur de Maers. *Moriarty, The Plantagenet Ancestry of King Edward III, pages 37 and 64; Schwennicke, Europäische Stammtafeln, Volumes II, table 59, and III, table 716* **See line 83 (6)**

LINE 79 continued from line 78 (6)

7. **Renaud I, Count of Burgundy**, died September 4, 1057. He married Adelaide (Judith) of Normandy (45–7). She was the daughter of Richard II, Duke of Normandy, and Judith of Brittany. *Moriarty, The Plantagenet Ancestry of King Edward III, pages 37 and 62; Schwennicke, Europäische Stammtafeln, Volume II, tables 59 and 79* **See line 84 (6)**

LINE 80 continued from Line 75 (4)

5. **Gerberge of Lorraine**, born ca. 935. She married Albert I (37–3), Count of Vermandois, born 915/920, died 987/988. He was the son of Herbert II, Count of Vermandois, Soissons, and Troyes, and Hildebrante. *Moriarty, The Plantagenet Ancestry of King Edward III, pages 6, 39, and 134; Schwennicke, Europäische Stammtafeln, Volumes I, table 95, and III, table 49* **See line 91 (3)**

LINE 81 continued from Line 75 (3)

4. **Reginar II, Count of Hainaut**, born ca. 890, died 932. He married Adelaide of Burgundy. She was the daughter of Richard, Duke of Burgundy, and Adelaide. *Moriarty, The Plantagenet Ancestry of King Edward III, pages 39 and 50; Schwennicke, Europäische Stammtafeln, Volumes I, table 95, and II, table 59*

5. **Reginar III, Count of Hainaut**, born ca. 920, died 973. He married Adele, died 961. She may have been the daughter of Lambert, Count of Louvain. *Moriarty, The Plantagenet Ancestry of King Edward III, page 50; Schwennicke, Europäische Stammtafeln, Volumes I, table 95, and I/2, table 236*

6. **Reginar IV, Count of Hainaut**, died 1013. He married Hedwig (Edith) Capet (50–4). She was the daughter of Hugh Capet, King of the Franks, and Adelaide of Poitou. *Moriarty, The Plantagenet*

Ancestry of King Edward III, page 50; Schwennicke, Europäische Stammtafeln, Volumes I, table 95, I/2, table 236, and II, table 11

7. **Beatrix of Hainaut.** She married Ebles I (75–7), Count of Rheims and Roucy, Archbishop of Rheims, died 1033. He was the son of Giselbert, Count of Roucy. *Moriarty, The Plantagenet Ancestry of King Edward III, page 50; Schwennicke, Europäische Stammtafeln, Volumes I, table 95, I/2, table 236, and III, table 675A See line 50 (5)*

LINE 82 continued from Line 81 (5)

6. **Lambert I, Count of Louvain,** born ca. 950, died September 12, 1015. He married Gerberge of Lorraine (28–8), born ca. 975, died January 27, 1018. She was the daughter of Charles, Duke of Lower Lorraine, and Adelaide. *Moriarty, The Plantagenet Ancestry of King Edward III, pages 50 and 125; Schwennicke, Europäische Stammtafeln, Volumes I, table 95, I/2, table 236, and II, table 1*

7. **Matilda (Maud) of Louvain.** She married Eustace I, Count of Boulogne, died 1049. He was the son of Baudouin II, Count of Boulogne, and Adele of Holland. *Cokayne, The Complete Peerage, Volume I (Aumale), page 352 (a); Moriarty, The Plantagenet Ancestry of King Edward III, pages 125 and 165; Schwennicke, Europäische Stammtafeln, Volumes I, table 95, I/2, table 236, and III, table 621 See line 28 (9)*

LINE 83

1. **Berengar I, King of Italy,** born 850, died April 7, 924. He was the son of Eberhard, Marquis of Friuli, and Gisele of France (daughter of Louis I, King of the Franks). He married Bertila of Spoleto, died December, 915. She was the daughter of Suppo, Marquis of Spoleto, Count of Turin, and Berta. *Moriarty, The Plantagenet Ancestry of King Edward III, pages 18 and 19; Schwennicke, Europäische Stammtafeln, Volumes I/1, table 4, and II, table 188A*

2. **Gisele,** died 910. She married Adalbert I, Marquis of Ivrea in Turin, died 923. He was the son of Anchier (Anskar), Marquis of Ivrea. *Moriarty, The Plantagenet Ancestry of King Edward III, page 18; Schwennicke, Europäische Stammtafeln, Volume II, tables 59 and 188A; Weis, Ancestral Roots of Certain American Colonists, 146 (17)*

3. **Berengar II, King of Italy**, died August 6, 966. He married Willa of Tuscany (71–5), died after 966. She was the daughter of Boso, Count of Arles and Marquis of Tuscany, and Willa. *Moriarty, The Plantagenet Ancestry of King Edward III, pages 18 and 20; Schwennicke, Europäische Stammtafeln, Volume II, tables 59 and 186; Weis, Ancestral Roots of Certain American Colonists, 146 (18)*

4. **Adalbert, King of Italy**, born ca. 936, died ca. 971. He married Gerberge of Mâcon, died 986 or 991. She may have been the daughter of Lietaud, Count of Mâcon, and Ermengarde, or of Lambert I, Count of Mâcon, and Aelis. *Moriarty, The Plantagenet Ancestry of King Edward III, pages 1, 18, and 37; Schwennicke, Europäische Stammtafeln, Volume II, table 59*

5. **Otto William, Count of Mâcon and Burgundy**, born ca. 958, died September 21, 1026. He married Ermentrude de Roucy (78–6), died ca. 1002. She was the daughter of Renaud, Count of Rheims and Roucy, and Alberade of Lorraine. *Moriarty, The Plantagenet Ancestry of King Edward III, pages 37 and 39; Schwennicke, Europäische Stammtafeln, Volumes II, table 59, and III, table 675A*

6. **Matilda of Burgundy**, died 1005. She married Landry III, Count of Nevers and Auxerre, died 1028. He was the son of Bodo, Seigneur de Maers. *Moriarty, The Plantagenet Ancestry of King Edward III, pages 37 and 64; Schwennicke, Europäische Stammtafeln, Volumes II, table 59, and III, table 716*

7. **Renaud I, Count of Nevers**, died May 29, 1040. He married Aelis of France (48–5), Countess of Auxerre, died ca. 1063. She was the daughter of Robert II, King of the Franks, and Constance of Provence. *Moriarty, The Plantagenet Ancestry of King Edward III, pages 24 and 64; Schwennicke, Europäische Stammtafeln, Volumes II, table 11, and III, table 716 (Note: Moriarty makes Adele the daughter of Hugh Capet, and therefore the sister of King Robert II.)*

8. **William I, Count of Nevers**, born ca. 1030, died June 20, 1100. He married Ermengarde, Countess of Tonnerre. She was the daughter of Renaud, Count of Tonnerre, and Helvise. *Moriarty, The Plantagenet Ancestry of King Edward III, pages 64–65; Schwennicke, Europäische Stammtafeln, Volume III, tables 716 and 730* **See line 48 (6)**

6. **Renaud I, Count of Burgundy,** died September 4, 1057. He married Adelaide (Judith) of Normandy (45–7). She was the daughter of Richard II, Duke of Normandy, and Judith of Brittany. *Moriarty, The Plantagenet Ancestry of King Edward III, pages 13, 37, and 62; Schwennicke, Europäische Stammtafeln, Volume II, tables 59 and 79*

7. **William I, Count of Burgundy,** died November 12, 1087. He married Etienne (Stephanie). *Moriarty, The Plantagenet Ancestry of King Edward III, page 62; Schwennicke, Europäische Stammtafeln, Volume II, table 59*

8. **Ermentrude of Burgundy.** She married Thierry (Dietrich) I (53–7), Count of Montbéliard and Bar-le-Duc, died 1105. He was the son of Louis, Count of Montbéliard, and Sophia, Countess Bar-le-Duc. *Moriarty, The Plantagenet Ancestry of King Edward III, pages 62 and 193; Schwennicke, Europäische Stammtafeln, Volumes I/2, table 226, II, table 59, and VI, table 146*

9. **Renaud I, Count of Bar, and Mousson,** died 1150. He married Gisele of Vaudemont. She was the daughter of Gerhard, Count of Vaudemont, and Heilwig of Egisheim. *Moriarty, The Plantagenet Ancestry of King Edward III, pages 193 and 194; Schwennicke, Europäische Stammtafeln, Volumes I/2, table 226, and VI, table 146*

10. **Clemence of Bar-le-Duc, Countess Dammartin**. She married Renaud II (51–8), Count of Clermont, died ca. 1162. He was the son of Hugh, Count of Clermont, and Marguerite de Roucy. *Moriarty, The Plantagenet Ancestry of King Edward III, page 194; Schwennicke, Europäische Stammtafeln, Volumes I/2, table 227, and III, table 653*

11. **Maud de Clermont,** died after October 1200. She married Alberic II, Count of Dammartin, died September 19, 1200. He was the son of Alberic I, Count of Dammartin. *Schwennicke, Europäische Stammtafeln, Volume III, tables 649 and 653; Weis, Ancestral Roots of Certain American Colonists, 144 (25–26) (Note: Moriarty makes Maud the daughter of Clemence's first husband, Lancelin I, Count of Dammartin, but Weis says Lancelin died d.s.p. Schwennicke agrees that Maud was the daughter of Clemence's second husband.) See line 51 (9)*

LINE 85 continued from line 83 (3)

4. **Rosala (Susanna) of Ivrea**, died 1003. She married (first) Arnold II (5–6), Count of Flanders, died March 30, 987. He was the son of Baldwin III, Count of Flanders, and Mathilda of Saxony. *Moriarty, The Plantagenet Ancestry of King Edward III, pages 14 and 18; Schwennicke, Europäische Stammtafeln, Volume II, tables 5 and 59*

5. **Baldwin IV, Count of Flanders**, born 980, died May 30, 1035. He married Ogiva of Luxembourg (114–3), died February 21, 1030. She was the daughter of Frederick I, Count of Luxembourg, and (possibly) Ermentrude of Gleiberg. *Moriarty, The Plantagenet Ancestry of King Edward III, pages 14, 22, and 24; Schwennicke, Europäische Stammtafeln, Volumes II, table 5, and VI, table 128 See line 5 (7)*

LINE 86 continued from line 85 (4)

5. **Eudes, Count of Cambrai**. He married Odele of Bois Ferrand. She was the daughter of Thebaud, Seigneur de Bois Ferrand. *Moriarty, The Plantagenet Ancestry of King Edward III, pages 240 and 277; Stuart, Royalty for Commoners, 184 (34) See line 6 (7)*

LINE 87

1. **Boso I, Count of Arles and Tuscany**. *Moriarty, The Plantagenet Ancestry of King Edward III, page 19*

2. **Boso II, Count of Arles and Tuscany**. *Moriarty, The Plantagenet Ancestry of King Edward III, page 19*

3. **Boso III "the Old", Count of Arles and Tuscany**, died 855. *Moriarty, The Plantagenet Ancestry of King Edward III, page 19; Schwennicke, Europäische Stammtafeln, Volume II, table 186*

4. **Richilde of Arles**. She married Bouvin, Count of Metz, died ca. 864. He was the son of Richard, Count of Amiens and Meaux. *Moriarty, The Plantagenet Ancestry of King Edward III, pages 19 and 51; Schwennicke, Europäische Stammtafeln, Volume II, table 189*

5. **Richilde (Richaut) of Metz.** She married Charles II "the Bald" (33–3), King of the Franks, born June 13, 823, died October 6, 877. He was the son of Louis I, King of the Franks, and Judith of Bavaria. *Moriarty, The Plantagenet Ancestry of King Edward III, pages 16 and 234; Schwennicke, Europäische Stammtafeln, Volumes I/1, table 4, and II, tables 1 and 189*

6. **Richilde (Rothilde) of France,** died ca. 928. She married (as her second husband) Roger, Count of Maine, died October 31, 900. *Moriarty, The Plantagenet Ancestry of King Edward III, page 37; Schwennicke, Europäische Stammtafeln, Volumes I/1, table 6, and II, table 1; Weis, Ancestral Roots of Certain American Colonists, 49 (17)* **See line 33 (4)**

LINE 88 continued from line 87 (4)

5. **Boso, King of Provence, King of Burgundy,** born 835, died November 1, 887. He married Ermengarde (64–3), born ca. 855. She was the daughter of Louis II, Emperor of the West, and Engelberge. *Moriarty, The Plantagenet Ancestry of King Edward III, page 51; Schwennicke, Europäische Stammtafeln, Volumes I/1, table 4, and II, table 189*

6. **Louis III, "the Blind", Emperor of the West, King of Italy,** born ca. 883, died June 5, 928. He married Anna of Byzantium (117–3), born ca. 886, died ca. 914. She was the daughter of Leo VI, Emperor of Byzantium, and Zoe Tzautzina. *Schwennicke, Europäische Stammtafeln, Volume II table 189; Weis, Ancestral Roots of Certain American Colonists, 141A (17), and 141B (18); Norwich, A Short History of Byzantium, page 161, and chart V (xxvi)* **See line 64 (4)**

LINE 89 continued from line 88 (5)

6. **Willa of Vienna.** She married Rudolph I, King of Burgundy, born 847, died October 25, 912. He was the son of Conrad II, Duke of Burgundy, and Waldrada. *Moriarty, The Plantagenet Ancestry of King Edward III, page 51; Schwennicke, Europäische Stammtafeln, Volumes I, table 57 and III, table 736* **See line 68 (4)**

Seal from Heinrich "the Fowler", King of the Saxons

Germania

1. **Heinrich "the Fowler", King of the Saxons,** born 876, died July
   2, 936. He was the son of Otto "the Illustrious", Duke of Saxony,
   and Hedwig. He married St. Mathilda (74–5 and 111–9), died March
   14, 968. She was the daughter of Dietrich, Count of Ringelheim,
   and Reginhilde of Friesland. *Moriarty, The Plantagenet Ancestry*
   of King Edward III, pages 25 and 26; Schwennicke, Europäische
   Stammtafeln, Volumes I, table 3, and I/1, table 10

2. **Gerberge of Saxony,** died May 5, 984. She married (first) Giselbert
   (75–4), Duke of Lorraine, born ca. 880, died 939. He was the
   son of Reginar I, Count of Hainaut, and Alberade. *Moriarty,*
   The Plantagenet Ancestry of King Edward III, pages 25 and 39;
   Schwennicke, Europäische Stammtafeln, Volumes I, tables 3 and
   95, and I/1, table 10

3. **Alberade of Lorraine.** She married Renaud, Count of Rheims and
   Roucy, died March 15, 973. *Moriarty, The Plantagenet Ancestry*
   of King Edward III, pages 38 and 39; Schwennicke, Europäische
   Stammtafeln, Volumes I, table 95, I/2, table 236, and III, table
   675A See line 75 (5)

LINE 91 continued from line 90 (2)

3. **Gerberge of Lorraine,** born ca. 935. She married Albert I (37–3),
   Count of Vermandois, born 915 or 920, died ca. 988. He was the
   son of Herbert II, Count of Vermandois, Soissons, and Troyes, and
   Hildebrante of France. *Moriarty, The Plantagenet Ancestry of*
   King Edward III, pages 6, 39, and 134; Schwennicke, Europäische
   Stammtafeln, Volumes I, table 95, and III, table 49

4. **Herbert III, Count of Vermandois,** born ca. 955, died 993. He
   married Ermengarde of Bar. She was the daughter of Renaud,
   Count of Bar-sur-Seine. *Moriarty, The Plantagenet Ancestry of*
   King Edward III, pages 134 and 135; Schwennicke, Europäische
   Stammtafeln, Volume III, table 49 See line 37 (4)

2. **Gerberge of Saxony** married (second) Louis IV "the Transmarine" (25–6), King of the Franks, born September 10, 920, died September 10, 954. He was the son of Charles III "the Simple", King of the Franks, and Ædgifu of England. *Moriarty, The Plantagenet Ancestry of King Edward III, pages 25 and 39; Schwennicke, Europäische Stammtafeln, Volumes I, table 3, and I/1, tables 6 and 10*

3. **Matilda of France**, born 943, died November 26, 981. She married Conrad I, King of Burgundy, born 925, died October 19, 993. He was the son of Rudolph II, King of Burgundy, and Bertha of Swabia. *Moriarty, The Plantagenet Ancestry of King Edward III, pages 33, 34, and 35; Schwennicke, Europäische Stammtafeln, Volumes I, table 57, I/1, table 6, II, table 1, and III, table 736 See line 25 (7)*

3. **Charles, Duke of Lower Lorraine**, born 951, died June 22, 991 or 994. He married Adelaide. *Moriarty, The Plantagenet Ancestry of King Edward III, pages 35 and 125; Schwennicke, Europäische Stammtafeln, Volumes I/1, table 6, and II, table 1; Weis, Ancestral Roots of Certain American Colonists, 148 (19) See line 27 (7)*

2. **Hedwig of Saxony**, born 921, died May 10, 965. She married Hugh "the Great", (47–2) Count of Paris, Orleans, the Vexin, and Le Mans, Duke of France, born ca. 895, died June 16, 956. He was the son of Robert I, King of the Franks, and Beatrice de Vermandois. *Moriarty, The Plantagenet Ancestry of King Edward III, pages 9, 24, and 25; Schwennicke, Europäische Stammtafeln, Volumes I, table 3, I/1, table 10, and II, tables 10 and 11*

3. **Hugh Capet, King of the Franks**, born 941, died October 24, 996. He married Adelaide of Poitou (21–8 and 97–12), born 945, died June 15, 1006. She was the daughter of William I, Count of Poitou, and Duc d'Aquitaine, and Gerloc (Adele) of Normandy. *Moriarty, The Plantagenet Ancestry of King Edward III, pages 24 and 27; Schwennicke, Europäische Stammtafeln, Volume II, tables 11 and 76 See line 47 (3)*

3. **Beatrice**, died after 987. She married Friedrich I (29–7), Count of
Bar, Duke of Upper Lorraine, died 978. He was the son of Wigeric,
Count d'Ardennes, and Kunegunde. *Moriarty, The Plantagenet
Ancestry of King Edward III, pages 24 and 160; Schwennicke,
Europäische Stammtafeln, Volumes I/2, table 202, II, table 11, and
VI, table 127 See line 53 (3)*

*Descendants of Heinrich the Fowler and Mathilda
from the Pedigree of the Ottonian dynasty, in Cologne*

Rollo "the Viking", (Ganger Rolf) Duke of Normandy
from a French manuscript in the Library of Toulouse

Scandinavia

LINE 96

1. **Bjørn I, King of Uppsala (Sweden)**. He was the son of Ragnar Sigurdsson, a Danish king at Lethra, and Aslag Sigurdsdotter of Denmark. *Turton, The Plantagenet Ancestry, page 27; Stuart, Royalty for Commoners, 240 (40–39); Ashley, The Mammoth Book of British Kings and Queens, page 458*

2. **Eric III, King of Uppsala**. *Turton, The Plantagenet Ancestry, page 27; Stuart, Royalty for Commoners, 240 (38); Ashley, The Mammoth Book of British Kings and Queens, page 458*

3. **Edmund I, King of Uppsala**. *Moriarty, The Plantagenet Ancestry of King Edward III, page 54; Turton, The Plantagenet Ancestry, page 27; Stuart, Royalty for Commoners, 240 (37); Ashley, The Mammoth Book of British Kings and Queens, page 458*

4. **Eric V, King of Uppsala, King of Sweden and Scotland, Lord of Finland**. *Moriarty, The Plantagenet Ancestry of King Edward III, page 54; Sturlason, Heimskringlas, page 63; Turton, The Plantagenet Ancestry, page 27*

5. **Bjørn III, King of Uppsala**. *Moriarty, The Plantagenet Ancestry of King Edward III, page 54; Sturlason, Heimskringlas, page 64; Turton, The Plantagenet Ancestry, page 27*

6. **Eric VI, "the Victorious", King of Sweden and Denmark**, died ca. 994. He married Sigrid Storrada. She was the daughter of Skoglar Toste. *Moriarty, The Plantagenet Ancestry of King Edward III, page 54; Schwennicke, Europäische Stammtafeln, Volume II, table 114; Sturlason, Heimskringlas, pages 64 and 110; Turton, The Plantagenet Ancestry, page 27*

7. **Olav II, King of Sweden**, died ca. 1022. He married Estrid, a princess of the Obotrites, died ca. 1065. *Moriarty, The Plantagenet Ancestry of King Edward III, page 54; Schwennicke, Europäische Stammtafeln, Volume II, table 114*

8. **Ingegarde of Sweden**, died February 10, 1050. She married Yaroslav I (116–5 and 132–4), Grand Prince of Kiev, born 979, died February 20, 1054. He was the son of St. Vladimir I, Grand Prince of Kiev, and Rogneda. *Moriarty, The Plantagenet Ancestry of King Edward III, pages 53 and 54; Schwennicke, Europäische Stammtafeln, Volume II, tables 114 and 128*

9. **Anna of Kiev, Queen of the Franks**, born 1036, died after 1075. She married Henri I (47–5 and 65–9), King of the Franks, born May 17, 1008, died August 4, 1060. He was the son of Robert II, King of the Franks, and Constance of Provence. *Moriarty, The Plantagenet Ancestry of King Edward III, pages 51 and 53; Schwennicke, Europäische Stammtafeln, Volume II, tables 11 and 128*

10. **Hugh Magnus, Duke of France and Burgundy, Marquis of Orleans, Count of Amiens, Chaumont, Paris, Valois, and Vermandois,** born 1057, died October 18, 1101. He married Adelaide, Countess of Vermandois (24–11 and 37–7), born 1050, died September 28, 1124. She was the daughter of Herbert IV, Count of Vermandois, and Adele of Valois. *Moriarty, The Plantagenet Ancestry of King Edward III, pages 51, 134, and 135; Schwennicke, Europäische Stammtafeln, Volume III, table 55* **See line 47 (6)**

LINE 97

1. **Olav "Tree Hewer", King of Vermaland in Sweden.** He was the son of Ingjald Braut-Onundsson, King of Uppsala in Sweden. He married Solveig Halfdansdotter. She was the daughter of Halfdan "Gold Tooth" of Sweden. *Moriarty, The Plantagenet Ancestry of King Edward III, page 170; Hughes, The British Chronicles, Volume II, page 535; Stuart, Royalty for Commoners, 166 (42)*

2. **Halfdan "White Leg" King of the Upplands, Salver and Vestfold.** He married Asa Eysteinsdotter. She was the daughter of Eystein, King of the Upplands. *Moriarty, The Plantagenet Ancestry of King Edward III, page 170; Sturlason, Heimskringlas, pages 32–33; Hughes, The British Chronicles, Volume II, page 535*

3. **Eystein, King of Vestfold and Raumarik.** He married Hilde. She was the daughter of Erik Agnarsson, King of Vestfold. *Moriarty,*

The Plantagenet Ancestry of King Edward III, page 170; Sturlason, Heimskringlas, page 33; Hughes, the British Chronicles, Volume II, page 535

4. **Halfdan, King of Vestfold**. He married Liv. She was the daughter of Dag, King of Vestmar. *Moriarty, The Plantagenet Ancestry of King Edward III, page 170; Sturlason, Heimskringlas, page 33; Schwennicke, Europäische Stammtafeln, Volume II, table 104; Hughes, the British Chronicles, Volume II, page 535*

5. **Gudrød, King of Vestfold**. He married Alfhild. She was the daughter of Alvaren, King of Alvheim. *Sturlason, Heimskringlas, page 34; Schwennicke, Europäische Stammtafeln, Volume II, table 104; Hughes, the British Chronicles, Volume II, page 535*

6. **Olav, King of Vestfold.** *Sturlason, Heimskringlas, page 34; Schwennicke, Europäische Stammtafeln, Volume II, table 104; Hughes, the British Chronicles, Volume II, page 535*

7. **Ragnvald**. He married Thora. She was the daughter of Ragnar "the Raven". *Gjerset, History of the Norwegian People, page 119; Schwennicke, Europäische Stammtafeln, Volume II, table 104; Smyth, Scandinavian Kings in the British Isles, page 103; Hughes, The British Chronicles, Volumes I, page 274, and II, pages 528 and 535*

8. **Aseda**. She married Eystein Glumra (113–3), Jarl of the Upplands, born ca. 805. He was the son of Ivar Oplaendinge, Jarl of the Upplands. *Cokayne, The Complete Peerage, Volume X (Appendix A), page 3; Moriarty, The Plantagenet Ancestry of King Edward III, page 10; Hughes, The British Chronicles, Volume II, page 535; Turton, The Plantagenet Ancestry, page 6*

9. **Ragnvald, "the Wise", Jarl of the North and South Møre, and of Ramsdal in Norway,** died 890. He married Hiltrude (or Raginhilde). She was the daughter of Hrolf Nefja. *Cokayne, The Complete Peerage, Volume X (Appendix A), pages 3–4; Moriarty, The Plantagenet Ancestry of King Edward III, pages 10–11; Schwennicke, Europäische Stammtafeln, Volume II, table 79; Hughes, The British Chronicles, Volume II, pages 529, 530 and 535*

10. **Rollo "the Viking" (Ganger Rolf), Duke of Normandy,** born 870, died ca. 932. He married Poppa de Bayeux, born 872. She was the daughter of Berenger, Count of Bayeux. *Cokayne, The Complete Peerage, Volume X (Appendix A), page 3; Moriarty, The Plantagenet Ancestry of King Edward III, page 11; Schwennicke, Europäische Stammtafeln, Volume II, table 79*

11. **Gerloc (Adele) of Normandy,** died ca. 970. She married William I (21–7), Count of Poitou, Duc d'Aquitaine, born 900, died April 3, 963. He was the son of Ebles, Count of Poitou, and Aremburge. *Moriarty, The Plantagenet Ancestry of King Edward III, pages 11 and 27; Schwennicke, Europäische Stammtafeln, Volume II, tables 76 and 79*

12. **Adelaide of Poitou,** born ca. 945, died June 15, 1006. She married Hugh Capet (47–3), King of the Franks, born 939, died October 24, 996. He was the son of Hugh "the Great", Count of Paris, and Hedwig of Saxony. *Moriarty, The Plantagenet Ancestry of King Edward III, pages 24 and 27; Schwennicke, Europäische Stammtafeln, Volume II, tables 11 and 76*

13. **Robert II, "the Pious" King of the Franks,** born March 27, 972, died July 20, 1031. He married Constance of Provence (65–8), born ca. 986, died July 25, 1032. She was the daughter of William I, Count of Provence, and Adelaide of Anjou. *Moriarty, The Plantagenet Ancestry of King Edward III, pages 24 and 28; Schwennicke, Europäische Stammtafeln, Volume II, tables 11 and 187 See line 47 (4)*

LINE 98 continued from line 97 (12)

13. **Hedwig (Edith) Capet,** died 1013. She married Reginar IV (81–6), Count of Hainaut, died 1013. He was the son of Reginar III, Count of Hainaut, and Adele. *Moriarty, The Plantagenet Ancestry of King Edward III, pages 24 and 50; Schwennicke, Europäische Stammtafeln, Volumes I, table 95, and II, table 11 See line 50 (4)*

LINE 99 continued from line 97 (10)

11. **William "Longsword", Duke of Normandy,** born ca. 891, died December 17, 942. He married Sprota. *Moriarty, The Plantagenet*

Ancestry of King Edward III, page 11; Schwennicke, Europäische Stammtafeln, Volume II, table 79; Douglas, William the Conqueror, table 1

12. **Richard I, Duke of Normandy**, born August 28, 933, died November 20, 996. His mistress is unknown. *Moriarty, The Plantagenet Ancestry of King Edward III, page 11; Schwennicke, Europäische Stammtafeln, Volume II, table 79; Douglas, William the Conqueror, table 1*

13. **Godfrey, Count of Brionne and Eu,** illegitimate son. *Cokayne, The Complete Peerage, Volumes III (Clare), page 242, and IV (Devon), pages 308–309; Schwennicke, Europäische Stammtafeln, Volumes II, table 79, and III, table 156; Douglas, William the Conqueror, tables 1 and 5*

14. **Gilbert Crispin, Count of Brionne.** *Cokayne, The Complete Peerage, Volumes III (Clare), page 242, and IV (Devon), page 308; Schwennicke, Europäische Stammtafeln, Volume III, table 156*

15. **Richard FitzGilbert de Clare, Lord of Clare and Tonbridge,** born before 1035, died about 1090. He married Rohese de Giffard. She was the daughter of Walter de Giffard, Earl of Buckingham, and Agnes Ribemont. *Cokayne, The Complete Peerage, Volume III (Clare), page 242; Schwennicke, Europäische Stammtafeln, Volume III, table 156; Douglas, William the Conqueror, table 5*

16. **Gilbert FitzRichard de Clare, Earl of Clare,** born before 1066, died 1114 or 1117. He married Adelaide de Clermont (50–8). She was the daughter of Hugh, Count of Clermont, and Marguerite de Roucy. *Cokayne, The Complete Peerage, Volume III (Clare), pages 242–243; Schwennicke, Europäische Stammtafeln, Volume III, tables 156 and 653*

17. **Gilbert de Clare, Earl of Pembroke,** born ca. 1100, died January 6, 1147 or 1148. He married Isabel de Beaumont (37–9), born ca. 1102. She was the daughter of Robert de Beaumont, Count of Meulan, Earl of Leicester, and Isabel of Vermandois. *Cokayne, The Complete Peerage, Volume X (Pembroke), pages 348–352; Schwennicke, Europäische Stammtafeln, Volume III, tables 156 and 700 See line 50 (9)*

15. **Baldwin FitzGilbert, Seigneur de Meules,** died 1090. He married Emma. She was the cousin or niece of William the Conqueror. *Cokayne, The Complete Peerage, Volume IV (Devon), pages 308–309; Schwennicke, Europäische Stammtafeln, Volume III, table 156*

16. **(A daughter,** perhaps named **Emma).** She married William d'Avranches, died ca. 1087. He was the son of Guitmond. *Cokayne, The Complete Peerage, Volume IV (Devon), page 317; Turton, The Plantagenet Ancestry, page 127; Wright, Some Account of the Barony and Town of Okehampton, page 16 (Note: Cokayne does not name Emma.)*

17. **Robert d'Avranches.** He married a daughter of Gelduin (Godwin) de Dol. *Cokayne, The Complete Peerage, Volume IV (Devon), page 317; Wright, Some Account of the Barony and Town of Okehampton, page 16*

18. **Maud (Matilda) d'Avranches,** died September 21, 1173. She married (first) William de Courcy, dead by 1162. *Cokayne, The Complete Peerage, Volume IV (Devon), page 317; Weis, Ancestral Roots of Certain American Colonists, 138 (26); Wright, Some Account of the Barony and Town of Okehampton, page 16*

19. **Hawise de Courcy,** died July 31, 1219. She married Renaud de Courtenay (48–10), died September 27, 1194. He was the son of Renaud, Seigneur de Courtenay, and Maud. *Cokayne, The Complete Peerage, Volumes III (Courtenay), page 465 (c), and IV (Devon), pages 317–318; Schwennicke, Europäische Stammtafeln, Volume III, table 629; Weis, Ancestral Roots of Certain American Colonists, 138 (26)*

20. **Robert de Courtenay, Baron Oakhampton,** born 1183, died July 26, 1242. He married Mary Vernon (2–6). She was the daughter of William Vernon, Earl of Devon, and Maud de Beaumont. *Cokayne, The Complete Peerage, Volumes III (Courtenay), page 465 (c), and IV (Devon) page 317, and (Appendix H), chart VI; Schwennicke, Europäische Stammtafeln, Volume III, table 629* **See line 48 (11)**

LINE 101 continued from line 99 (14)

15. **Hesilia Crispin.** She married William Malet, Seigneur de Granville, died 1071. *Collinson, The History and Antiquities of the County of Somerset, Volume I (Curry-Mallett), page 32; Malet, Notices of an English Branch of the Malet Family, charts I and II, and pages 6–7; Skaife, Domesday Book for Yorkshire, page 123*

16. **Gilbert Malet**, died 1078. *Malet, Notices of an English Branch of the Malet Family, charts I and II, and pages 16–17 and 68–72; Skaife, Domesday Book for Yorkshire, page 123; Burke, Burke's Peerage (Malet), page 1511*

17. **Robert Malet, Baron of Curry Malet**, died ca. 1150. *Malet, Notices of an English Branch of the Malet Family, chart I, and pages 71–73; Weis, Ancestral Roots of Certain American Colonists, 234A (25); Sanders, English Baronies, page 38*

18. **William Malet, Baron of Curry Malet**, died ca. 1169. He married Maud Mortimer. She was the daughter of Robert Mortimer. *Malet, Notices of an English Branch of the Malet Family, chart I, and pages 73–74; Weis, Ancestral Roots of Certain American Colonists, 234A (26); Sanders, English Baronies, page 38*

19. **Gilbert Malet, Baron of Curry Malet**, died 1189/1194. He married Alice Picot. She was the daughter of Ralph Picot. *Malet, Notices of an English Branch of the Malet Family, chart I, and pages 74–76; Weis, Ancestral Roots of Certain American Colonists, 234A (27); Sanders, English Baronies, page 38*

20. **William Malet, Baron of Curry Malet**, died 1215. He married Alice Basset. She was the daughter of Thomas Basset, Lord of Headington in Oxfordshire and Colynton and Whitford in Devonshire, and Philippa Malbank. William probably had an earlier, unknown wife. *Cokayne, The Complete Peerage, Volume X (Poyntz), page 672; Malet, Notices of an English Branch of the Malet Family, pages 77–83; Weis, Ancestral Roots of Certain American Colonists, 234A (27–28); Sanders, English Baronies, page 38* **See line 123 (1)**

16. Robert Malet, Great Chamberlain of England, died ca. 1106. He married Elisée de Brionne, who may have been the mother of his son William (102–17, next). *Collinson, The History and Antiquities of the County of Somerset, Volume I (Enmore), page 91; Malet, Notices of an English Branch of the Malet Family, charts I and II, and pages 18–22; Burke, Burke's Peerage (Malet), page 1511*

17. William Malet, Sire de Granville. *Collinson, The History and Antiquities of the County of Somerset, Volume I (Enmore), page 91; Malet, Notices of an English Branch of the Malet Family, chart I, and pages 22–23; Burke, Burke's Peerage (Malet), page 1511 (Note: Collinson says William's relationship to Robert Malet is uncertain.)*

18. Hugh Malet "Fitchet", died 1150. He married Basilea. *Collinson, The History and Antiquities of the County of Somerset, Volume I (Enmore), page 91; Malet, Notices of an English Branch of the Malet Family, chart I, and pages 24–27; Burke, Burke's Peerage (Malet), page 1512*

19. Baldwin Malet, died 1195. He married Emma Neville. She was the daughter of Hugh Neville. *Collinson, The History and Antiquities of the County of Somerset, Volume I (Enmore), page 91; Malet, Notices of an English Branch of the Malet Family, chart I, and pages 27–28; Burke, Burke's Peerage (Malet), page 1512*

20. William Malet, died ca. 1252. He married Sara de Sully. She was the daughter of Raymond de Sully. *Collinson, The History and Antiquities of the County of Somerset, Volume I (Enmore), page 91; Malet, Notices of an English Branch of the Malet Family, chart I, and pages 28–29; Burke, Burke's Peerage (Malet), page 1512 (Note: Collinson calls Sara's father Robert.)*

21. William Malet. He married Mary. *Collinson, The History and Antiquities of the County of Somerset, Volume I (Enmore), page 91; Weaver, The Visitation of Somerset, page 45; Malet, Notices of an English Branch of the Malet Family, chart I, and pages 29–30; Burke, Burke's Peerage (Malet), page 1512*

22. **Baldwin Malet**, died ca. 1285. He married Mabel de Deandon. She was the daughter of Hamelyn de Deandon and Aubrea de Punchardon. *Collinson, The History and Antiquities of the County of Somerset, Volume I (Enmore), page 91; Malet, Notices of an English Branch of the Malet Family, pages 30–31; Burke, Burke's Peerage (Malet), page 1512*

23. **John Malet**, died ca. 1287. He married Sibylla de St. Cleere. She was the daughter of Robert (or John) de St. Cleere. *Collinson, The History and Antiquities of the County of Somerset, Volume I (Enmore), page 91; Malet, Notices of an English Branch of the Malet Family, pages 32–33; Burke, Burke's Peerage (Malet), page 1512*

24. **Baldwin Malet**, born 1284, died ca. 1340. He married Avicia (Hawise) Raleigh. She was the daughter of Simon Raleigh. *Collinson, The History and Antiquities of the County of Somerset, Volume I (Enmore), page 91; Malet, Notices of an English Branch of the Malet Family, pages 33–34; Burke, Burke's Peerage (Malet), page 1512*

25. **John Malet**. He married Elizabeth Kingston. She was the daughter of Sir John Kingston. *Collinson, The History and Antiquities of the County of Somerset, Volume I (Enmore), page 91; Weaver, The Visitation of Somerset, page 45; Malet, Notices of an English Branch of the Malet Family, chart I, and pages 34–35; Burke, Burke's Peerage (Malet), page 1512*

26. **Baldwin Malet**, died 1416. He married Amice Lyffe (2–13), born ca. 1360. She was the daughter of Richard Lyffe and Margery Stawell. *Collinson, The History and Antiquities of the County of Somerset, Volume I (Enmore), page 91; Weaver, The Visitation of Somerset, page 45; Malet, Notices of an English Branch of the Malet Family, pages 35–36; Burke, Burke's Peerage (Malet), page 1512*

27. **Hugh Malet**, died ca. 1466. He married Joan Roynon. She was the daughter of John Roynon and Joan Longland. *Collinson, The History and Antiquities of the County of Somerset, Volume I (Enmore), page 91; Weaver, The Visitation of Somerset, page 45; Malet, Notices of an English Branch of the Malet Family, pages 38–40; Burke, Burke's Peerage (Malet), page 1512; Richardson, Plantagenet Ancestry, page 13* **See line 2 (14)**

LINE 103 continued from line 99 (12)

13. **Richard II, Duke of Normandy,** died August 28, 1026. He married Judith of Brittany (41–6), born 982, died June 16, 1017. She was the daughter of Conan I, Duke of Brittany, and Ermengarde of Anjou. *Moriarty, The Plantagenet Ancestry of King Edward III, pages 13 and 14; Schwennicke, Europäische Stammtafeln, Volume II, tables 75 and 79; Douglas, William the Conqueror, tables 1 and 5*

14. **Robert I, Duke of Normandy,** died July 22, 1035. His mistress was Herleve. She was the daughter of Fulbert. *Cokayne, The Complete Peerage, Volume I (Aumale), page 351; Moriarty, The Plantagenet Ancestry of King Edward III, page 13; Schwennicke, Europäische Stammtafeln, Volume II, table 79; Douglas, William the Conqueror, tables 1 and 5 See line 41 (7)*

LINE 104 continued from line 103 (13)

14. **Richard III, Duke of Normandy,** died August 6, 1028. His mistress is unknown. *Schwennicke, Europäische Stammtafeln, Volume II, table 79; Douglas, William the Conqueror, table 1; Weis, Ancestral Roots of Certain American Colonists, 132A (23) See line 43 (7)*

LINE 105 continued from line 103 (13)

14. **Papia of Normandy.** She married Gilbert de St. Valeri (Vallery) *Schwennicke, Europäische Stammtafeln, Volume II, table 79; Aungier, History and Antiquities of Syon Monastery, pages 193–194; Forester, The Ecclesiastical History of England and Normandy, page 266; Planché, The Conqueror and his Companions, Volume II, page 208 See line 46 (7)*

LINE 106 continued from line 103 (13)

14. **Adelaide of Normandy.** She married Renaud I (79–7 and 84–6), Count of Burgundy, died September of 1057. He was the son of Otto William, Count of Burgundy, and Ermentrude de Roucy. *Moriarty, The Plantagenet Ancestry of King Edward III, pages 13, 37, and 62; Schwennicke, Europäische Stammtafeln, Volume II, tables 59 and 79; Douglas, William the Conqueror, table 5 See line 45 (7)*

13. **Robert, Count d'Evreux**, died March 16, 1037. He married Herleve. *Moriarty, The Plantagenet Ancestry of King Edward III, page 11; Schwennicke, Europäische Stammtafeln, Volume II, table 79; Douglas, William the Conqueror, tables 1 and 5*

14. **Richard, Count d'Evreux**, died 1067. He married Godehut. She was the widow of Roger de Toeni. *Cokayne, The Complete Peerage, Volumes VII (Appendix D), page 709, and XIII/1 (Tony), page 757; Moriarty, The Plantagenet Ancestry of King Edward III, page 11; Schwennicke, Europäische Stammtafeln, Volumes II, table 79, and III, table 705; Douglas, William the Conqueror, table 5*

15. **Agnes of Evreux.** She married Simon de Montfort, Seigneur de Montfort, died about 1087. He was the son of Amauri de Montfort and Bertrade. *Cokayne, The Complete Peerage, Volumes VII (Appendix D), pages 708–709, and XIII/1 (Tony), page 760 (a); Moriarty, The Plantagenet Ancestry of King Edward III, pages 10 and 11; Schwennicke, Europäische Stammtafeln, Volume II, table 79*

16. **Amauri de Montfort, Count d'Evreux.** He married Agnes de Garlande. She may have been the daughter of Anseau de Garlande. *Cokayne, The Complete Peerage, Volume VII (Appendix D), pages 709 and 713; Moriarty, The Plantagenet Ancestry of King Edward III, page 10*

17. **Agnes de Montfort**, died December 15, 1181. She married Waleran de Beaumont (38–9), Count of Meulan, Earl of Leicester, Earl of Worcester, born 1104, died April, 1166. He was the son of Robert de Beaumont, Count of Meulan, and Isabel of Vermandois, Countess of Leicester. *Cokayne, The Complete Peerage, Volumes III (Appendix D), page 714, VII (Leicester), page 527 (b), (Appendix D), page 714, (Appendix I), pages 737–738, and XII/2 (Worcester), pages 829–837*

18. **Robert de Beaumont, Count of Meulan**, died 1207. He married Maud of Cornwall (2–4). She was the daughter of Reginald FitzRoy, Earl of Cornwall, (the illegitimate son of Henry I, King of England), and Maud de Mortain. *Cokayne, The Complete Peerage, Volume VII (Leicester), page 520, and (Appendix I), page 740; Schwennicke, Europäische Stammtafeln, Volume III, table 700*

19. **Maud (Mabel) de Beaumont**, died 1204. She married William Vernon, Earl of Devon, born 1155, died September 14, 1217. He was the son of Baldwin de Redvers, Earl of Devon, and Adelise. *Cokayne, The Complete Peerage, Volumes IV (Devon), pages 315–316, and VII (Leicester), page 520, and (Appendix I) (i), page 740 See line 2 (5)*

LINE 108 continued from line 99 (12)

13. **Hawise of Normandy**, died February 21, 1034. She married Geoffrey (40–6), Duke of Brittany, died November 20, 1008. He was the son of Conan I, Duke of Brittany, and Ermengarde of Anjou. *Cokayne, The Complete Peerage, Volume X (Richmond), page 780; Schwennicke, Europäische Stammtafeln, Volumes II, tables 75 and 79, and III, table 116; Douglas, William the Conqueror, table 9*

14. **Alan III, Duke of Brittany**, died October 1, 1040. He married Bertha of Blois (36–6 and 64–10), died 1085. She was the daughter of Eudes II, Count of Blois, and Ermengarde d'Auvergne. *Cokayne, The Complete Peerage, Volume X (Richmond), page 780; Schwennicke, Europäische Stammtafeln, Volume II, tables 46 and 75; Douglas, William the Conqueror, table 9 See line 40 (7)*

LINE 109 continued from line 97 (8)

9. **Ragnvald, "the Wise", Jarl of the North and South Møre, and of Ramsdal in Norway**, died 890. His mistress is unnamed. *Cokayne, The Complete Peerage, Volume X (Appendix A), pages 3–4; Moriarty, The Plantagenet Ancestry of King Edward III, pages 10 and 11; Schwennicke, Europäische Stammtafeln, Volume II, table 79*

10. **Hrollaug**. A son. *Cokayne, The Complete Peerage, Volume X (Appendix A), page 4; Sturlason, Heimskringlas, page 59; Hughes, The British Chronicles, Volume II, page 530*

11. **Hrolf Turstan**. He married Gerlotte of Blois. She was the daughter of Thebaud, Count of Chartres, and Richilde. *Planché, The Conqueror and his Companions, Volume II, page 18; Stuart, Royalty for Commoners, 295 (37), and 340 (36); Hughes, The British Chronicles, Volume II, page 530*

12. **Ansfred "the Dane", Count of Hiesmer**, died after 978. *Moriarty, The Plantagenet Ancestry of King Edward III, page 111; Planché, The Conqueror and his Companions, Volume II, page 18; Hughes, The British Chronicles, Volume II, page 530*

13. **Ansfred, Vicomte d'Hiesmer**, died 1013. *Moriarty, The Plantagenet Ancestry of King Edward III, page 111; Planché, The Conqueror and his Companions, Volume II, page 18; Hughes, The British Chronicles, Volume II, page 530*

14. **Thurstan le Goz, Vicomte d'Avranches.** His wife was perhaps Judith de Monterolier. *Cokayne, The Complete Peerage, Volume III (Chester), page 164; Moriarty, The Plantagenet Ancestry of King Edward III, page 111; Hughes, The British Chronicles, Volume II, page 530*

15. **Richard le Goz, Vicomte d'Avranches.** He married Emma. *Cokayne, The Complete Peerage, Volume III (Chester), pages 164–165; Moriarty, The Plantagenet Ancestry of King Edward III, page 111; Schwennicke, Europäische Stammtafeln, Volume III, table 694B; Hughes, The British Chronicles, Volume II, page 530*

16. **Marguerite d'Avranches.** She married Ranulph II (43–9), Vicomte de Bayeux. He was the son of Ranulph I, Vicomte of the Bessin, and Alice of Normandy. *Cokayne, The Complete Peerage, Volume III (Chester), pages 164–166; Schwennicke, Europäische Stammtafeln, Volume III, table 694B; Farrer, Early Yorkshire Charters, Volume II, page 195*

17. **Ranulph le Meschin, Vicomte de Bayeux, Earl of Chester**, died ca. 1129. He married Lucy. *Cokayne, The Complete Peerage, Volumes III (Chester), page 166, and VII (Appendix J), pages 743–746; Sanders, English Baronies, pages 32–33; Farrer, Early Yorkshire Charters, Volume II, page 195* **See line 43 (10)**

LINE 110 continued from line 109 (16)

17. **William le Meschin, Lord of Skipton-in-Craven.** He married Cecily de Romilly. She was the daughter of Robert de Romilly. *Cokayne, The Complete Peerage, Volume IX (Mortimer), pages 270–272; Farrer, Early Yorkshire Charters, Volumes II, page 195, and III, page 470* **See line 44 (10)**

4. **Geva of Vestfold**. She married Widukind (Wittekind), the Saxon leader of Westphalia, died ca. 809. He was the son of Warnechin, Duke of Engern. *Moriarty, The Plantagenet Ancestry of King Edward III, pages 25 and 170; Schwennicke, Europäische Stammtafeln, Volume II, table 104*

5. **Wicbert, Count of Westphalia**, died ca. 843. He married Ordrad. *Moriarty, The Plantagenet Ancestry of King Edward III, page 26; Schwennicke, Europäische Stammtafeln, Volume XIX, table 1A*

6. **Walbert, Count of Threkwitigau**, died ca. 891. He married Altburg. *Moriarty, The Plantagenet Ancestry of King Edward III, page 26; Schwennicke, Europäische Stammtafeln, Volume XIX, table 1A*

7. **Unknown (possibly Reginhert, Count of Ringelheim)**. He married Mathilda. She may have been the daughter of Egbert of Saxony. *Moriarty, The Plantagenet Ancestry of King Edward III, page 26; Schwennicke, Europäische Stammtafeln, Volume XIX, table 1A*

8. **Dietrich, Count of Ringelheim**, died December 8, 917. He married Reginhilde of Friesland. She was the daughter of Godefrid, King of Haithabu, and Gisele of Lorraine. *Moriarty, The Plantagenet Ancestry of King Edward III, page 26; Schwennicke, Europäische Stammtafeln, Volumes I, table 3, I/1, table 10, and XIX, table 1B*

9. **St. Mathilda (Mechtilda)**, born ca. 890, died March 14, 968. She married Heinrich "the Fowler" (90–1), Duke of Saxony, King of the Saxons, born 876, died July 2, 936. He was the son Otto "the Illustrious", Duke of Saxony, and Hedwig, the daughter of Arnulf, Emperor of Germany. *Moriarty, The Plantagenet Ancestry of King Edward III, pages 25 and 26; Schwennicke, Europäische Stammtafeln, Volumes I, table 3, and XIX, table 1B; Engelbert, The Lives of the Saints, pages 101–102*

10. **Gerberge of Saxony,** died May 5, 984. She married (first) Giselbert (75–4), Duke of Lorraine, born ca. 880, died 939. He was the son of Reginar I, Count of Hainaut, and Alberade. *Moriarty, The Plantagenet Ancestry of King Edward III, pages 25 and 39;*

Schwennicke, Europäische Stammtafeln, Volumes I, tables 3 and 95, and I/1, table 10 See line 90 (2)

LINE 112 continued from Line 111 (9)

10. **Gerberge of Saxony** married (second) Louis IV "the Transmarine" (25–6), King of the Franks, born September 10, 920, died September 10, 954. He was the son of Charles III "the Simple", King of the Franks, and Ædgifu of England. *Moriarty, The Plantagenet Ancestry of King Edward III, pages 25 and 39; Schwennicke, Europäische Stammtafeln, Volumes I, table 3, and I/1, tables 6 and 10 See line 92 (2)*

LINE 113

1. **Halfdan "the Old", King of Denmark.** *Cokayne, The Complete Peerage, Volume X (Appendix A), pages 3–4; Moriarty, The Plantagenet Ancestry of King Edward III, page 10*

2. **Ivar Oplaendinge, Jarl of the Upplands.** *Cokayne, The Complete Peerage, Volume X (Appendix A), pages 3–4; Moriarty, The Plantagenet Ancestry of King Edward III, page 10*

3. **Eystein Glumra, Jarl of the Upplands.** He married Aseda (97–8), born ca. 812. She was the daughter of Ragnvald (the son of Olav, King of Jutland), and Thora. *Cokayne, The Complete Peerage, Volume X (Appendix A), pages 3–4; Moriarty, The Plantagenet Ancestry of King Edward III, page 10; Schwennicke, Europäische Stammtafeln, Volume II, table 79; Hughes, The British Chronicles, Volume II, page 535*

4. **Ragnvald, "the Wise", Jarl of the North and South Møre, and of Ramsdal in Norway,** died 890. He married Hiltrude (or Raginhilde). She was the daughter of Hrolf Nefja. *Cokayne, The Complete Peerage, Volume X (Appendix A), pages 3–4; Moriarty, The Plantagenet Ancestry of King Edward III, pages 10 and 11; Schwennicke, Europäische Stammtafeln, Volume II, table 79; Hughes, The British Chronicles, Volume II, pages 529, 530, and 535 **See lines 97 (9) and 109 (9)***

Siegfried, Count of Luxembourg
from a stained glass in the Cathedral of Luxembourg

Luxembourg

1. **Siegfried, Count of Luxembourg**, born ca. 922, died October 28, 998. He was the son of either Wigeric, Count d'Ardennes, or Richwin, Count of Verdun, and Kunegunde, (a granddaughter of Louis II "the Stammerer", King of the Franks; Kunegunde was married to both Wigeric and Richwin). He married Hedwig, died December 13, 992. She may have been the daughter of Eberhard, Count in the Nordgau. *Moriarty, The Plantagenet Ancestry of King Edward III, pages 21 and 22; Schwennicke, Europäische Stammtafeln, Volumes I/2, table 203, and VI, tables 127 and 128; Weis, Ancestral Roots of Certain American Colonists, 143 (18–19) (Note: Schwennicke makes Siegfried the son of Wigeric, but Weis says he more probably was the son of Kunegunde's second husband, Richwin, Count of Verdun.)*

2. **Frederick I, Count of Luxembourg**, born ca. 965, died 1019. He married (possibly) Ermentrude of Gleiberg. She was the daughter of Herbert, Count of Gleiberg, and Ermentrude. *Moriarty, The Plantagenet Ancestry of King Edward III, pages 22 and 24; Schwennicke, Europäische Stammtafeln, Volumes I/2, table 203, and VI, table 128*

3. **Ogiva of Luxembourg**, born ca. 995, died February 21, 1030. She married Baldwin IV (5–7 and 85–5), Count of Flanders, born 980, died May 30, 1035. He was the son of Arnold II, Count of Flanders, and Rosala of Ivrea. *Moriarty, The Plantagenet Ancestry of King Edward III, pages 22 and 248; Schwennicke, Europäische Stammtafeln, Volumes I/2, table 203, II, table 5, and VI, table 128*

4. **Baldwin V, Count of Flanders**, born ca. 1012, died September 1, 1067. He married Adele of France (49–5 and 67–9), Countess of Contentin, died January 8, 1079, widow of Richard III, Duke of Normandy. She was the daughter of Robert II, King of the Franks, and Constance of Provence. *Moriarty, The Plantagenet Ancestry of King Edward III, pages 15 and 24; Schwennicke, Europäische Stammtafeln, Volume II, tables 11 and 79 See line 5 (8)*

2. **Liutgarde of Luxembourg,** died 1005. She married Arnulf, Count of Holland (7–6), born ca. 950, died 993. He was the son of Dietrich II (Dirk II), Count of Holland, and Hildegarde of Flanders. *Moriarty, The Plantagenet Ancestry of King Edward III, pages 22 and 55; Schwennicke, Europäische Stammtafeln, Volumes I, table 158, and II, table 2; Turton, The Plantagenet Ancestry, page 176*

3. **Adele of Holland (Ada of Ghent)**, born ca. 985. She married Baudouin II (32–9), Count of Boulogne, born 976, died 1033. He was the son of Arnulf II, Count of Boulogne. *Schwennicke, Europäische Stammtafeln, Volume II, table 2; Turton, The Plantagenet Ancestry, page 105; Tanner, Families, Friends and Allies, pages 290 and 299* **See line 7 (7)**

*Dietrich II, Count of Holland
from the Egmond Gospels*

The Counts of Flanders and their families
Top: Mathilda of Saxony, wife of Boudouin III, Count of
Flanders; Arnulf II, Count of Flanders; Suzanna (Rosala), wife
of Arnulf II. Bottom: Boudouin IV, Count of Flanders; Ogiva
of Luxembourg, wife of Boudouin IV; Gisla of Luxembourg,
sister of Ogiva (married to Rudolf of Ghent)

Yaroslav the Wise, Grand Prince of Kiev

Russia

1. **Oleg, Prince of Kiev**, a Danish prince, died 912. *Moriarty, The Plantagenet Ancestry of King Edward III, page 221; Weis, Ancestral Roots of Certain American Colonists, 241 (2)*

2. **St. Olga, Regent of Kiev**, died 969. She married Igor, Prince of Kiev, died 945, a relative of Rurik the Viking, founder of the house of Rurikovitch which ruled Russia until the end of the 16th century. *Moriarty, The Plantagenet Ancestry of King Edward III, pages 52 and 221; Schwennicke, Europäische Stammtafeln, Volume II, table 128*

3. **Sviatoslav I, Prince of Kiev**, died 972 or 973. He married Malusha, died 1002. She may have been the daughter of Mal or Malfred, Prince of the Drevianes. *Moriarty, The Plantagenet Ancestry of King Edward III, pages 52 and 221; Schwennicke, Europäische Stammtafeln, Volume II, table 128*

4. **St. Vladimir, Grand Prince of Kiev**, born ca. 955, died July 15, 1015. He married Rogneda. She was the daughter of Rogvolod, Prince of Polotsk. *Moriarty, The Plantagenet Ancestry of King Edward III, pages 53 and 221; Schwennicke, Europäische Stammtafeln, Volume II, table 128*

5. **Yaroslav I, "the Wise", Grand Prince of Kiev**, born 979, died February 20, 1054. He married Ingegarde (96–8), died February 10, 1050. She was the daughter of Olav II, King of Sweden, and Estrid. *Moriarty, The Plantagenet Ancestry of King Edward III, pages 53 and 54; Schwennicke, Europäische Stammtafeln, Volume II, table 128*

6. **Anna of Kiev, Queen of the Franks**, born 1036, died after 1075. She married Henri I (47–5), King of the Franks, born May 17, 1008, died August 4, 1060. He was the son of Robert II, King of the Franks, and Constance of Provence. *Moriarty, The Plantagenet Ancestry of King Edward III, pages 51 and 53; Schwennicke, Europäische Stammtafeln, Volume II, tables 11 and 128* **See line 96 (9)**

Coin depicting Leo VI, Emperor of Byzantium

Byzantium

1. **Basil I, Emperor of Byzantium**, died August 29, 866. He married Eudocia Ingerina, born ca. 840, died 882 or 883. She was the mistress of Michael III, Emperor of Byzantium (generation 1A)

1A. **Michael III, Emperor of Byzantium**, born ca. 840, died September 24, 867. He was the son of Theophilus, Emperor of Byzantium, and Theodora. His mistress was Eudocia Ingerina, the wife of Emperor Basil I (generation 1, above). It is not certain which of the two emperors was the father of Leo VI (generation 2). *Norwich, A Short History of Byzantium, pages 132, 135–141, 148–149, 151, 157, and charts VI (xxv) and VII (xxvi); Weis, Ancestral Roots of Certain American Colonists, 141A (15)*

2. **Leo VI, Emperor of Byzantium**, born September 1, 866, died May 12, 912. He married Zoe Tzautsina, died 899. She was the daughter of Stylian Zautses. *Norwich, A Short History of Byzantium, pages 149, 157, and 161, and chart VII (xxvi); Weis, Ancestral Roots of Certain American Colonists, 141A (16)*

3. **Anna of Byzantium**, born ca. 887, died ca. 914. She married Louis III (64–4 and 88–6), Emperor of the West, and King of Italy, born ca. 883, died June 5, 928. He was the son of Boso, King of Provence, King of Burgundy, and Count of Vienne, and Ermengarde. *Norwich, A Short History of Byzantium, page 161, and chart VII (xxvi); Schwennicke, Europäische Stammtafeln, Volume II, table 189; Weis, Ancestral Roots of Certain American Colonists, 141A (17), and 141B (17–18)*

4. **Charles Constantine, Count of Vienne**, died 962. He married Teutberga of Troyes (73–5), died ca. 960. She was the daughter of Garnier, Count of Troyes and Vicomte de Sens, and Teutberga of Arles. *Schwennicke, Europäische Stammtafeln, Volume II, table 189; Weis, Ancestral Roots of Certain American Colonists, 141A (18); Norwich, A Short History of Byzantium, page 161, and chart V (xxvi)* **See line 64 (5)**

Arnoldus, Bishop of Metz
from the Chapelle Sainte-Glossinde

Other Historic Figures
Roman Empire

1. **Flavius Afranius Syagrius,** living 380. Gallo Roman Senator of the Roman Empire. *Moriarty, The Plantagenet Ancestry of King Edward III, page 7; Weis, Ancestral Roots of Certain American Colonists, 180 (1)*

2. **(daughter).** She married Ferreolus. *Moriarty, The Plantagenet Ancestry of King Edward III, page 7; Weis, Ancestral Roots of Certain American Colonists, 180 (2)*

3. **Tonantius Ferreolus,** Praetorian Prefect. He married Papianilla, a relative of Avitus, Roman Emperor from July 455 to October 456. *Moriarty, The Plantagenet Ancestry of King Edward III, page 7; Weis, Ancestral Roots of Certain American Colonists, 180 (3)*

4. **Tonantius Ferreolus,** Roman Senator. He married Industria. *Moriarty, The Plantagenet Ancestry of King Edward III, page 7; Weis, Ancestral Roots of Certain American Colonists, 180 (4)*

5. **Ferreolus,** Roman Senator. He married Dode. *Weis, Ancestral Roots of Certain American Colonists, 180 (5). (Note, Moriarty skips this generation.)*

6. **Ansbertus,** Gallo-Roman Senator. He may have married Blichilde. *Moriarty, The Plantagenet Ancestry of King Edward III, page 7; Weis, Ancestral Roots of Certain American Colonists, 180 (6)*

7. **Arnoldus,** Bishop of Metz. *Moriarty, The Plantagenet Ancestry of King Edward III, page 8; Weis, Ancestral Roots of Certain American Colonists, 180 (7)*

8. **Clotilde (Dode).** She married St. Arnulf (126–3), born 582, died August 16, 641. He was the son of Bodegeisel II and Oda. *Moriarty, The Plantagenet Ancestry of King Edward III, pages 5 and 7–8; Schwennicke, Europäische Stammtafeln, Volume I, table 2; Weis, Ancestral Roots of Certain American Colonists, 180 (8)*

9. **Ansegius,** born 602, died 685. He married St. Begga (127–1). She was the daughter of Pepin I, Mayor of the Palace in Austrasia, and St. Itta. *Moriarty, The Plantagenet Ancestry of King Edward III, pages 5, 8, and 224; Schwennicke, Europäische Stammtafeln, Volume I, table 2; Engelbert, The Lives of the Saints, page 479* **See line 126 (4)**

Medieval Great Britain and Europe

LINE 119

1. **Herleve,** died December 2, 1050. She was the daughter of Fulbert. She was the mistress of Robert I (41–7), Duke of Normandy, died July 22, 1035. He was the son of Richard II, Duke of Normandy, and Judith of Brittany. She and Robert were the parents of William the Conqueror. *Cokayne, The Complete Peerage, Volumes I (Aumale), pages 351–352, and XIII/1 (Appendix K), pages 30–34; Moriarty, The Plantagenet Ancestry of King Edward III, page 13; Schwennicke, Europäische Stammtafeln, Volume II, table 79; Douglas, William the Conqueror, tables 1, 2, and 6; Planché, The Conqueror and his Companions, Volume I, page 88*

2. **Adelaide of Normandy, Countess of Aumale,** born 1030, died before 1090. She was the full sister of William the Conqueror. She married Lambert (28–10), Count of Lens, died 1054. He was the son of Eustace I, Count of Boulogne, and Matilda of Louvain. *Cokayne, The Complete Peerage, Volumes I (Aumale), pages 351–352, and XIII/1 (Appendix K), pages 30–34; Moriarty, The Plantagenet Ancestry of King Edward III, pages 13, 165, and 184; Schwennicke, Europäische Stammtafeln, Volume II, table 79; Douglas, William the Conqueror, tables 2 and 6; Planché, The Conqueror and his Companions, Volume I, pages 118 and 122* **See line 42 (8)**

LINE 120 continued from line 119 (1)

1. **Herleve,** died December 2, 1050, mistress of Robert I (41–7), Duke of Normandy. She married Herluin de Conteville, Viscount of Conteville, died 1066. *Cokayne, The Complete Peerage, Volumes III (Cornwall), page 427; and XIII/1 (Appendix K), pages 30–34; Moriarty, The Plantagenet Ancestry of King Edward III, page 44; Douglas, William the Conqueror, tables 1, 2, and 6*

2. **Robert, Count of Mortain, Earl of Cornwall**, born ca. 1031, died December 8, 1090. He married Maud Montgomery. She was the daughter of Roger Montgomery, Earl of Shrewsbury, and Mabel d'Alençon. *Cokayne, The Complete Peerage, Volumes III (Cornwall), pages 427–428, XI (Mortain), page 243, and XII/1 (Appendix K), pages 30–34; Moriarty, The Plantagenet Ancestry of King Edward III, page 44; Douglas, William the Conqueror, tables 1 and 6*

3. **William, Count of Mortain, Earl of Cornwall**, born before 1084, died after 1140. He married Adilidis. *Cokayne, The Complete Peerage, Volume III (Cornwall), pages 428–429; Moriarty, The Plantagenet Ancestry of King Edward III, page 44*

4. **Maud of Mortain**, died by 1162. She married Reginald FitzRoy (2–3), Earl of Cornwall, died July 1, 1175. He was the illegitimate son of Henry I, King of England, and his mistress, Sybilla Corbet. *Cokayne, The Complete Peerage, Volumes III (Cornwall), page 429, and XII/2 (Worcester), pages 837–838; Weis, Ancestral Roots of Certain American Colonists, 121 (26) [Note: in both "Cornwall" and "Worcester", Cokayne refers to her as Beatrice, while Weis calls her Maud]*

5. **Maud of Cornwall**. She married Robert de Beaumont (38–10 and 107–18), Count of Meulan, died 1207. He was the son of Waleran de Beaumont, Earl of Worcester, and Agnes de Montfort. *Cokayne, The Complete Peerage, Volumes IV (Devon), pages 315–316, VII (Leicester), page 520, and (Appendix I), page 740, and XII/2 (Worcester), pages 837–838; Weis, Ancestral Roots of Certain American Colonists, 50 (26) See line 2 (4)*

LINE 121 continued from line 120 (4)

5. **Joan of Cornwall**. She married Roger (or possibly Ralph) Valletort. He was the son of Robert (or possibly Reginald) Valletort. *Benson, in Devon and Cornwall Notes and Queries, Volume XX, pages 247-254; Pole, Collections Towards a Description of the County of Devon, page 21 See line 3 (4)*

1. **Lady Godiva,** born ca. 1010, died September 10, 1067. Her ancestry is uncertain. She is the Lady Godiva of legend, who rode naked through the streets of Coventry. She married Leofric, Earl of Mercia, born 975, died August 31, 1057. He was the son of Leowine, Earl of Mercia. *Baxter, The Earls of Mercia, figure 2.1; Weis, Ancestral Roots of Certain American Colonists, 176A (2)*

2. **Ælfgar, Earl of Mercia,** died ca. 1063. He married Ælfgifu. *Baxter, The Earls of Mercia, figure 2.1; Weis, Ancestral Roots of Certain American Colonists, 176A (3)*

3. **Ældgyth (Edith) of Mercia.** She married Gruffydd ap Llewellyn (9–18 and 10–17), Prince of North Wales, King of Gwynedd, Powys, and Deheubarth, died August 5, 1063. He was the son of Llewellyn ap Seisyll, King of Deheubarth and Gwynedd, and Prince of North Wales, and Angharad verch Maredudd. *Baxter, The Earls of Mercia, figure 2.1; Weis, Ancestral Roots of Certain American Colonists, 176 (2), 176A (3–4), and 177 (1)*

4. **Nesta of North Wales,** born ca. 1055. She married Osborn FitzRichard, sheriff of Hereford. He was the son of Richard FitzScrob. *Maund, The Welsh Kings, page 68; Baxter, The Earls of Mercia, figure 2.1; Weis, Ancestral Roots of Certain American Colonists, 176 (3), and 177 (2)* **See line 9 (19)**

Magna Charta Surety

1. **William Malet, Baron of Curry Malet, a Magna Charta Surety** (101–20), died 1215. He was the son of Gilbert Malet, Baron of Curry Malet, and Alice Picot. He married Alice Basset. She was the daughter of Thomas Basset, Lord of Headington in Oxfordshire, and Colynton and Whitford in Devonshire, and Philippa Malbank. William probably had an earlier, unknown wife, who was the mother of generation 2. *Cokayne, The Complete Peerage, Volume X (Poyntz), page 672; Malet, Notices of an English Branch of the Malet Family, pages 77–83; Weis, Ancestral Roots of Certain American Colonists, 234A (27–28); Sanders, English Baronies, page 38*

2. Hawise Malet. She married Sir Hugh Poyntz (43–14), died April 4, 1220. He was the son of Nicholas Poyntz, Lord of Tockington, and Juliana Bardolf. *Cokayne, The Complete Peerage, Volume X (Poyntz), page 672; Malet, Notices of an English Branch of the Malet Family, page 79; Collinson, The History and Antiquities of the County of Somerset, Volume I (Enmore), page 91; Sanders, English Baronies, page 39*

3. Nicholas Poyntz, born ca. 1220, died 1273. He married Elizabeth Dyall. She was the daughter of Timothy Dyall. *Cokayne, The Complete Peerage, Volume X (Poyntz), page 673; Metcalfe, The Visitation of Essex, page 268; Sanders, English Baronies, page 39*
See line 43 (15)

Saints

LINE 124

1. St. Clotildus *Feast Day, June 3*
Born 474, died 545. She was the daughter of Chilperic, King of Burgundy. She married Clovis I, King of the Franks, born 466, died 511. *Schwennicke, Europäische Stammtafeln, Volume I, table 1; Weis, Ancestral Roots of Certain American Colonists, 240A (3); Engelbert, The Lives of the Saints, page 215*

St. Clotildus, a miniature from the Great Chronicles of France

2. Clotaire I, King of the Franks, born 497, died 561. He married Arnégonde, born 515, died 573. *Schwennicke, Europäische Stammtafeln, Volume I, table 1; Weis, Ancestral Roots of Certain American Colonists, 240A (4)*

3. **Chilpéric I, King of Soissons**, born 539, died 584. He married Frédégonde, born 543, died 597. *Schwennicke, Europäische Stammtafeln, Volume I, table 1; Weis, Ancestral Roots of Certain American Colonists, 240A (5)*

4. **Clotaire II, King of the Franks**, born 584, died 629. He married Bertrade, born 582, died 618. *Schwennicke, Europäische Stammtafeln, Volume I, table 1; Weis, Ancestral Roots of Certain American Colonists, 240A (6)*

5. **Dagobert I, King of the Franks**, died 639. He married Nantilde, died 642. *Schwennicke, Europäische Stammtafeln, Volume I, table 1; Weis, Ancestral Roots of Certain American Colonists, 240A (7)*

6. **Clovis II, King of Soissons**, died 657. He married Bathilde, born 626, died ca. 680. *Schwennicke, Europäische Stammtafeln, Volume I, table 1; Weis, Ancestral Roots of Certain American Colonists, 240A (8)*

7. **Thierry III, King of Soissons**, born 654, died 691. He married Clotilde, born 650, died 699. *Schwennicke, Europäische Stammtafeln, Volume I, table 1; Weis, Ancestral Roots of Certain American Colonists, 240A (9)*

8. **Berthe**. Her husband is unknown. *Moriarty, The Plantagenet Ancestry of King Edward III, pages 5 and 232; Weis, Ancestral Roots of Certain American Colonists, 240A (10)*

9. **Charibert, Count of Laon.** He married Gisele (Bertrada). *Moriarty, The Plantagenet Ancestry of King Edward III, pages 5 and 232; Weis, Ancestral Roots of Certain American Colonists, 240A (11)*

10. **Bertrada of Laon**, died July 12, 783. She married Pepin "the Short" (54–2), King of the Franks, born 714, died 768. He was the son of Charles Martel, and Rotrou. *Moriarty, The Plantagenet Ancestry of King Edward III, pages 5 and 232; Schwennicke, Europäische Stammtafeln, Volume I, table 2; Weis, Ancestral Roots of Certain American Colonists, 190 (11), and 240A (12)*

11. Charlemagne, King of the Franks, born April 2, 747, died January 28, 814. *Moriarty, The Plantagenet Ancestry of King Edward III, pages 5, 7, and 220; Schwennicke, Europäische Stammtafeln, Volumes I, table 2, and I/1, table 4* **See lines 17 (1)** *for descents from Himiltrude,* **and 19 (1)** *for descents from Hildegarde*

LINE 125

1. St. Gondolfus *Feast Day, July 16*
born 524, died July 6, 607. Bishop of Tongres. He was the son of Munderic of Vitry-en-Perthois. *Moriarty, The Plantagenet Ancestry of King Edward III, page 5; Weis, Ancestral Roots of Certain American Colonists, 190 (6)*

2. Bodegeisel II. He married Oda. They were the parents of St. Arnulf of Metz (126–3). *Moriarty, The Plantagenet Ancestry of King Edward III, page 5; Weis, Ancestral Roots of Certain American Colonists, 190 (7) (Note: Moriarty makes Bodegeisel the son of Godegeisel I, St. Gondolfus' brother. Weis corrects this with source citations.)* **Continued on line 126 (3) next**

LINE 126 continued from line 125 (2)

3. St. Arnulf of Metz *Feast Day, July 18*
Born 582, died August 16, 641. He was the son of Bodegeisel II (125-2) and Oda. He married Clotilde (Dode) (118–8). She was the daughter of Arnoldus, Bishop of Metz. *Moriarty, The Plantagenet Ancestry of King Edward III, page 5; Schwennicke, Europäische Stammtafeln, Volume I, table 2; Weis, Ancestral Roots of Certain American Colonists, 190 (7–8); Engelbert, The Lives of the Saints, page 276*

4. Ansegius, born 602, died 685. He married St. Begga (127–1). She was the daughter of Pepin I, Mayor of the Palace in Austrasia, and St. Itta. *Moriarty, The Plantagenet Ancestry of King Edward III, pages 5, 8, and 224; Schwennicke, Europäische Stammtafeln, Volume I, table 2; Engelbert, The Lives of the Saints, page 479* **Continued with St. Begga on line 127 (1) next**

1. **St. Begga** *Feast Day, December 17*
   Died 693. She was the daughter of Pepin I, Mayor of the Palace in Austrasia, and St. Itta. She married Ansegius (118–9 and 126–4). *Moriarty, The Plantagenet Ancestry of King Edward III, pages 5, 8, and 224; Schwennicke, Europäische Stammtafeln, Volume I, table 2; Engelbert, The Lives of the Saints, page 479*

2. **Pepin II, Mayor of the Palace,** born ca. 645. His mistress was Aupais. *Moriarty, The Plantagenet Ancestry of King Edward III, pages 5 and 8; Schwennicke, Europäische Stammtafeln, Volume I, table 2*

3. **Charles Martel, Mayor of the Palace of Austrasia,** born 689, died 741. He married Rotrou, died 724. *Moriarty, The Plantagenet Ancestry of King Edward III, page 5; Schwennicke, Europäische Stammtafeln, Volume I, table 2* **See line 54 (1)**

LINE 128 continued from line 126 (3)

4. **St. Clodoule** *Feast Day, June 8*
   Born 602, died 685. Bishop of Metz. It is not known whom St. Clodoule married. *Moriarty, The Plantagenet Ancestry of King Edward III, page 5*

5. **Gunza**. She married Warin, Count of Poitiers and of Paris, died 677. They were the parents of St. Liutwin (129–6). *Moriarty, The Plantagenet Ancestry of King Edward III, pages 1 and 5* **Continued on line 129 (6) next**

LINE 129 continued from line 128 (5)

6. **St. Liutwin** *Feast Day, September 23 (moved from September 29)*
   Count and Bishop of Treves, died ca. 722. He was the son of Warin, Count of Poitiers, and Gunza (128–5). *Moriarty, The Plantagenet Ancestry of King Edward III, pages 1, 5, and 74*

7. **Gui, Count of Hornbach**. *Moriarty, The Plantagenet Ancestry of King Edward III, page 74*

8. **Lambert, Count of Hornbach**, died ca. 783. *Moriarty, The Plantagenet Ancestry of King Edward III, pages 74 and 233*

9. **Waldrada**. She married Hadrian, Count of Orleans, died ca. 824. He was the son of Gerald I, Duke of Alemania, Count in the Vinzgau, and Imma. *Moriarty, The Plantagenet Ancestry of King Edward III, pages 74 and 233*

10. **Eudes, Count of Orleans**, born 798, died 834. He married Engeltrude (17–4). She was the daughter of Leutaud, Count of Paris. *Moriarty, The Plantagenet Ancestry of King Edward III, pages 9, 23, and 233; Schwennicke, Europäische Stammtafeln, Volumes I, table 2, I/1, table 4, and II, table 1*

11. **Ermentrude of Orleans**, born September 27, 823, died October 6, 869. She married Charles II "the Bald" (25–3 and 33–3), King of the Franks, born June 13, 823, died October 6, 877. He was the son of Louis I, "the Pious", King of the Franks, and Judith of Bavaria. *Moriarty, The Plantagenet Ancestry of King Edward III, pages 16, 23 and 233; Schwennicke, Europäische Stammtafeln, Volumes I, table 2, I/1, table 4, and II, table 1* **See line 17 (5)**

LINE 130

1. **St. Itta** *Feast Day, May 8*
Died 652. She was the daughter of Arnoldus, Bishop of Metz (118–7). She married Pepin I, Mayor of the Palace in Austrasia. *Moriarty, The Plantagenet Ancestry of King Edward III, pages 5, 8, and 224; Engelbert, The Lives of the Saints, page 652; Stuart, Royalty for Commoners, 171 (45)*

2. **St. Begga** *Feast Day, December 17*
Died 693. She married Ansegius (118–9 and 126–4), born 602, died 685. He was the son of St. Arnulf and Clotilde (Dode). *Moriarty, The Plantagenet Ancestry of King Edward III, pages 5, 8, and 224; Schwennicke, Europäische Stammtafeln, Volume I, table 2; Engelbert, The Lives of the Saints, page 479* **See line 127 (1)**

LINE 131

1. **St. Olga** *Feast Day, July 11*
   Died 969. She married Igor, Prince of Kiev, born ca. 875, died 945, a relative of Rurik the Viking. *Moriarty, The Plantagenet Ancestry of King Edward III, pages 52 and 221; Schwennicke, Europäische Stammtafeln, Volume II, table 128*

2. **Sviatoslav I, Prince of Kiev,** died 972 or 973. He married Malusha, died 1002. She may have been the daughter of Mal or Malfred, Prince of the Drevianes. *Moriarty, The Plantagenet Ancestry of King Edward III, pages 52 and 221; Schwennicke, Europäische Stammtafeln, Volume II, table 128* **Continued on line 132 (3) next**

LINE 132 continued from line 131 (2)

3. **St. Vladimir, Grand Prince of Kiev.** *Feast Day, July 15*
   Died July 15, 1015. He was the son of Sviatoslav I, Prince of Kiev (131-2) and Malusha. He married Rogneda. She was the daughter of Rogvolod, Prince of Polotsk. *Moriarty, The Plantagenet Ancestry of King Edward III, pages 53 and 221; Schwennicke, Europäische Stammtafeln, Volume II, table 128*

4. **Yaroslav I, "the Wise", Grand Prince of Kiev,** born 979, died February 20, 1054. He married Ingegarde (96–8), died February 10, 1050. She was the daughter of Olav II, King of Sweden, and Estrid. *Moriarty, The Plantagenet Ancestry of King Edward III, pages 53 and 54; Schwennicke, Europäische Stammtafeln, Volume II, table 128* **See line 116 (5)**

LINE 133

1. **St. Mathilda (Mechtilda)** *Feast Day, March 14*
   Born ca. 890, died March 14, 968. She was the daughter of Dietrich, Count of Ringelheim, and Reginhilde of Friesland. She married Heinrich "the Fowler" (90–1), Duke of Saxony, King of the Saxons, born 876, died July 2, 936. He was the son Otto "the Illustrious", Duke of Saxony, and Hedwig, the daughter of Arnulf, Emperor of Germany. *Moriarty, The Plantagenet Ancestry of King Edward III, pages 25 and 26; Schwennicke, Europäische Stammtafeln, Volume I, table 3; Engelbert, The Lives of the Saints, pages 101–102*

2. **Hedwig of Saxony**, born 921, died May 10, 965. She married Hugh "the Great" (47–2 and 61–6), Count of Paris, Orleans, the Vexin, and Le Mans, Duke of France, born ca. 895, died June 16, 956. He was the son of Robert I, King of the Franks, and Beatrice of Vermandois. *Moriarty, The Plantagenet Ancestry of King Edward III, pages 9, 24, and 25; Schwennicke, Europäische Stammtafeln, Volumes I, table 3, and II, tables 10 and 11* **See line 94 (2)**

LINE 134 continued from line 133 (1)

2. **Gerberge of Saxony,** died May 5, 984. She married (first) Giselbert (75–4), Duke of Lorraine, born ca. 880, died 939. He was the son of Reginar I, Count of Hainaut, and Alberade. She married (second) Louis IV (25–6), King of the Franks, born September 10, 920, died September 10, 954. He was the son of Charles III "the Simple", King of the Franks, and Ædgifu of England. *Moriarty, The Plantagenet Ancestry of King Edward III, pages 25, 35, and 39; Schwennicke, Europäische Stammtafeln, Volumes I, tables 3 and 95, and I/1, table 10* **See lines 90 (2) and 92 (2)**

LINE 135

1. **St. Pabo Post Prydain** *Feast Day, November 9*
Born ca. 474, died 530. He was the son of Arthwys ap Mar ap Ceneu ap Coel. *Griffith, Pedigrees of Anglesey and Carnarvonshire Families, page 309: Baring-Gould and Fisher, The Lives of the British Saints, Volume IV, pages 38–39* **Continued on line 136 (2) next**

LINE 136 continued from line 135 (1)

2. **St. Arddun**
She was the daughter of St. Pabo Post Prydain (135–1). She married Brochwel Ysgythrog (9–1), King of Powys, died 617. He was the son of Cynan ab Cadell Deyrnllwg. *Griffith, Pedigrees of Anglesey and Carnarvonshire Families, page 309: Baring-Gould and Fisher, The Lives of the British Saints, Volume II, page 326*

3. **Cynan Garwyn ap Brochwel, King of Powys.** *Griffith, Pedigrees of Anglesey and Carnarvonshire Families, page 309; Lloyd, A History of Wales, page 181* **See line 9 (2)**

Prater

Descents to Later Prater/Prather Lines from Judith Ivye

Judith Ivye provides a noble ancestry for her Prater/Prather descendants, as shown in the preceding pages. It is also thought that her husband, Anthony Prater was of noble descent, though nothing yet has been found to provide a direct link to any specific royal or peer. However, Anthony Prater's mother, Jane Plott, was the daughter of Alice Malet. Proving Alice's connection to the Malet family would then provide a descent from Henry II to Anthony Prater. Jane Plott was born in 1515, her mother Alice around 1490. A likely choice for Alice's parents could be William Malet (1471–1511) of Somerset, and his wife Alice, the daughter of Thomas Young. If William Malet and Alice Young can be proven to be the parents of Alice Malet, then Alice would be a sister of Hugh Malet (2–18), the husband of Isabel Michell. Hugh and Isabel were the maternal grandparents of Judith Ivye.

The Praters are suspected of descending from the Carews of Beddington. If this relationship can be proven, it could provide descents to the Praters from the Rollo the Viking, Robert I, King of the Franks, and Rhodri Mawr, King of Gwynedd.

Some of Anthony Prater's relatives married into families with royal connections of their own. His brother Richard married Margaret Ashfield, a descendant of Henry I. His sister Alice (wife of Thomas Walrond) was the mother of Elizabeth, who married Richard Goddard, a descendant of King John.

In the 18th century, American descendants of Anthony Prater and Judith Ivye married into families whose ancestors also originated from English or European royalty. The following pages trace two of those families with royal descents through lineages that culminated in marriages with Prater descendants: Anne Yates (137–25) who married William Prater (ca. 1670–1748), and Martha Riley (147–15), who married Brice Bazel Prater (1776–1859).

Coronation of William the Conqueror
from the Flores Historiarum

England

1. **William the Conqueror, King of England**, born October 14, 1025, died September 9, 1087. He was the son of Robert I, Duke of Normandy, and Herleve. He married Mathilda of Flanders, born 1031, died November 2, 1083. She was the daughter of Baldwin V, Count of Flanders, and Adele of France, Countess of Contentin. *Cokayne, The Complete Peerage, Volumes I (Aumale), page 351, and XII/1 (Appendix K), pages 30–34; Moriarty, The Plantagenet Ancestry of King Edward III, pages 13 and 15; Schwennicke, Europäische Stammtafeln, Volume II, tables 79 and 81; Burke, Burke's Peerage (The Royal Lineage), page 28; Douglas, William the Conqueror, page 15, and tables 1, 2, 5, and 6*

2. **Adela of England**, born 1062, died 1137. She married Etiene (Stephen), Count of Champagne, Brie, Blois and Chartres, born 1045, died 1102. He was the son of Thebaud III, Count of Blois, and Alix de Crepi. *Cokayne, The Complete Peerage, Volume V (Eu), page 156; Moriarty, The Plantagenet Ancestry of King Edward III, pages 13 and 117; Schwennicke, Europäische Stammtafeln, Volume II, tables 46 and 81*

3. **William of Champagne, Sire de Sully.** He married Agnes de Sully. She was the daughter of Giles de Sully and Eldeburge of Bourges. *Cokayne, The Complete Peerage, Volume V (Eu), page 156; Schwennicke, Europäische Stammtafeln, Volume II, table 46; Weis, Ancestral Roots of Certain American Colonists, 139 (24)*

4. **Marguerite of Champagne**, died December 15, 1145. She married Henry, Count of Eu, died July 12, 1140. He was the son of William, Count of Eu, Lord of Hastings, and Beatrice de Builly. *Cokayne, The Complete Peerage, Volume V (Eu), page 156; Schwennicke, Europäische Stammtafeln, Volume III, table 110*

5. **John, Count of Eu, Lord of Hastings**, died June 26, 1170. He married Alice d'Aubigny, died September 11, 1188. She was the daughter of William d'Aubigny, Earl of Arundel, and Adeliz of Louvain, Queen of England, widow of Henry I, King of England. *Cokayne, The Complete Peerage, Volume V (Eu), page 156*

6. **Ida of Eu**. She married William Hastings. He was the son of Hugh de Hastings and Erneburga de Flamville. *Roberts, The Royal Descents of 600 Immigrants, page 519*

7. **Thomas Hastings**. *Roberts, The Royal Descents of 600 Immigrants, page 519; Burke, Dormant and Extinct Peerages, page 266*

8. **Hugh Hastings**. He married Helen Alveston. *Roberts, The Royal Descents of 600 Immigrants, page 519*

9. **Thomas Hastings**. He married Amicia. *Roberts, The Royal Descents of 600 Immigrants, page 519*

10. **Sir Nicholas Hastings**. He married Emmeline Heron. *Cokayne, The Complete Peerage, Volume IV (Darcy), page 58; Roberts, The Royal Descents of 600 Immigrants, page 519*

11. **Alice Hastings**. She married Walter Heron. He was the son of Sir William Heron and Christian de Notton. *Cokayne, The Complete Peerage, Volume IV (Darcy), page 58 (d); Weis, Ancestral Roots of Certain American Colonists, 88 (33)*

12. **Emmeline Heron**. She married Sir John Darcy, Baron Darcy, died May 30, 1347. He was the son of Roger Darcy and Isabel d'Aton. *Cokayne, The Complete Peerage, Volume IV (Darcy), pages 54–58*

13. **John Darcy, Baron Darcy**, died March 5, 1355 or 1356. He married Elizabeth de Meinill, born October 15, 1331, died July 9, 1368. She was the daughter of Nicholas de Meinill and Alice de Ros. *Cokayne, The Complete Peerage, Volumes IV (Darcy), pages 58–60, and VIII (Meinill), page 634*

14. **Alice Darcy**, She married Sir John Colville, died August 20, 1405. He was the son of Sir William Colville and Joan de Fauconberg. *Weis, The Magna Charta Sureties, 117 (7); Roberts, The Royal Descents of 500 Immigrants, page 342**

*This descent, which appears in Roberts' earlier work, *The Royal Descents of 500 Immigrants*, is entirely replaced by a separate and distinct line in his later work, *The Royal Descents of 600 Immigrants*. However, in a personal correspondence, Mr. Roberts assured the author that both lines of descent remain valid.

15. **Isabel Colville**, She married John Wandesford, died ca. 1400. He was the son of John Wandesford and Elizabeth Musters. *Weis, Ancestral Roots of Certain American Colonists, 208 (34); Weis, The Magna Charta Sureties, 117 (8); Roberts, The Royal Descents of 500 Immigrants, page 342*

16. **Thomas Wandesford**, died October 13, 1448. He married Idonea. *Weis, The Magna Charta Sureties, 117 (9); Roberts, The Royal Descents of 500 Immigrants, page 342*

17. **Joan Wandesford**. She married John Tichborne. He was the son of John Tichborne and Margaret Moking. *Roberts, The Royal Descents of 500 Immigrants, page 342; Munday, The Visitation of Hampshire, (Tichborne), page 125; Burke, Burke's Peerage (Tichborne), page 2202*

18. **Sir John Tichborne**. He married Margaret Martin. She was the daughter of Richard Martin and Margaret Wallis. *Roberts, The Royal Descents of 500 Immigrants, page 342; Burke, Burke's Peerage (Tichborne), page 2202*

19. **Nicholas Tichborne**, died 1513. He married Anne White. She was the daughter of Robert White and Margaret Gainsford. *Roberts, The Royal Descents of 500 Immigrants, page 342; Burke, Burke's Peerage (Tichborne), page 2202; Faris, Plantagenet Ancestry of Seventeenth Century Colonists, (Yate), page 387*

20. **Nicholas Tichborne**, died 1555. He married Elizabeth Rythe. She was the daughter of William Rythe and Margery Cowdray. *Roberts, The Royal Descents of 500 Immigrants, page 342; Burke, Burke's Peerage (Tichborne), page 2202; Faris, Plantagenet Ancestry of Seventeenth Century Colonists, (Yate), page 388*

21. **Jane Tichborne**. She married Francis Yate, died 1588. He was the son of John Yate and Alice Hyde. *Roberts, The Royal Descents of 500 Immigrants, page 342; Faris, Plantagenet Ancestry of Seventeenth Century Colonists, (Yate), page 388*

22. **Thomas Yate**, died between 1654 and 1660. He married Dorothy Stephens. She was the daughter of Nicholas Stephens. *Roberts, The Royal Descents of 500 Immigrants, page 342; Faris, Plantagenet Ancestry of Seventeenth Century Colonists, (Yate), page 388; Boyan and Lamb, Francis Tregian: Cornish Recusant, pages 135–137*

23. **John Yate**, born ca. 1613, died 1654. He married Elizabeth Tattershall. She was the daughter of George Tattershall and Elizabeth Biggs. *Roberts, The Royal Descents of 500 Immigrants, page 342; Faris, Plantagenet Ancestry of Seventeenth Century Colonists, (Yate), page 388*

24. **George Yates**, born ca. 1640. He married Mary Wells, died January 21, 1698 or 1699, widow of Captain Thomas Stockett. She was the daughter of Richard Wells. *Roberts, The Royal Descents of 500 Immigrants, page 342; Doliante, Maryland and Virginia Colonials, Volume II, page 659; Faris, Plantagenet Ancestry of Seventeenth Century Colonists, (Yate), pages 388–389*

25. **Anne Yates**, born ca. 1672, died 1719. She married William Prather, died 1748. He was the son of Jonathan Prather (a descendant of Judith Ivye) and Jane, possibly the daughter of Robert MacKay. *Doliante, Maryland and Virginia Colonials, Volume II, page 659; Prather, Praters in Wiltshire, page 13 0*

Children of Anne Yates and William Prather:
   a. William Prather, March 8, 1700 – September 20, 1780
      married his first cousin Martha Prather
   b. Jane Prather, September 12, 1703 – December 5, 1782
      married (1) William Ward, and (2) Solomon Turner
   c. Priscilla Prather, born September 21, 1707
      married William Brashears
   d. Margaret Prather, born September 8, 1709
   e. Joseph Prather, born July 11, 1711
   f. John Prather, June 12, 1715 – November 3, 1796
      married Rachel O'Dell
   g. Sarah Prather, born March 23, 1716
      married her cousin William Prather
   h. Elizabeth Prather, born 1718

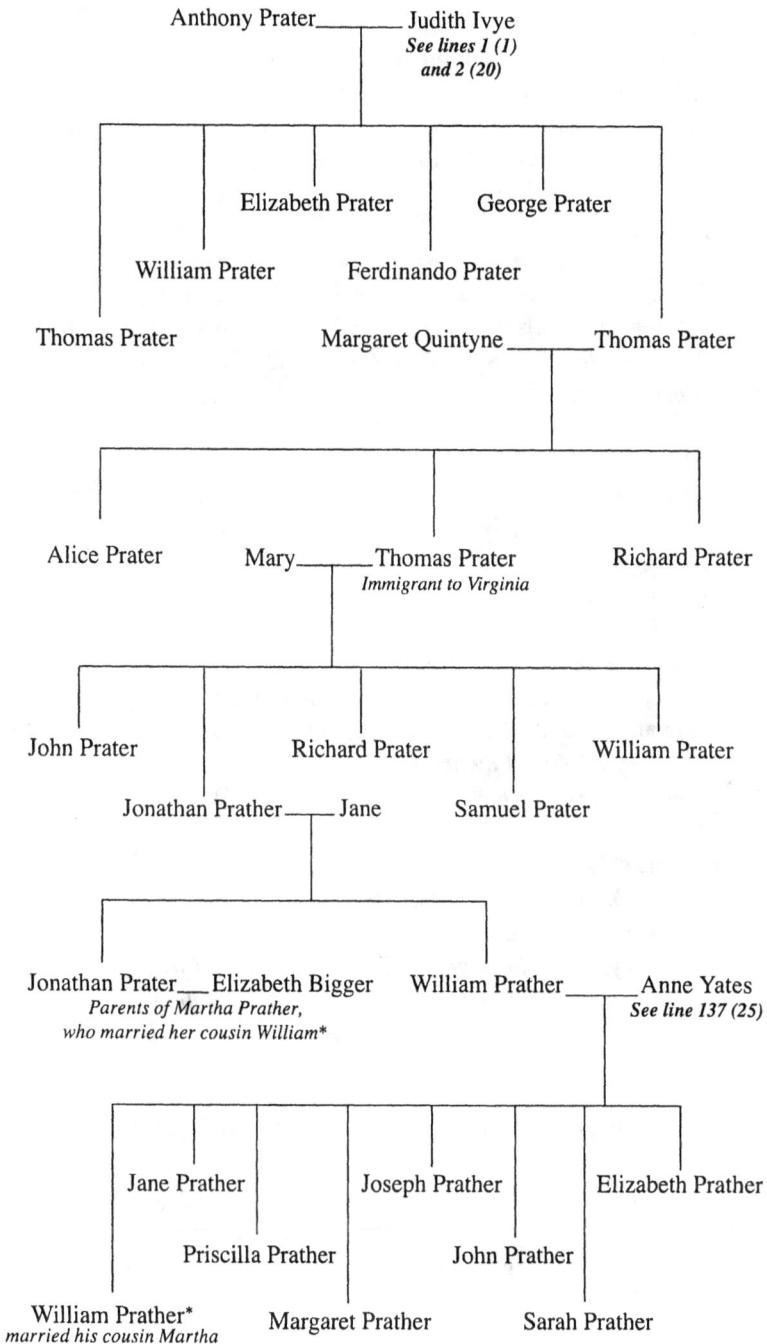

Anthony Prater———— Judith Ivye
See lines 1 (1)
and 2 (20)

Elizabeth Prater   George Prater

William Prater   Ferdinando Prater

Thomas Prater   Margaret Quintyne————Thomas Prater

Alice Prater   Mary————Thomas Prater   Richard Prater
Immigrant to Virginia

John Prater   Richard Prater   William Prater

Jonathan Prather———— Jane   Samuel Prater

Jonathan Prater——Elizabeth Bigger   William Prather————Anne Yates
Parents of Martha Prather,   *See line 137 (25)*
*who married her cousin William**

Jane Prather   Joseph Prather   Elizabeth Prather

Priscilla Prather   John Prather

William Prather*   Margaret Prather   Sarah Prather
married his cousin Martha

133

1. **Henry I, King of England**, born September, 1068, died December 1, 1135. He was the son of William the Conqueror, King of England, and Mathilda of Flanders. His mistress was Edith. *Cokayne, The Complete Peerage, Volume XI (Appendix D), pages 112–113; Moriarty, The Plantagenet Ancestry of King Edward III, page 13*

2. **Matilda, Countess of Perche**, born ca. 1086, died November 25, 1120. She married Rotrou II, Count of Perche, died 1144. He was the son of Geoffrey II, Count of Perche, and Beatrix. *Cokayne, The Complete Peerage, Volume XI (Appendix D), pages 112–113; Moriarty, The Plantagenet Ancestry of King Edward III, page 49*

3. **Maud (Matilda)**, born 1105, died 1143. She married Raymond I, Viscount of Turenne, died 1122. He was the son of Boso I, Viscount of Turenne. *Moriarty, The Plantagenet Ancestry of King Edward III, pages 47 and 48; Weis, Ancestral Roots of Certain American Colonists, 153 (25)*

4. **Marguerite of Turenne**. She married William IV, Count of Angoulême, died 1178. He was the son of Wulgrim II, Count of Angoulême, and Poncia de la Marche. *Moriarty, The Plantagenet Ancestry of King Edward III, pages 47 and 48; Weis, Ancestral Roots of Certain American Colonists, 117 (26), and 153 (26)*

5. **Aymer "Taillifer" de Valence, Count of Angoulême**, died June 16, 1202. He married Alice de Courtenay, died 1218. She was the daughter of Pierre de Courtenay and Elizabeth de Courtenay. *Moriarty, The Plantagenet Ancestry of King Edward III, page 47; Schwennicke, Europäische Stammtafeln, Volume II, table 17; Weis, Ancestral Roots of Certain American Colonists, 117 (26), and 153 (27)*

6. **Isabel of Angoulême**, born 1188, died May 31, 1236. She married John, King of England, born December 24, 1167, died October 18, 1216. He was the son of Henry II, King of England, and Eleanor of Aquitaine. *Cokayne, The Complete Peerage, Volume III (Cornwall), page 430; Moriarty, The Plantagenet Ancestry of King Edward III, page 47*

7. **Sir Richard Plantagenet, Earl of Cornwall, Count of Poitou, King of the Romans**, born January 5, 1209, died April 2, 1272. *Cokayne, The Complete Peerage, Volume III (Cornwall), page 430; Weis, Ancestral Roots of Certain American Colonists, 258 (27); See line 141 (2)*

LINE 139

1. **Empress Matilda, Lady of the English**, born ca. 1103, died September 10, 1167. She was the daughter of Henry I, King of England, and Mathilda of Flanders. She married Geoffrey Plantagenet, Count of Anjou and Duke of Normandy, born November 23, 1113, died September 7, 1151. He was the son of Fulk V, Count of Anjou, and Erembourg, Countess of Maine. *Moriarty, The Plantagenet Ancestry of King Edward III, pages 2 and 13; Schwennicke, Europäische Stammtafeln, Volume II, table 81; Burke, Burke's Peerage (The Royal Lineage), page 28*

2. **Henry II, King of England**, born March 5, 1132, died July 6, 1189. He married Eleanor of Aquitaine, Queen of France, born 1123, died March 3, 1204. She was the daughter of William, Duc d'Aquitaine, and Eleanor de Chatellerault. *Moriarty, The Plantagenet Ancestry of King Edward III, pages 2 and 36; Burke, Burke's Peerage (The Royal Lineage), page 29*

3. **Eleanor of England, Queen of Castile**, born October 13, 1162, died October 31, 1214. She married Alfonso VIII, King of Castile, born November 11, 1155, died October 6, 1214. He was the son of Sancho III, King of Castile, and Blanca of Navarre. *Moriarty, The Plantagenet Ancestry of King Edward III, page 108; Burke, Burke's Peerage (The Royal Lineage), page 29*

4. **Berengaria of Castile, Queen of León**, born ca. 1180, died November 8, 1246. She married Alfonso IX, King of León, born August 15, 1171, died September 23, 1230. He was the son of Fernando II, King of León, and Urraca of Portugal, daughter of Alfonso I, King of Portugal. *Moriarty, The Plantagenet Ancestry of King Edward III, page 108; Weis, Ancestral Roots of Certain American Colonists, 110 (28), and 114 (27)*

5. **Berengaria of León, Queen of Jerusalem**, born 1204, died April 12, 1237. She married Jean de Brienne, Emperor of Constantinople and King of Jerusalem, born ca. 1168, died March 21, 1237. He was the son of Erard II, Count of Brienne, and Agnes de Montfauçon. *Cokayne, The Complete Peerage, Volume II (Beaumont), page 59 (b); Weis, Ancestral Roots of Certain American Colonists, 114 (28)*

6. **Louis de Brienne, Viscount Beaumont-au-Maine**, died 1297. He married Agnes de Beaumont. She was the daughter of Raoul VIII, Vicomte of Maine, and Agnes. *Cokayne, The Complete Peerage, Volume II (Beaumont), page 59 (b); Weis, Ancestral Roots of Certain American Colonists, 114 (29)*

7. **Henry de Beaumont, Baron Beaumont, Earl of Buchan**, died March 10, 1339. He married Alice Comyn, died 1349. She was the daughter of Alexander Comyn, Earl of Buchan, and Joan Latimer. *Cokayne, The Complete Peerage, Volume II (Beaumont), page 60, and (Buchan), page 375*

8. **John de Beaumont, Baron Beaumont**, died 1342. He married Eleanor Plantagenet, born 1318, died January 11, 1372. She was the daughter of Henry Plantagenet, Earl of Lancaster, and Maud de Chaworth. *Cokayne, The Complete Peerage, Volumes II (Beaumont), pages 60–61, and VII (Lancaster), page 401 (b)*

9. **Henry de Beaumont, Baron Beaumont**, born 1340, died June 17, 1369. He married Margaret de Vere, died June 15, 1398. She was the daughter of John de Vere, Earl of Oxford, and Maud de Badlesmere. *Cokayne, The Complete Peerage, Volumes II (Beaumont), page 61, and X (Oxford), pages 223–224 (b)*

10. **Sir John de Beaumont, Baron Beaumont**, born ca. 1361, died September 9, 1396. He married Catherine Everingham, died 1426. She was the daughter of Thomas Everingham. *Cokayne, The Complete Peerage, Volume II (Beaumont), page 61, and (Botreaux) page 242*

11. **Elizabeth de Beaumont**. She married William Botreaux, Baron Botreaux, born February 20, 1388, died May 16, 1462. He was the

son of William Botreaux, Baron Botreaux, and Elizabeth de St. Lo. *Cokayne, The Complete Peerage, Volumes II (Botreaux), page 242, and VI, (Hungerford), page 617*

12. **Margaret Botreaux, Baroness Botreaux**, died February 7, 1477. She married Robert Hungerford, Baron Hungerford, died May 18, 1459. He was the son of Walter Hungerford, Baron Hungerford, and Catherine Peverell. *Cokayne, The Complete Peerage, Volumes II (Botreaux), page 242, and VI, (Hungerford), pages 613–618*

13. **Eleanor Hungerford**. She married John White, died 1469. He was the son of Robert White and Alice. *Faris, Plantagenet Ancestry of Seventeenth Century Colonists, (Yate), page 387; Weis, Ancestral Roots of Certain American Colonists, 51A (36)* **See line 141 (9)**

LINE 140

1. **Henry II, King England**, born March 5, 1132, died July 6, 1189. He was the son of Geoffrey Plantagenet, Count of Anjou and Duke of Normandy, and Empress Matilda, Lady of the English. He married Eleanor of Aquitaine, Queen of the Franks, born 1123, died March 3, 1204. She was the daughter of William, Duc d'Aquitaine, and Eleanor de Chatellerault. *Moriarty, The Plantagenet Ancestry of King Edward III, page 2; Burke, Burke's Peerage (The Royal Lineage), page 29*

2. **Eleanor of England, Queen of Castile**, born October 13, 1162, died October 31, 1214. She married Alfonso VIII, King of Castile, born November 11, 1155, died October 6, 1214. He was the son of Sancho III, King of Castile, and Blanca of Navarre. *Moriarty, The Plantagenet Ancestry of King Edward III, page 108; Burke, Burke's Peerage (The Royal Lineage), page 29*

3. **Blanca of Castile, Queen of the Franks**, born March 4, 1188, died November 27, 1252. She married Louis VIII "the Lion", King of the Franks, born September 3, 1187, died November 8, 1226. He was the son of Philip II Augustus, King of the Franks, and Isabella of Hainaut. *Moriarty, The Plantagenet Ancestry of King Edward III, pages 108 and 116; Weis, Ancestral Roots of Certain American Colonists, 101 (27), and 113 (28)*

4. **Robert I, Count of Artois**, born September 1216, died February 9, 1250. He married Mathilda of Brabant, died September 29, 1288. She was the daughter of Henry II, Duke of Brabant, and Marie von Hohenstauffen. *Cokayne, The Complete Peerage, Volume VII (Lancaster), page 386; Moriarty, The Plantagenet Ancestry of King Edward III, page 154*

5. **Blanche of Artois, Queen of Navarre**, born 1245, died May 2, 1302. She married Edmund "Crouchback" Plantagenet, Earl of Lancaster, born January 16, 1244, died June 5, 1296. He was the son of Henry III, King of England, and Eleanor of Provence. *Cokayne, The Complete Peerage, Volume VII (Lancaster), pages 378–387; Moriarty, The Plantagenet Ancestry of King Edward III, pages 148 and 154*

6. **Henry Plantagenet, Earl of Lancaster**, born 1281, died September 22, 1345. He married Maud de Chaworth, born 1282, died ca. 1322. She was the daughter of Patrick de Chaworth and Isabella Beauchamp. *Cokayne, The Complete Peerage, Volume VII (Lancaster), pages 396–401; Weis, Ancestral Roots of Certain American Colonists, 17 (29), and 72 (32)* **See line 143 (3)**

LINE 141

1. **John, King of England**, born December 24, 1167, died October 18, 1216. He was the son of Henry II, King of England, and Eleanor of Aquitaine. He married Isabel of Angoulême, born 1188, died May 31, 1246. She was the daughter of Aymer "Taillifer" de Valence, Count of Angoulême, and Alice de Courtenay. *Cokayne, The Complete Peerage, Volume III (Cornwall), page 430; Burke, Burke's Peerage (The Royal Lineage), page 29*

2. **Sir Richard Plantagenet, Earl of Cornwall, Count of Poitou, King of the Romans**, born January 5, 1209, died April 2, 1272. His mistress was Joan Valletort. She was the daughter of Reginald Valletort. She may have been the mother of generation 3. *Cokayne, The Complete Peerage, Volume III (Cornwall), pages 430–432; Weis, Ancestral Roots of Certain American Colonists, 258 (27)*

3. **Sir Walter of Cornwall**, illegitimate son, born 1245, died 1313. *Peter, The Journal of the Royal Institution of Cornwall, page 414; Richardson, Plantagenet Ancestry, (Yate), page 789*

John, King of England
from the British Library

4. **Margaret of Cornwall**. She married James Peverell. *Richardson, Plantagenet Ancestry, (Yate), page 789; Weaver, in Notes and Queries for Somerset and Dorset, Volume VII, pages 64–65 (Note: Weaver says Margaret's husband was named Hugh, not James.)*

5. **Hugh Peverell**. He married Margaret Cobham. She was the daughter of John Cobham. *Richardson, Plantagenet Ancestry, (Yate), page 789; Weaver, in Notes and Queries for Somerset and Dorset, Volume VII, pages 64–65 (Note: Weaver says Hugh Peverell's wife was named Elizabeth, not Margaret.)*

6. **Thomas Peverell**. He married Margaret de Courtenay, died 1422. She was the daughter of Sir Thomas de Courtenay and Muriel Moels. *Cokayne, The Complete Peerage, Volume VI (Hungerford), page 615; Weis, Ancestral Roots of Certain American Colonists, 51A (33)*

7. **Catherine Peverell**. She married Sir Walter Hungerford, Baron Hungerford, born 1378, died August 9, 1449. He was the son of Sir Thomas Hungerford and Joan Hussey. *Cokayne, The Complete Peerage, Volume VI (Hungerford), pages 613–616*

8. **Robert Hungerford, Baron Hungerford,** died May 14, 1459. He married Margaret Botreaux, Baroness Botreaux, died February 7, 1477. She was the daughter of William Botreaux, Baron Botreaux, and Elizabeth Beaumont. *Cokayne, The Complete Peerage, Volumes II (Botreaux), pages 242–243, and VI (Hungerford), pages 613–616; Faris, Plantagenet Ancestry of Seventeenth Century Colonists, (Yate), page 387*

9. **Eleanor Hungerford**. She married John White, died 1469. He was the son of Robert White and Alice. *Roberts, The Royal Descents of 600 Immigrants, page 374; Faris, Plantagenet Ancestry of Seventeenth-Century Colonists, (Yate), page 387*

10. **Robert White**, died 1512. He married Margaret Gainsford. She was the daughter of Nicholas Gainsford and Margaret Sidney. *Roberts, The Royal Descents of 600 Immigrants, page 374; Faris, Plantagenet Ancestry of Seventeenth-Century Colonists, (Yate), page 387*

11. **Anne White**. She married Nicholas Tichborne, died 1513. He was the son of John Tichborne and Margaret Martin. *Roberts, The Royal Descents of 600 Immigrants, page 374; Faris, Plantagenet Ancestry of Seventeenth-Century Colonists, (Yate), page 387; Burke, Burke's Peerage (Tichborne) page 2202*

12. **Nicholas Tichborne**, died 1555. He married Elizabeth Rythe. She was the daughter of William Rythe and Margery Cowdray. *Roberts, The Royal Descents of 600 Immigrants, page 374; Faris, Plantagenet Ancestry of Seventeenth-Century Colonists, (Yate), page 388; Burke, Burke's Peerage (Tichborne), page 2202; Richardson, Plantagenet Ancestry, (Yate), page 789* **See line 137 (20)**

LINE 142 continued from line 141 (10)

11. **Robert White**, born ca. 1475. He married Elizabeth Inglefield. She was the daughter of Sir Thomas Inglefield. *Mundy, The Visitation of Hampshire, page 82*

12. **Thomas White**, born ca. 1490. He married Agnes White, died 1571. She was the daughter of Robert White. *Mundy, The Visitation of Hampshire, page 82; Faris, Plantagenet Ancestry of Seventeenth-Century Colonists, (Yate), page 388; Burke, Dormant and Extinct Peerages, page 592*

13. **Frances White**, died 1580. She married Thomas Yate. He was the son of John Yate and Alice Hyde. *Metcalfe, The Visitation of Berkshire, page 32; Mundy, The Visitation of Hampshire, page 82; Faris, Plantagenet Ancestry of Seventeenth-Century Colonists, (Yate), page 388*

14. **Francis Yate**, died 1588. He married Jane Tichborne. She was the daughter of Nicholas Tichborne and Elizabeth Rythe. *Roberts, The Royal Descents of 600 Immigrants, page 374; Faris, Plantagenet Ancestry of Seventeenth-Century Colonists, (Yate), page 388*

15. **Thomas Yate**, died between 1654 and 1660. He married Dorothy Stephens. She was the daughter of Nicholas Stephens. *Roberts, The Royal Descents of 600 Immigrants, page 374; Faris, Plantagenet Ancestry of Seventeenth-Century Colonists, (Yate), page 388; Boyan and Lamb, Francis Tregian: Cornish Recusant, pages 135–137 See line 137 (22)*

LINE 143

1. **Henry III, King of England**, born October 1, 1207, died November 16, 1272. He was the son of John, King of England, and Isabel of Angoulême. He married Eleanor of Provence (152-9), born 1217, died June 24, 1291. She was the daughter of Raymond V, Count of Provence, and Beatrice of Savoy. *Cokayne, The Complete Peerage, Volume VII (Lancaster), page 378; Moriarty, The Plantagenet Ancestry of King Edward III, pages 2 and 68; Schwennicke, Europäische Stammtafeln, Volume II, table 83*

2. **Edmund "Crouchback" Plantagenet, Earl of Lancaster**, born January 16, 1244, died June 5, 1296. He married Blanche of Artois, Queen of Navarre, born 1245, died May 2, 1302. She was the daughter of Robert I, Count of Artois (son of Louis VIII, King of the Franks), and Mathilda of Brabant. *Cokayne, The Complete Peerage, Volume VII (Lancaster), pages 378–387; Moriarty, The Plantagenet Ancestry of King Edward III, pages 148 and 154*

3. **Henry Plantagenet, Earl of Lancaster**, born 1281, died September 22, 1345. He married Maud de Chaworth, born 1282, died ca. 1322. She was the daughter of Patrick de Chaworth and Isabella Beauchamp. *Cokayne, The Complete Peerage, Volumes II (Beaumont), page 61, and VII (Lancaster), pages 396–401; Weis, Ancestral Roots of Certain American Colonists, 17 (29), and 72 (32)*

4. **Eleanor Plantagenet**, born 1318, died January 11, 1372. She married John de Beaumont, Baron Beaumont, born 1318, died 1342. He was the son of Henry de Beaumont, Earl of Buchan, and Alice Comyn. *Cokayne, The Complete Peerage, Volumes II (Beaumont), pages 60–61, and VII (Lancaster), page 401 (b); Weis, Ancestral Roots of Certain American Colonists, 17 (30), and 114 (31)*

5. **Henry de Beaumont, Baron Beaumont**, born 1340, died June 17, 1369. He married Margaret de Vere, died June 15, 1398. She was the daughter of John de Vere, Earl of Oxford, and Maud de Badlesmere. *Cokayne, The Complete Peerage, Volumes II (Beaumont), page 61, and X (Oxford), pages 223–224* **See line 139 (9)**

LINE 144

1. **Edward I, King of England**, born June 17, 1239, died July 7, 1307. He was the son of Henry III, King of England, and Eleanor of Provence. He married (first) Elenora of Castile, born 1241, died November 28, 1290. She was the daughter of St. Fernando, King of Castile and León, and Joanna Dammartin, Countess of Ponthieu. *The Complete Peerage, Volume V, (Gloucester), pages 707–708; Moriarty, The Plantagenet Ancestry of King Edward III, pages 2 and 109*

2. **Joan Plantagenet**, died April 23, 1307. She married Gilbert de Clare, Earl of Gloucester and Hertford, born September 2, 1243, died December 7, 1295. He was the son of Richard de Clare, Earl

of Hertford, and Maud de Lacy. *Cokayne, The Complete Peerage, Volumes III (Clare), page 244, V, (Gloucester), pages 696–707, and VI (Hertford), page 503*

3. **Elizabeth de Clare**, born September 16, 1295, died November 4, 1360. She married John de Burgh, born 1290, died June 18, 1313. He was the son of Richard de Burgh, Earl of Ulster, and Margaret de Couci. *Cokayne, The Complete Peerage, Volumes V, (Gloucester), page 708 (a), and XII/2 (Ulster), pages 173–178*

4. **William de Burgh, Earl of Ulster**, born September 17, 1312, died June 6, 1333. He married Maud Plantagenet, born 1310, died May 5, 1377. She was the daughter of Henry Plantagenet, Earl of Lancaster, and Maud de Chaworth. *Cokayne, The Complete Peerage, Volumes III (Clarence), page 257, and XII/2 (Ulster), pages 178–179*

5. **Elizabeth de Burgh, Countess of Ulster**, born 1332, died 1363. She married Lionel of Antwerp, Duke of Clarence, born November 29, 1338, died October 17, 1368. He was the son of Edward III, King of England, and Philippa of Hainaut. *Cokayne, The Complete Peerage, Volumes III (Clarence) pages 257–258, and XII/2 (Ulster), page 180*

6. **Philippa Plantagenet, Countess of Ulster**, born August 16, 1355, died January 1377. She married Edmund Mortimer, Earl of March, born February 1, 1351, died December 27, 1381. He was the son of Roger Mortimer, Earl of March, and Philippa Montagu. *Cokayne, The Complete Peerage, Volumes III (Clarence), page 258 (d), VIII (March), pages 445–448, and XII/2 (Ulster), page 180*

7. **Roger Mortimer, Earl of March**, died 1398. He married Eleanor Holand, died October 1405. She was the daughter of Thomas Holand, Earl of Kent, and Alice FitzAlan. *Cokayne, The Complete Peerage, Volumes VII (Kent), page 156 (e), VIII (March), pages 448–450, and XII/2 (Ulster), page 180*

8. **Anne Mortimer**, died September 1411. She married Richard Plantagenet, Duke of York, born 1375, died August 5, 1415. He was the son of Edmund of Langley, Duke of York (son of Edward III, King of England), and Isabella of Castile (daughter of Pedro I, King of Castile and León). *Cokayne, The Complete Peerage, Volume XII/2 (York), pages 895–899*

9. **Richard Plantagenet, Duke of York**, born September 21, 1411, died December 30, 1460. He married Cecily Neville, born May 3, 1415, died May 31, 1495. She was the daughter of Ralph Neville, Earl of Westmoreland, and Joan Beaufort. *Cokayne, The Complete Peerage, Volume XII/2 (Westmoreland), page 547 (h), and (York), pages 905–909*

10. **Edward IV, King of England**, born April 28, 1442, died April 9, 1483. He married Elizabeth Wydville, born 1437, died June 8, 1492. She was the daughter of Richard Wydville, Earl Rivers, and Jacquetta de St. Pol, Duchess of Bedford. *Cokayne, The Complete Peerage, Volumes II (Bedford), page 72, and XII/2 (Westmoreland), page 547 (h); Burke, Burke's Peerage (The Royal Lineage), page 33; Weir, Britain's Royal Families, pages 133–141* **See line 147 (1)**

LINE 145

1. **Edward II, King of England**, born April 25, 1284, died September 21, 1327. He was the son of Edward I, King of England, and Elenora of Castile. He married Isabella of France, born 1293, died August 22, 1358. She was the daughter of Philip IV, "the Fair", King of the Franks, and Jeanne, Queen of Navarre. *Moriarty, The Plantagenet Ancestry of King Edward III, pages 2 and 116; Schwennicke, Europäische Stammtafeln, Volume II, table 84; Burke, Burke's Peerage (The Royal Lineage), page 30*

2. **Edward III, King of England**, born November 13, 1312, died June 21, 1377. He married Philippa of Hainaut, born June 24, 1311, died August 14, 1369. She was the daughter of William III, Count of Hainaut and Holland, and Jeanne of Valois. *The Complete Peerage, Volume III (Clarence), pages 257–258; Moriarty, The Plantagenet Ancestry of King Edward III, pages 2 and 176; Burke, Burke's Peerage (The Royal Lineage), page 31*

3. **Lionel of Antwerp, Duke of Clarence**, born November 29, 1338, died October 17, 1368. He married Elizabeth de Burgh, Countess of Ulster, born July 6, 1332, died December 10, 1363. She was the daughter of William de Burgh, Earl of Ulster, and Maud Plantagenet. *Cokayne, The Complete Peerage, Volumes III (Clarence), pages 257–258, and XII/2 (Ulster), page 180*

4. **Philippa Plantagenet, Countess of Ulster**, born August 16, 1355, died January 1377. She married Edmund Mortimer, Earl of March, born February 1, 1351, died December 27, 1381. He was the son of Roger Mortimer, Earl of March, and Philippa Montagu. *Cokayne, The Complete Peerage, Volumes III (Clarence) page 258 (d), VIII (March), pages 445–448, and XII/2 (Ulster), page 180* **See line 144 (6)**

LINE 146

1. **Edward III, King of England**, born November 13, 1312, died June 21, 1377. He was the son of Edward II, King of England, and Isabella of France. He married Philippa of Hainaut, born June 24, 1311, died August 14, 1369. She was the daughter of William III, Count of Hainaut and Holland, and Jeanne of Valois. *Cokayne, The Complete Peerage, Volume VII (Lancaster), page 410; Moriarty, The Plantagenet Ancestry of King Edward III, pages 2 and 176; Schwennicke, Europäische Stammtafeln, Volume II, table 84*

2. **John of Gaunt, Duke of Lancaster**, born June 24, 1340, died February 3, 1399. He married his mistress, Katherine de Roelt, born 1350, died May 10, 1403. She was the daughter of Payne de Roelt. *Cokayne, The Complete Peerage, Volumes VII (Lancaster), pages 410–416, and XII/2 (Westmoreland), page 547; Schwennicke, Europäische Stammtafeln, Volume III/1, table 157; Burke, Burke's Peerage (The Royal Lineage), page 31*

3. **Joan Beaufort**, died November 13, 1440. She married Ralph Neville, Earl of Westmoreland, born 1364, died October 21, 1425. He was the son of John Neville and Maud de Percy. *Cokayne, The Complete Peerage, Volumes VII (Lancaster), pages 415–416 (i), and XII/2 (Westmoreland), pages 544–547 (h), and (York), page 908; Schwennicke, Europäische Stammtafeln, Volume III/1, table 157*

4. **Cecily Neville**, born May 3, 1415, died May 31, 1495. She married Richard Plantagenet, Duke of York, born September 21, 1411, died December 30, 1460. He was the son of Richard Plantagenet, Duke of York, and Anne Mortimer. *Cokayne, The Complete Peerage, Volume XII/2 (Westmoreland), page 547 (h), and (York), pages 905–909*

5. **Edward IV, King of England**, born April 28, 1442, died April 9, 1483. He married Elizabeth Wydville, born 1437, died June 8, 1492. She was the daughter of Richard Wydville, Earl Rivers, and Jacquetta de St. Pol, Duchess of Bedford. *Cokayne, The Complete Peerage, Volumes II (Bedford), page 72, XII/2 (Westmoreland), pages 544–547 (h). and (York), page 909; Burke, Burke's Peerage (The Royal Lineage), page 33* **See line 147 (1)**

LINE 147

1. **Edward IV, King of England**, born April 28, 1442, died April 9, 1483. He was the son of Richard Plantagenet, Duke of York, and Cecily Neville. He had several mistresses, one of whom, Elizabeth Waite, may have been the mother of line 2. *Cokayne, The Complete Peerage, Volume XII/2 (Westmoreland), pages 544–547 (h); Schwennicke, Europäische Stammtafeln, Volume II, table 86; Weis, Ancestral Roots of Certain American Colonists, 225 (35); Burke, Burke's Peerage (The Royal Lineage), page 33*

2. **Mary Plantagenet**. She married Henry Harman, died 1502. *Bruce, The Visitation of Kent, Volume 74, page 61; Trabue, in The Augustan, Volume XXVII:4, No. 116, The Arms and Ancestry of the Stocketts of Maryland, page 15*

3. **Henry Harman**. *Bruce, The Visitation of Kent, Volume 74, page 61; Trabue, in The Augustan, Volume XXVII:4, No. 116, The Arms and Ancestry of the Stocketts of Maryland, page 15*

4. **Alice Harman**. She married John Somer. *Trabue, in The Augustan, Volume XXVII:4, No. 116, The Arms and Ancestry of the Stocketts of Maryland, page 14*

5. **Elizabeth Somer**. She married John Ashton. *Trabue, in The Augustan, Volume XXVII:4, No. 116, The Arms and Ancestry of the Stocketts of Maryland, pages 13–14*

6. **Elizabeth Ashton**. She married John Aylesworth. *Bruce, The Visitation of Kent, (Ayleworth), page 149; Trabue, in The Augustan, Volume XXVII:4, No. 116, The Arms and Ancestry of the Stocketts of Maryland, pages 13–14; Barnes, British Roots of Maryland Families, page 31*

7. **Walter Aylesworth**. He married Jane Stockett. She was the daughter of Lewis Stockett. *Bruce, The Visitation of Kent, (Ayleworth), page 150; Barnes, British Roots of Maryland Families, page 31*

8. **Frances Aylesworth**. She married Thomas Stockett, born 1595. He was the son of Thomas Stockett and Joanna Biggs. *Bruce, The Visitation of Kent, (Ayleworth), page 150; Barnes, British Roots of Maryland Families, pages 31 and 410*

9. **Captain Thomas Stockett**, born 1635, died 1671. He married Mary Wells, died January 21, 1697. She was the daughter of Richard Wells. *Newman, Anne Arundel Gentry, Volume II, page 377; Barnes, British Roots of Maryland Families, page 410; Richardson, Plantagenet Ancestry, YATE, page 790*

10. **Elizabeth Stockett**, died 1700. She married Thomas Plummer, died ca. 1694. *Jourdan, Early Families of Southern Maryland, Volume II, page 2; Newman, Anne Arundel Gentry, Volume II, page 377*

11. **Margaret Plummer**. She married Aodh (Hugh) Riley, died ca. 1740. He was probably the son of Maolmordha (Miles) Riley. *Jourdan, Early Families of Southern Maryland, Volume II, page 2; Riley, The Colonial Riley Families of the Tidewater Frontier, Volume I, pages 209–212*

12. **Eliphaz Riley**, born ca. 1688, died May, 1760. He married Elizabeth (possibly Burkett). She may have been the daughter of John Burkett and Jane Abbott. *Riley, The Colonial Riley Families of the Tidewater Frontier, Volume I, pages 216–217*

13. **Samuel Riley**, died after 1792. He married Eleanor Wallace. She may have been the daughter of Samuel Wallace and "Jane", probably a member of the Pekowi-Metis Shawnee Indian tribe. *Riley, The Colonial Riley Families of the Tidewater Frontier, Volume I, pages 288–290. [In his book <u>Shawnee Heritage</u>, Don Greene includes the following: "Riley, Milcah – 1/4th Pekowi-Metis, daughter of Samuel Riley & Eleanor Wallace." We know that Samuel Riley was Irish, the son of Eliphaz Riley and Elizabeth Burkett, so the only other ancestor that could provide 1/4 Shawnee blood to Milcah Riley would have been his grandmother, "Jane", the mother of Eleanor, wife of Samuel Riley.]*

14. Eliphaz Riley, born January 27, 1749, died October 20, 1834. He married Sarah Mahan. She was the daughter of James Mahan and Sarah. *Riley, The Colonial Riley Families of the Tidewater Frontier, Volume I, pages 308–310*

15. Martha Riley. She married Brice Bazel Prater, born ca. 1776, died 1859. He was the son of Bazel Prater and Priscilla (possibly Swearingen). *Riley, The Colonial Riley Families of the Tidewater Frontier, Volume I, page 357; Prather, Prater, Prather, Prator, Praytor in America, Volume II, page 144: Doliante, Maryland and Virginia Colonials, Volume II, page 664*

Children of Martha Riley and Brice Bazel Prater:
a. Charles, 1800–1800
b. Holloway, 1802–1862
c. Andrew, 1804–1858
   married Mary Liddia
d. Martin, born 1806
   married Minerva Hester
e. Eliphaz, born August 6, 1808
   married Kesiah Skelly
f. Bazel, 1810 – January 28, 1887
   married Nancy Cooper Crawford
g. Josiah, born 1811
   married Sarah Elizabeth Harpoole
h. Isaac, born 1815
i. King, October 18, 1818 – March 28, 1900
   married Nancy Riley
j. Samuel, 1822–1880
   married Elizabeth Rebecca Riley
k. Nancy, born 1824
l. Jenkins, 1826–1910
   married Elizabeth Carter Lloyd
m. Cassandra, 1828–1859
   married Isom Turnbough
n. Brison, born 1829
o. Ninian, 1831–1885
   married Nancy Permelia Ann Battles Walker

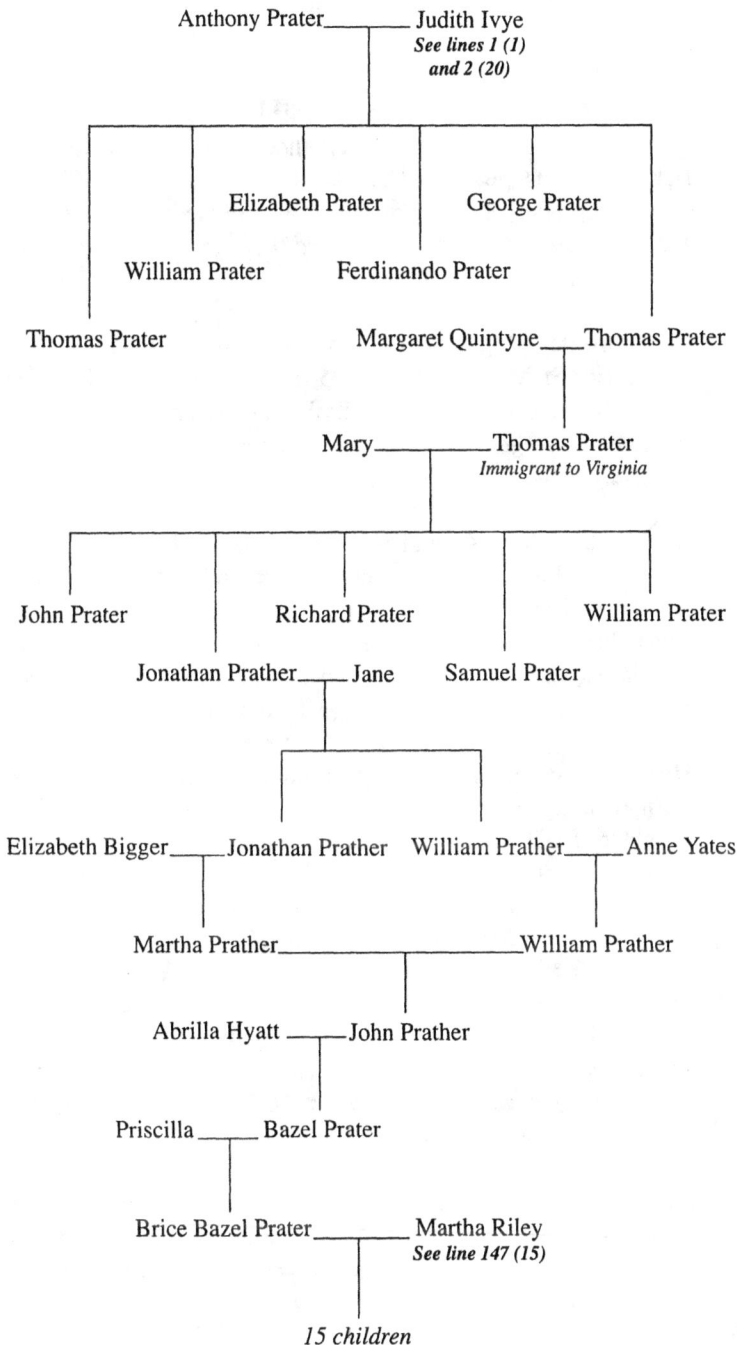

Anthony Prater_____ Judith Ivye
See lines 1 (1)
and 2 (20)

Elizabeth Prater   George Prater

William Prater   Ferdinando Prater

Thomas Prater   Margaret Quintyne____Thomas Prater

Mary_____Thomas Prater
Immigrant to Virginia

John Prater   Richard Prater   William Prater

Jonathan Prather_____ Jane   Samuel Prater

Elizabeth Bigger_____Jonathan Prather   William Prather_____Anne Yates

Martha Prather_____William Prather

Abrilla Hyatt _____John Prather

Priscilla _____ Bazel Prater

Brice Bazel Prater_____ Martha Riley
See line 147 (15)

15 children

149

Scotland

1. **Duncan, I, King of Scots**, born 1001, died August 14, 1040. He was the son of Crinan "the Thane", and Bethoc, the daughter of Malcolm II, King of Scots. He married Sybilla. She was the daughter of Sigurd "the Strong", Earl of Northumberland, and Ælflaeda. *Moriarty, The Plantagenet Ancestry of King Edward III, page 30; Weir, Britain's Royal Families, pages 178 and 180–181*

2. **Malcolm, III, King of Scots**, born 1031, died November 13, 1093. He married St. Margaret, born 1045, died November 16, 1093. She was the daughter of Edward "the Exile", and Agatha. *Cokayne, The Complete Peerage, Volume VI (Huntingdon), page 641; Moriarty, The Plantagenet Ancestry of King Edward III, page 30*

3. **David "the Saint", King of Scots**, died May 24, 1153. He married Matilda of Huntingdon, Countess of Northumberland, born 1072, died 1131. She was the daughter of Waltheof II, Earl of Huntingdon, and Judith of Lens. *Cokayne, The Complete Peerage, Volume VI (Huntingdon), pages 639 and 641–642; Moriarty, The Plantagenet Ancestry of King Edward III, pages 30 and 182*

4. **Henry of Scotland, Earl of Northumberland**, died June 12, 1152. He married Ada de Warenne, born 1120, died 1178. She was the daughter of William II, Earl of Surrey, and Isabel of Vermandois. *Cokayne, The Complete Peerage, Volumes VI (Huntingdon), pages 642–643, and XII/1 (Surrey), page 496 (g); Roberts, The Royal Descents of 600 Immigrants, pages 463, 466, and 469*

5. **William, I, "the Lion" King of Scots**, born 1143, died December 4, 1214. His mistress was a daughter of Richard Avenal. *Cokayne, The Complete Peerage, Volumes VI (Huntingdon), pages 644–645, and XI (Ros), pages 92–93; Roberts, The Royal Descents of 500 Immigrants, page 342*

6. **Isabel of Scotland**. She married Robert de Ros, died December 23, 1226. He was the son of Everard de Ros and Roese Trussebut. *Cokayne, The Complete Peerage, Volume XI (Ros), pages 92–93; Roberts, The Royal Royal Descents of of 500 Immigrants, pages 342 and 367*

7. **Sir William de Ros**, died ca. 1264. He married Lucy. She may have been the daughter of Reginald FitzPiers. *Cokayne, The Complete Peerage, Volume XI (Ros), pages 93–94; Roberts, The Royal Descents of 500 Immigrants, page 342*

8. **Sir Robert de Ros**, died May 17, 1285. He married Isabel d'Aubigny, died June 15, 1301. She was the daughter of William d'Aubigny, probably by his second wife, Isabel. *Cokayne, The Complete Peerage, Volume XI (Ros), pages 95–96; Roberts, The Royal Descents of 500 Immigrants, page 342*

9. **William de Ros, Baron Ros**, died 1316. He married Maud de Vaux. She was the daughter of John de Vaux. *Cokayne, The Complete Peerage, Volume XI (Ros), pages 96–97; Roberts, The Royal Descents of 500 Immigrants, page 342; Burke, Dormant and Extinct Peerages, page 459*

10. **William de Ros, Baron Ros**, died February 3, 1342. He married Margery de Badlesmere, died 1363. She was the daughter of Bartholomew de Badlesmere, Baron Badlesmere, and Margaret de Clare. *Cokayne, The Complete Peerage, Volume XI (Ros), pages 98–99; Weis, Ancestral Roots of Certain American Colonists, 54 (33); Burke, Dormant and Extinct Peerages, page 459*

11. **Alice de Ros**, died ca. 1344. She married Nicholas Meinill, Baron Meinill, died ca. 1341. He was the illegitimate son of Nicholas Meinill, Baron Meinill, and Lucy Thweng. *Cokayne, The Complete Peerage, Volume VIII (Meinill), pages 627–634; Weis, Ancestral Roots of Certain American Colonists, 54 (34); Roberts, The Royal Descents of 500 Immigrants, page 342 (Note: Roberts makes Alice a daughter of #9, William Ros and Maud Vaux. Weis makes her a daughter of #10, William Ros and Margery Badlesmere. Cokayne says only that she was the daughter of William Ros, Baron Ros.)*

12. **Elizabeth Meinill, Baroness Meinill**, born October 15, 1331, died July 9, 1368. She married John Darcy, Baron Darcy, died March 5, 1355 or 1356. He was the son of Sir John Darcy, Baron Darcy, and Emmeline Heron. *Cokayne, The Complete Peerage, Volumes IV (Darcy), pages 58–60, and VIII (Meinill), pages 634–635; Roberts, The Royal Descents of 500 Immigrants, page 342*

13. Alice Darcy, She married Sir John Colville, died August 20, 1405. He was the son of Sir William Colville and Joan de Fauconberg. *Weis, The Magna Charta Sureties, 117 (7); Roberts, The Royal Descents of 500 Immigrants, page 342* **See line 137 (14)**

LINE 149 continued from line 148 (8)

9. **Isabel de Ros**. She married Walter Fauconberg, Baron Fauconberg, died December 31, 1318. He was the son of Sir Walter Fauconberg, Baron Fauconberg, and Agnes de Brus. *Cokayne, The Complete Peerage, Volume V (Fauconberg), pages 268–270; Roberts, The Royal Descents of 500 Immigrants, page 342; Burke, Dormant and Extinct Peerages, page 459*

10. **John Fauconberg, Baron Fauconberg**, born 1290, died September, 1349. He married Eve Bulmer. She was probably the daughter of Sir Ralph Bulmer. *Cokayne, The Complete Peerage, Volume V (Fauconberg), pages 271–272; Weis, Ancestral Roots of Certain American Colonists, 208 (31); Roberts, The Royal Descents of 500 Immigrants, page 342*

11. **Joan Fauconberg**. She married Sir William Colville, died ca. 1380. *Cokayne, The Complete Peerage, Volume IV (Darcy), pages 58–60; Weis, Ancestral Roots of Certain American Colonists, 208 (32); Roberts, The Royal Descents of 500 Immigrants, page 342*

12. **John Colville**, died August 20, 1405. He married Alice Darcy. She was the daughter of John Darcy, Baron Darcy, and Elizabeth Meinill. *Weis, Ancestral Roots of Certain American Colonists, 208 (33); Weis, The Magna Charta Sureties, 117 (7); Roberts, The Royal Descents of 500 Immigrants, page 342*

13. **Isabel Colville**, She married John Wandesford, died ca. 1400. He was the son of John Wandesford and Elizabeth Musters. *Weis, Ancestral Roots of Certain American Colonists, 208 (34); Weis, The Magna Charta Sureties, 117 (8); Roberts, The Royal Descents of 500 Immigrants, page 342; Burke, Dormant and Extinct Peerages, page 567* **See line 137 (15)**

France

1. **Philip I, King of the Franks**, born 1053, died July 29, 1108. He was the son of Henri I, King of the Franks, and Anna of Kiev. He married Bertha of Holland, born 1055, died 1094. She was the daughter of Florence I, Count of Holland, and Gertrude of Saxony. *Moriarty, The Plantagenet Ancestry of King Edward III, page 51; Schwennicke, Europäische Stammtafeln, Volume II, tables 2 and 11*

2. **Louis VI, King of the Franks**, born 1081, died August 1, 1137. He married Adela of Savoy, born 1092, died November 18, 1154. She was the daughter of Umberto II, Duke of Savoy, and Gisele of Burgundy. *Moriarty, The Plantagenet Ancestry of King Edward III, pages 51 and 59; Schwennicke, Europäische Stammtafeln, Volume II, table 11*

3. **Louis VII, King of the Franks**, born 1120, died September 13, 1180. He married Alix of Champagne, born 1140, died June 4, 1206. She was the daughter of Thebaud IV, Count of Blois, and Matilda of Carinthia. *Moriarty, The Plantagenet Ancestry of King Edward III, pages 51, 116, and 117; Schwennicke, Europäische Stammtafeln, Volume II, table 11*

4. **Phillip II (Augustus), King of the Franks**, born August 22, 1165, died July 14, 1223. He married Isabella of Hainaut, born 1170, died March 15, 1190. She was the daughter of Baldwin V, Count of Hainaut, and Marguerite of Lorraine. *Moriarty, The Plantagenet Ancestry of King Edward III, pages 116 and 124; Schwennicke, Europäische Stammtafeln, Volume II, table 11*

5. **Louis VIII, King of the Franks**, born September 3, 1187, died November 8, 1226. He married Blanca of Castile (151-6), born 1188, died November 27, 1252. She was the daughter of Alfonso VIII, King of Castile, and Eleanor of England, the daughter of Henry II, King of England. *Moriarty, The Plantagenet Ancestry of King Edward III, pages 108 and 116; Schwennicke, Europäische Stammtafeln, Volume II, table 12*

6. **Robert I, Count of Artois,** born September 1216, died February 9, 1250. He married Mathilda of Brabant, died September 29, 1288. She was the daughter of Henry II, Duke of Brabant, and Marie von Hohenstauffen. *Cokayne, The Complete Peerage, Volume VII (Lancaster), page 386; Moriarty, The Plantagenet Ancestry of King Edward III, pages 116 and 154* **See line 140 (4)**

Spain

LINE 151

1. **Rodrigo "El Cid" Díaz de Vivar, Count of Valencia,** born ca. 1042, died July 10, 1099. He was the son of Diego Lainez. He married Jimena, died ca. 1115. She was the daughter of Diego, Count of Orviedo, and Cristina Gundemariz. *Moriarty, The Plantagenet Ancestry of King Edward III, page 110*

2. **Cristina,** born ca. 1077. She married Ramiro, Count of Monçon, died after 1116. He was the son of Sancho Ramirez and Constanza. *Moriarty, The Plantagenet Ancestry of King Edward III, page 110*

3. **Garcia VII, King of Navarre,** died 1150. He married Marguerite de l'Aigle, died May 25, 1141. She was the daughter of Gilbert, Seigneur de l'Aigle, and Juliana of Mortagne and Perche. *Moriarty, The Plantagenet Ancestry of King Edward III, pages 109 and 111*

4. **Blanca of Navarre,** died August 1156 or 1158. She married Sancho III, King of Castile, born 1134, died August 31, 1158. He was the son of Alfonso VII, King of Castile and León, and Berengaria of Barcelona. *Moriarty, The Plantagenet Ancestry of King Edward III, page 108; Schwennicke, Europäische Stammtafeln, Volume II, table 62*

5. **Alfonso VIII, King of Castile,** born 1155, died 1214. He married Eleanor of England, born 1162, died 1214. She was the daughter of Henry II, King of England, and Eleanor of Aquitaine. *Moriarty, The Plantagenet Ancestry of King Edward III, page 108; Schwennicke, Europäische Stammtafeln, Volume II, table 62*

6. **Blanca of Castile,** died November 27, 1252. She married Louis VIII (150-5), King of the Franks, died 1226. He was the son of Philip II

(Augustus), King of the Franks, and Isabella of Hainaut. *Moriarty, The Plantagenet Ancestry of King Edward III, pages 108 and 116; Schwennicke, Europäische Stammtafeln, Volume II, table 62*

7. **Robert I, Count of Artois,** born 1216, died 1250. He married Mathilda of Brabant, died September 29, 1288. She was the daughter of Henry II, Duke of Brabant, and Marie von Hohenstauffen. *Cokayne, The Complete Peerage, Volume VII (Lancaster), page 386; Moriarty, The Plantagenet Ancestry of King Edward III, pages 116 and 154*

8. **Blanche of Artois, Queen of Navarre,** born ca. 1250, died May 2, 1302. She married Edmund "Crouchback" Plantagenet, (143–2) Earl of Lancaster, born January 16, 1244, died June 5, 1296. He was the son of Henry III, King of England, and Eleanor of Provence. *Cokayne, The Complete Peerage, Volume VII (Lancaster), pages 378–387; Moriarty, The Plantagenet Ancestry of King Edward III, page 154*

9. **Henry Plantagenet, Earl of Lancaster,** born 1281, died September 22, 1345. He married Maud de Chaworth, born 1282, died ca. 1322. She was the daughter of Patrick de Chaworth and Isabella Beauchamp. *Cokayne, The Complete Peerage, Volume VII (Lancaster), pages 396–401; Weis, Ancestral Roots of Certain American Colonists, 17 (29), and 72 (32)* **See line 143 (3)**

LINE 152

1. **Sancho Garcia III, "the Great", King of Aragon, Castile and Navarre,** died October 15, 1035. He was the son of Garcia Sanchez, King of Navarre, and Ximena. His mistress was Munia, died July 13, 1066. She was the daughter of Sancho Garcia, Count of Castile. *Moriarty, The Plantagenet Ancestry of King Edward III, page 78; Schwennicke, Europäische Stammtafeln, Volume II, table 55*

2. **Ramiro I, King of Aragon,** died May 8, 1063. He married Gilberge of Couserans, died 1054. She was the daughter of Bernard Roger, Count of Couserans, and Gersinda of Bigorre. *Moriarty, The Plantagenet Ancestry of King Edward III, pages 78 and 80; Schwennicke, Europäische Stammtafeln, Volumes II, table 58, and III/1, table 145*

3. **Sancho Ramirez I, King of Aragon**, born 1045, died July 6, 1094. He married Felicia de Roucy, died April 24, 1086. She was the daughter of Hildouin, Count of Roucy, and Adelaide. *Moriarty, The Plantagenet Ancestry of King Edward III, pages 49 and 78*

4. **Ramiro II, King of Aragon**, died August 16, 1147. He married Agnes of Aquitaine. She was the daughter of William IX, Duc d'Aquitaine, and Philippa of Toulouse. *Moriarty, The Plantagenet Ancestry of King Edward III, pages 36 and 78; Schwennicke, Europäische Stammtafeln, Volume II, table 76*

5. **Petronilla of Aragon**, born 1135, died October 13, 1173. She married Ramón Berenger IV, Count of Barcelona, born ca. 1115, died August 6, 1162. He was the son of Ramón Berenger III, Count of Barcelona, and Dulce de Gevaudan. *Moriarty, The Plantagenet Ancestry of King Edward III, pages 68 and 78; Schwennicke, Europäische Stammtafeln, Volume II, tables 69 and 70*

6. **Alfonso II, King of Aragon**, born April 4, 1152, died April 25, 1196. He married Sancha of León, died November 9, 1208. She was the daughter of Alfonso VII, King of Castile and León, and Richilde of Poland. *Moriarty, The Plantagenet Ancestry of King Edward III, pages 68 and 81; Schwennicke, Europäische Stammtafeln, Volume II, table 70*

7. **Alfonso II, Count of Provence**, born 1180, died February of 1209. He married Gersinda de Sabran. She was the daughter of Rainier, Count of Forcalquier, and Gersinda. *Moriarty, The Plantagenet Ancestry of King Edward III, pages 68 and 99; Europäische Stammtafeln, Volume II, table 70*

8. **Raymond V, Count of Provence**, born 1198, died August 19, 1245. He married Beatrice of Savoy, died 1266. She was the daughter of Thomas I, Duke of Savoy, and Margaret. *Moriarty, The Plantagenet Ancestry of King Edward III, pages 68 and 104; Europäische Stammtafeln, Volume II, table 70*

9. **Eleanor of Provence, Queen of England**, born 1223, died June 24, 1291. She married Henry III (143-1), King of England, born October 1, 1207, died November 16, 1272. He was the son of John, King of England, and Isabel of Angoulême. *Moriarty, The Plantagenet*

Ancestry of King Edward III, pages 2 and 68; Europäische Stammtafeln, Volume II, table 70; Burke, Burke's Peerage (The Royal Lineage), page 29

10. **Edmund "Crouchback" Plantagenet, Earl of Lancaster**, born January 16, 1244, died June 5, 1296. He married Blanche of Artois, Queen of Navarre, died May 2, 1302. She was the daughter of Robert I, Count of Artois (son of Louis VIII, King of the Franks), and Mathilda of Brabant. *Cokayne, The Complete Peerage, Volume VII (Lancaster), pages 378–387; Moriarty, The Plantagenet Ancestry of King Edward III, pages 148 and 154 See line 143 (2)*

Hungary

LINE 153

1. **Bela III, King of Hungary**, born ca. 1148, died April 23, 1196. He was the son of Geza II, King of Hungary, and Euphrosyne of Kiev. He married Agnes de Chatillon. She was the daughter of Renaud de Chatillon, Prince of Antioch, and Constance of Antioch. *Moriarty, The Plantagenet Ancestry of King Edward III, pages 143 and 147; Schwennicke, Europäische Stammtafeln, Volume II, tables 154 and 179*

2. **Andreas II, King of Hungary**, born ca. 1170, died 1235. He married Gertrude von Meran, died November 23, 1213. She was the daughter of Berthold VI, Duke of Croatia, and Agnes von Rochlitz. *Moriarty, The Plantagenet Ancestry of King Edward III, pages 143 and 198; Schwennicke, Europäische Stammtafeln, Volume II, table 155*

3. **Bela IV, King of Hungary**, born 1206, died May 3, 1270. He married Maria of Byzantium, died 1270. She was the daughter of Theodoros I, Emperor of Byzantium, and Anna Angela. *Moriarty, The Plantagenet Ancestry of King Edward III, pages 174 and 198; Schwennicke, Europäische Stammtafeln, Volume II, table 155*

4. **István V, King of Hungary**, born 1239, died August 1, 1272. He married Erzsebet of Cumania (Elizabeth of Bosnia). She was the daughter of Kuthan, Khan of the Cumanians. *Moriarty, The Plantagenet Ancestry of King Edward III, page 198; Schwennicke, Europäische Stammtafeln, Volume II, table 155*

5. **Maria of Hungary**, died March 25, 1323. She married Charles II, King of Naples, born 1248, died May 6, 1309. He was the son of Charles I, King of Sicily, and Beatrice of Provence. *Moriarty, The Plantagenet Ancestry of King Edward III, pages 197 and 198; Schwennicke, Europäische Stammtafeln, Volume II, table 155*

6. **Margaret of Naples, Countess of Anjou**, died December 31, 1299. She married Charles of Valois, Count of Valois, born March 12, 1270, died December 16, 1325. He was the son of Philip III "the Bold", King of the Franks, and Isabella of Aragon. *Moriarty, The Plantagenet Ancestry of King Edward III, page 197; Schwennicke, Europäische Stammtafeln, Volume II, table 115*

7. **Jeanne of Valois** died March 7, 1352. She married William III, Count of Hainaut, born 1286, died June 7, 1342. He was the son of Jean II, Count of Hainaut and Holland, and Philippa of Luxembourg. *Moriarty, The Plantagenet Ancestry of King Edward III, page 175; Schwennicke, Europäische Stammtafeln, Volume II, table 4*

8. **Philippa of Hainaut**, born 1313, died August 15, 1369. She married Edward III, King of England, born November 13, 1312, died June 21, 1377. He was the son of Edward II, King of England, and Isabella of France. *Cokayne, The Complete Peerage, Volume VII (Lancaster), page 410; Moriarty, The Plantagenet Ancestry of King Edward III, pages 2, 175, and 176*

9. **John of Gaunt, Duke of Lancaster**, born June 24, 1340, died February 3, 1399. He married his mistress, Katherine de Roelt, born 1350, died May 10, 1403. She was the daughter of Payne de Roelt. *Cokayne, The Complete Peerage, Volume VII (Lancaster), pages 410–416; Burke, Burke's Peerage (The Royal Lineage), page 31* **See line 146 (2)**

Poland

1. **Mieszko II, King of Poland**, born 990, died March 25, 1034. He was the son of Boleslav I, King of Poland, and Emmilda of Silesia. He married Richeza of Lorraine, died March 31, 1063. She was the daughter of Ezzo, Count of Palatine. *Moriarty, The Plantagenet Ancestry of King Edward III, page 84; Schwennicke, Europäische Stammtafeln, Volume II, table 120*

2. **Kazimierz I, King of Poland**, born 1016, died November 28, 1058. He married Maria Dobronega, died 1087. She was the daughter of St. Vladimir (116-4), Grand Prince of Kiev, and Rogneda. *Moriarty, The Plantagenet Ancestry of King Edward III, pages 53 and 84; Schwennicke, Europäische Stammtafeln, Volume II, table 120*

3. **Vladislav I, King of Poland**, born 1040, died June 4, 1102. He married Judith of Bohemia. She was the daughter of Vladislav II, King of Bohemia, and Adelaide of Hungary. *Moriarty, The Plantagenet Ancestry of King Edward III, pages 84 and 85; Schwennicke, Europäische Stammtafeln, Volume II, table 120*

4. **Boleslav III, Grand Prince of Poland**, born 1086, died October 28, 1138. He married Zbyslava of Kiev, died 1010. She was the daughter of Michael II (Sviatpolk), Grand Prince of Kiev. *Moriarty, The Plantagenet Ancestry of King Edward III, pages 84 and 87; Schwennicke, Europäische Stammtafeln, Volume II, table 120*

5. **Vladislav II, King of Poland**, died May 30, 1159. He married Agnes of Austria, died January 25, 1157 or 1163. She was the daughter of St. Leopold, Margave of Austria, and Agnes. *Moriarty, The Plantagenet Ancestry of King Edward III, pages 84 and 90; Schwennicke, Europäische Stammtafeln, Volume II, table 120*

6. **Richilde**, died June 16, 1185. She married Alfonso VII, King of Castile and León, died August 21, 1157. He was the son of Raymond, Count of Burgundy, and Urraca, Queen of Castile. *Moriarty, The Plantagenet Ancestry of King Edward III, pages 84 and 90; Schwennicke, Europäische Stammtafeln, Volume II, table 62*

7. **Sancha of León**, died November 9, 1208. She married Alfonso II, King of Aragon, born April 4, 1152, died April 25, 1196. He was the son of Ramón IV, Count of Barcelona, and Petronilla of Aragon. *Moriarty, The Plantagenet Ancestry of King Edward III, pages 68 and 81; Schwennicke, Europäische Stammtafeln, Volume II, tables 62 and 70*

8. **Alfonso II, Count of Provence**, born 1180, died February of 1209. He married Gersinda de Sabran. She was the daughter of Rainier, Count of Forcalquier, and Gersinda. *Moriarty, The Plantagenet Ancestry of King Edward III, pages 68 and 99; Schwennicke, Europäische Stammtafeln, Volume II, table 70* **See line 152 (7)**

Bulgaria

LINE 155

1. **Krum, Khan of the Bulgars**, died 814. *Moriarty, The Plantagenet Ancestry of King Edward III, page 139; Schwennicke, Europäische Stammtafeln, Volume II, table 167*

2. **Omurtag, Khan of the Bulgars**, died 831. *Moriarty, The Plantagenet Ancestry of King Edward III, page 139; Schwennicke, Europäische Stammtafeln, Volume II, table 167*

Note: Moriarty and Schwennicke disagree on four of the next five generations, as noted:

3. **Zvinitsa**, a son. *Moriarty, The Plantagenet Ancestry of King Edward III, page 139; Schwennicke, Europäische Stammtafeln, Volume II, table 167 (Note: Moriarty has N.N. (no name) for this generation.)*

4. **Presijan, Khan of the Bulgars**, died 852. *Schwennicke, Europäische Stammtafeln, Volume II, 167 (Note: Moriarty skips this generation.)*

5. **Boris-Michael, Tsar of the Bulgars**, died 907. He married Marija. *Moriarty, The Plantagenet Ancestry of King Edward III, page 139; Schwennicke, Europäische Stammtafeln, Volume II, table 167*

6. **Simon, Tsar of the Bulgars**, died 927. *Moriarty, The Plantagenet Ancestry of King Edward III, page 139 (Note: Schwennicke skips this generation.)*

7. **Nicolaus, Tsar of the Bulgars**, died 928. *Moriarty, The Plantagenet Ancestry of King Edward III, page 139; Schwennicke, Europäische Stammtafeln, Volume II, table 168 (Note: Moriarty calls him John (Ivan), dying 928.)*

8. **Aaron Amitopoulos**, died ca. 987. *Moriarty, The Plantagenet Ancestry of King Edward III, page 139; Schwennicke, Europäische Stammtafeln, Volume II, table 168*

9. **Ivan Vladislav, Tsar of West Bulgaria**, died 1018. He married Maria of Byzantium. *Moriarty, The Plantagenet Ancestry of King Edward III, page 139; Schwennicke, Europäische Stammtafeln, Volume II, table 168*

10. **Trojan, Tsar of West Bulgaria**. *Moriarty, The Plantagenet Ancestry of King Edward III, page 139; Schwennicke, Europäische Stammtafeln, Volume II, table 168*

11. **Maria of Bulgaria**. She married Andronikos Doukas, died 1077. He was the son of Caesar Ioannes Doukas and Irene Pergonita. *Moriarty, The Plantagenet Ancestry of King Edward III, pages 138 and 139; Schwennicke, Europäische Stammtafeln, Volume II, table 168*

12. **Irene Doukas, Empress of Byzantium**. She married Alexius I, Emperor of Byzantium. He was the son of Ioannes I, Duke of Durazzo. *Moriarty, The Plantagenet Ancestry of King Edward III, pages 137 and 138; Schwennicke, Europäische Stammtafeln, Volume II, table 179; Norwich, A Short History of Byzantium, Chart 11, "The Comneni"*

13. **Ioannes II, Emperor of Byzantium**, died 1143. He married Irene of Hungary, died 1137. She was the daughter of St. Ladislas I, King of Hungary, and Adelheid of Swabia. *Moriarty, The Plantagenet Ancestry of King Edward III, pages 138 and 140; Norwich, A Short History of Byzantium, Chart 11, "The Comneni"*

14. **Andronikos**, died 1142. He married Irene. *Schwennicke, Europäische Stammtafeln, Volume II, table 179; Norwich, A Short History of Byzantium, Chart 11, "The Comneni"*

15. **Euphrosyne**. She married Alexius III, Emperor of Byzantium, died ca. 1215. He was the son of Andronikos Doukas and Euphrosyne. *Schwennicke, Europäische Stammtafeln, Volume II, table 179; Norwich, A Short History of Byzantium, Chart 12*

16. **Anna Angela**. She married Theodoros I, Emperor of Byzantium, died 1222. *Schwennicke, Europäische Stammtafeln, Volume II, table 179; Norwich, A Short History of Byzantium, Chart 12*

17. **Maria of Byzantium**, died 1270. She married Bela IV, King of Hungary, born 1206, died May 3, 1270. He was the son of Andreas II, King of Hungary, and Gertrude von Meran. *Moriarty, The Plantagenet Ancestry of King Edward III, pages 174 and 198; Schwennicke, Europäische Stammtafeln, Volume II, table 155*

18. **István V, King of Hungary**, born 1239, died August 1, 1272. He married Erzsebet of Cumania (Elizabeth of Bosnia). She was the daughter of Kuthan, Khan of the Cumanians. *Moriarty, The Plantagenet Ancestry of King Edward III, page 198; Schwennicke, Europäische Stammtafeln, Volume II, table 155* **See line 153 (4)**

*Ioannes II, Emperor of Byzantium and Irene of Hungary
from the Church of St. Sophia in Istanbul*

An Ivye connection by marriage to English royalty

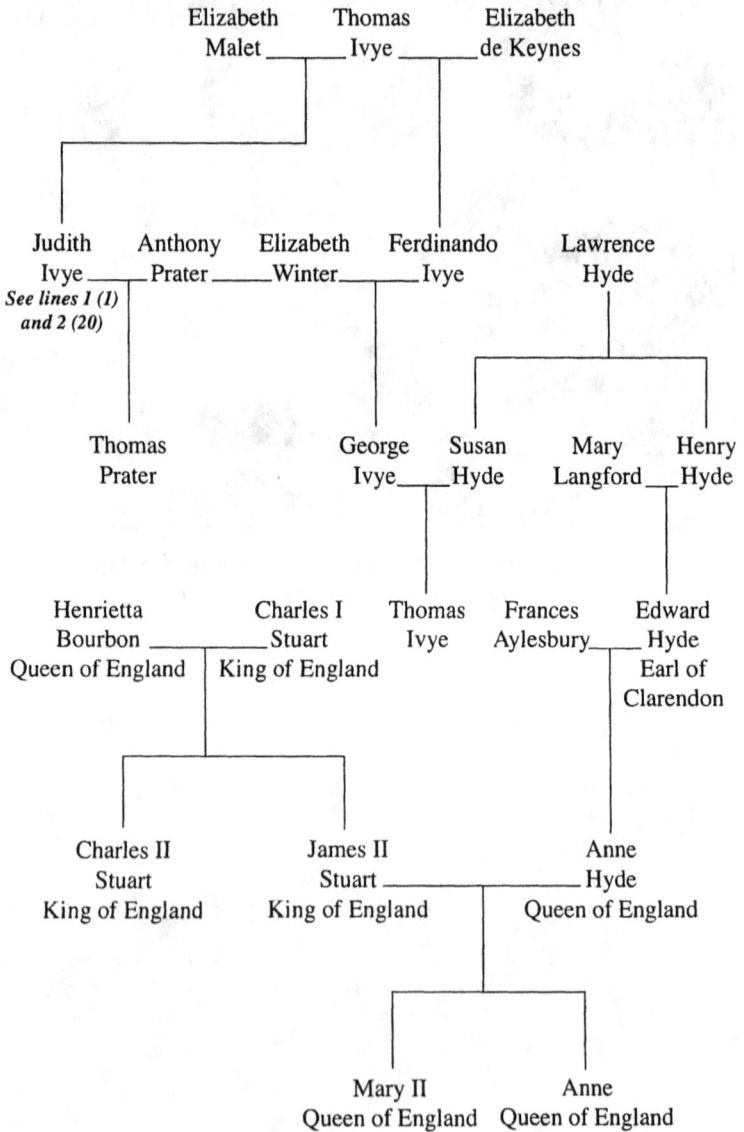

```
        Elizabeth      Thomas      Elizabeth
          Malet _____ Ivye _____ de Keynes


   Judith    Anthony   Elizabeth   Ferdinando    Lawrence
    Ivye ____ Prater ____ Winter _____ Ivye         Hyde
 See lines 1 (1)
 and 2 (20)


         Thomas            George  Susan     Mary    Henry
         Prater             Ivye __ Hyde   Langford __ Hyde


   Henrietta        Charles I   Thomas   Frances    Edward
   Bourbon _____ Stuart      Ivye   Aylesbury ____ Hyde
 Queen of England  King of England                 Earl of
                                                   Clarendon


      Charles II        James II                 Anne
       Stuart            Stuart _____ Hyde
   King of England    King of England       Queen of England


                        Mary II            Anne
                   Queen of England   Queen of England
```

Three Prater connections by marriage to English royalty

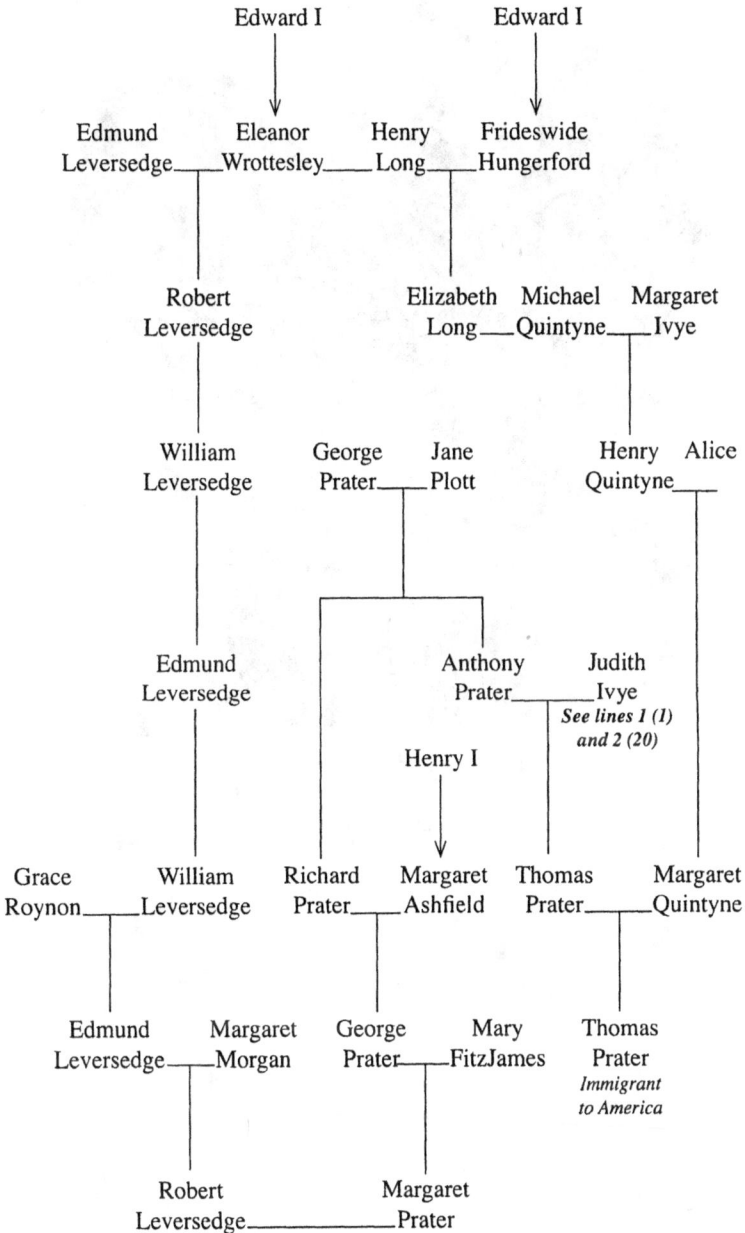

Edward I
↓

Edmund Leversedge —— Eleanor Wrottesley

Edward I
↓

Henry Long —— Frideswide Hungerford

Robert Leversedge

Elizabeth Long —— Michael Quintyne —— Margaret Ivye

William Leversedge

George Prater —— Jane Plott

Henry Quintyne   Alice

Edmund Leversedge

Anthony Prater —— Judith Ivye
*See lines 1 (1)
and 2 (20)*

Henry I
↓

Grace Roynon —— William Leversedge

Richard Prater —— Margaret Ashfield

Thomas Prater —— Margaret Quintyne

Edmund Leversedge —— Margaret Morgan

George Prater —— Mary FitzJames

Thomas Prater
*Immigrant
to America*

Robert Leversedge —— Margaret Prater

165

Ivye

Further Research

The preceding pages contain 155 lines of descent from royal, noble or historically significant persons to Judith Ivye, as well as to some of her descendants. All 155 lines are documented with citations that prove their validity, so the reader may follow up, expand, or pursue his own genealogical research.

Not all of Judith's ancestors have been traced successfully. Most of her remaining lines end at generations that simply have not — or can not be researched further. Others however, provide clues that can lead to important connections with well-known individuals.

The following pages contain documented lines of descent to Judith Ivye or to her husband, Anthony Prater. Each of these begins with someone who is suspected, though not proven, to descend from one or more of the royal families of Europe. This appendix is included, as genealogical research is an ongoing study, and more of Judith's and Anthony's ancestors may yet be discovered. When possible, references and citations are included for each line, so that others are free to explore these possibilities and further our understanding of the royal descents of both Judith Ivye and her husband, Anthony Prater.

Joan Wrottesley

In his book *A History of the Family of Wrottesley*, George Wrottesley refers to "the destruction of the Wrottesley muniments by the fire of December 1897". Much irreplaceable historical information singular to the Wrottesleys was lost, but other sources are still available.

There are many references that show that Judith Ivye's ancestor Joan, wife of Thomas Malet, was the daughter of Sir William Wadham and Margaret Chiselden. *The Complete Peerage, Volume XII/1 (Stourton), page 302*, states that this William Wadham was the son of John Wadham and Joan Wrottesley. *Wadham College,* by T. G.

Monumental brass of Joan Wrottesley and her son, William Wadham

Jackson, (pages 4 and 27), *The Worthies of Devon*, by John Prince (page 748) and *Collections Towards a Description of the County of Devon*, by Sir William Pole (page 141), all confirm that John Wadham of Somerset, and Joan Wrottesley were married, but none identifies Joan's parents.

Of the Wrottesleys living in Somerset at the time of Joan's marriage to John Wadham (ca. 1369), a promising candidate for Joan's father might be Hugh Wrottesley (ca. 1313–1381), a founding member and the 18th Knight of the Order of the Garter. Hugh was married three times. His first wife was Elizabeth de Hampton, contracted for marriage in 1325. She died in 1349. His second wife was Mabel, the daughter of Philip ap Rhys. She was born in 1344 or 1345 and died in 1370. Hugh's third wife was Isabel Arderne, whom he married by August 1372.

Chronologically, Joan Wrottesley can not be the daughter of Isabel Arderne. Mabel ap Rhys and Hugh had only one son, Hugh, who died young. If Joan was the daughter of Hugh's first wife, Elizabeth, then Joan had to have been born before Elizabeth died in 1349. As John Wadham's birth date was 1344, this is quite plausible.

If Joan's relationship to the Wrottesley family can be proven, she would bring two separate and distinct descents to Judith Ivye from Henry I, King of England,.

Joan Wrottesley

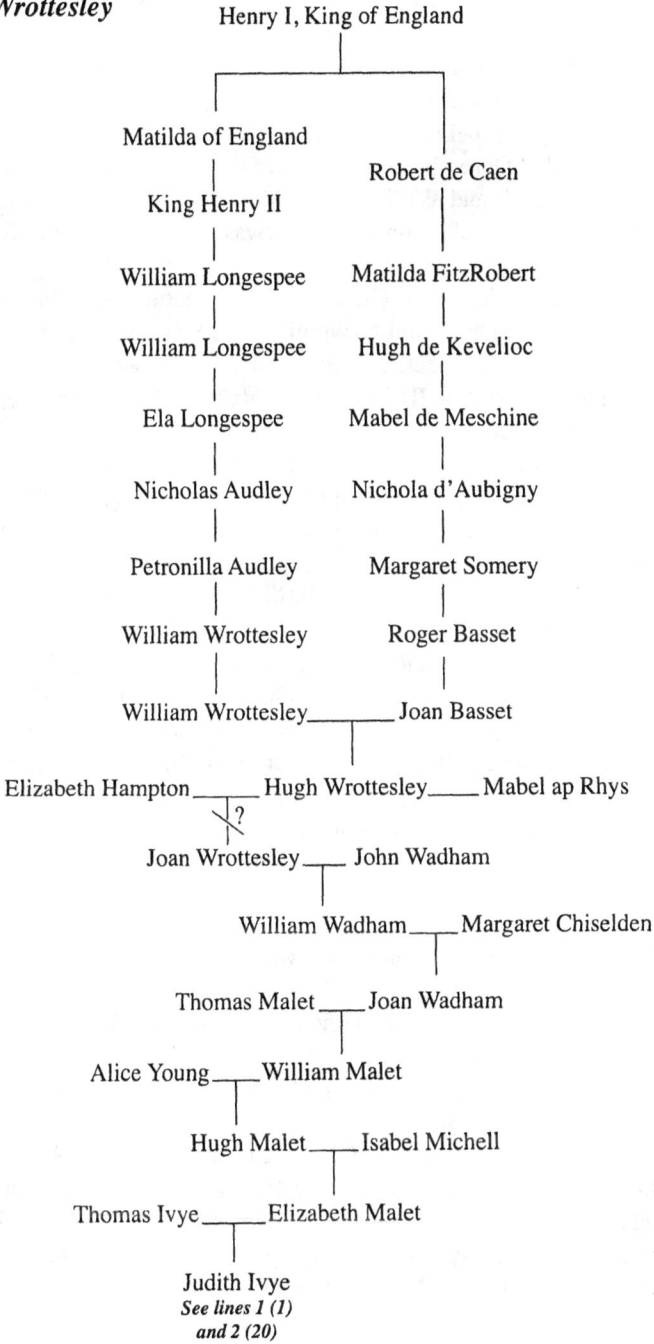

Henry I, King of England

Matilda of England
King Henry II
William Longespee
William Longespee
Ela Longespee
Nicholas Audley
Petronilla Audley
William Wrottesley
William Wrottesley_____ Joan Basset

Robert de Caen
Matilda FitzRobert
Hugh de Kevelioc
Mabel de Meschine
Nichola d'Aubigny
Margaret Somery
Roger Basset

Elizabeth Hampton_____ Hugh Wrottesley_____ Mabel ap Rhys

Joan Wrottesley____ John Wadham

William Wadham____ Margaret Chiselden

Thomas Malet____ Joan Wadham

Alice Young____ William Malet

Hugh Malet____ Isabel Michell

Thomas Ivye_____ Elizabeth Malet

Judith Ivye
See lines 1 (1)
and 2 (20)

Isabel (Plantagenet) FitzRoy

Isabel FitzRoy was an ancestor of Joan Roynon, the wife of Hugh Malet (see line 2–14). The descent leads to Elizabeth Malet (2–19), the mother of Judith Ivye. Isabel FitzRoy was married to Richard FitzIves (died ca. 1207), Lord of Degembris in Cornwall. Their three known children were Richard, Isabel, and William (died May 26, 1265). William married Rose, the daughter of Ralph Bevyle and was the ancestor of Joan Roynon.

It is speculated that Isabel FitzRoy was an illegitmate daughter of King John of England by an unknown mistress. In a paragraph about Isabel and her possible connection to King John, as well as her marriage and descendants, Douglas Richardson, in his book Plantagenet Ancestry, on page 13, references obituaries for the Fitz Ives family in the *Herald and Genealogist*, 7 (1873): 229–231: "Isabel styled filie Regis Joh'is" ("Isabel, styled daughter of King John"). The full texts read: "Obitus d'ni Ric'i fits yva militis Anno 1207," and "Obitus d'ne Isabelle uxoris sue filie Regis Joh'is." ("The death of Richard Fitz Ives, soldier, in the year 1207," and "The death of his wife Isabelle, the daughter of King John").

Chris Given-Wilson and Alice Curteis, in The Royal Bastards of Medieval England state on page 128 that John's only known illegitimate daughter was Joan, the wife of Llewelyn ap Iorwerth, Prince of North Wales. However, Allison Weir, in her book Britain's Royal Families: The Complete Genealogy lists twelve illegitimate children for John on pages 71 and 72 including, besides the aforementioned Joan, two more daughters, Matilda and Isabella la Blanche.

Finally, *The Visitations of Cornwall, 1530, 1573 and 1620,* page 30 shows "Isabell, da. of King John, styled Isabell le Blanche ... elsewhere Isabell, sister of K. Hen. III". This Isabell is married to Sir Robert Fitz Yvs, and they are shown to be the parents of a son, Richard.

If Isabel was the daughter of King John, her lineage would bring royal descent to Judith Ivye from the Norman king William the Conqueror, the Saxon king Alfred "the Great", and the Scots king Malcolm III through John's father King Henry II. Isabel would also bring royal descent from Robert I, King the Franks, Heinrich "the Fowler", King of the Saxons, Louis II, Emperor of the West, and Berengarius II, King of Italy, through King John's mother, Eleanor of Aquitaine.

Isabel FitzRoy

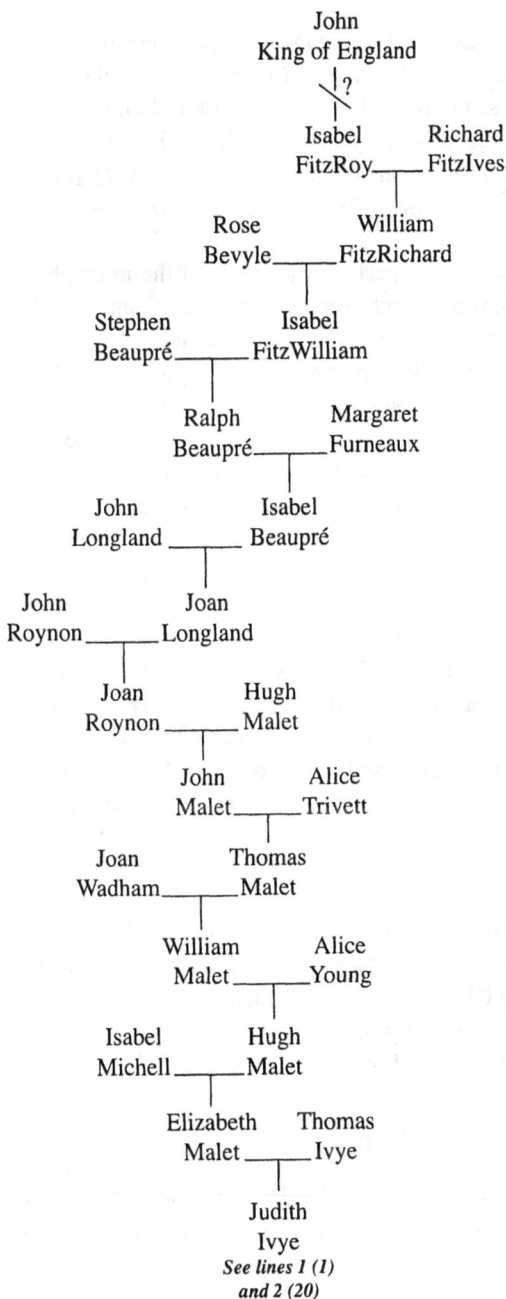

John
King of England
\?

Isabel   Richard
FitzRoy___ FitzIves

Rose   William
Bevyle___FitzRichard

Stephen   Isabel
Beaupré___ FitzWilliam

Ralph   Margaret
Beaupré___Furneaux

John   Isabel
Longland ___ Beaupré

John   Joan
Roynon___Longland

Joan   Hugh
Roynon ___ Malet

John   Alice
Malet___Trivett

Joan   Thomas
Wadham___Malet

William   Alice
Malet___Young

Isabel   Hugh
Michell___Malet

Elizabeth   Thomas
Malet ___Ivye

Judith
Ivye
See lines 1 (1)
and 2 (20)

Gladys de la Mare

It has been assumed by many that an ancestor of Anthony Prater, husband of Judith Ivye, was a de la Mare (Delamere or Delamare) heiress, possibly named Gladys. The de la Mare family had extensive land holdings at Nunney in the 1300s — it was Elias Delamare who began the construction of Nunney Castle. From A History of the County of Wiltshire, Volume 8 (1965, edited by Elizabeth Crittall):

> "Among the properties held freely of the lords of Warminster were several which were styled manors, and for which courts are known to have been held. The manor of Borham or Burton Delamare or Bishopstrow took its suffix from a family which was seated at Nunney Castle (Somerset). The de la Meres may have acquired the land ca. 1200 by the marriage of Nicholas de la Mere with Grace de Meysey, who was heir to considerable estates in Wiltshire and Somerset which apparently included Nunney. In 1217 Nicholas was given seisin of his land of Bishopstrow on returning to the king's service. He was succeeded by his son by Grace, Ellis de la Mere; he held the manor by 1227, and was still living, as was his mother, in 1263. He was dead by 1271, and succeeded by his son Nicholas; he or another Nicholas still held it in 1300, when the property was described as two carucates of land held at a rent of 3s. By 1330 the manor had passed to Thomas de la Mere, who then settled it on himself and his wife Margery. They were the parents of Sir John de la Mere from whom the manor descended in the same way as the manor of Fisherton de la Mere to the Paulet family."

Elias (Ellis) de la Mare (above) began the building of Nunney Castle (*1851 Report for the Somerset Archaeological and Natural History Society,* by Charles Edmund Giles, page 123), which was subsequently acquired, and lost, by the Prater family. Elias' successors finished the castle with "spoils of war obtained in France".

Judith Ivye was descended from Elias de la Mare, mentioned above. Her descent comes through her great-great-great grandmother, Alice Newburgh, who was married to John FitzJames. Alice Newburg's mother was Joan de la Mare, the daughter of John who was the great-grandson of Elias de la Mare.

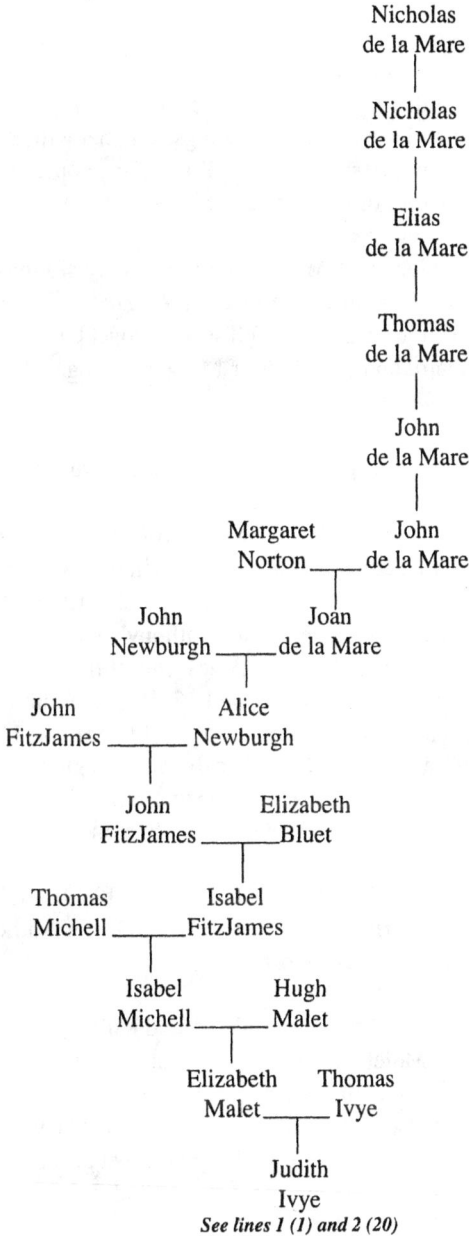

de la Mare

Nicholas
de la Mare
|
Nicholas
de la Mare
|
Elias
de la Mare
|
Thomas
de la Mare
|
John
de la Mare
|
Margaret   John
Norton _____ de la Mare

John   Joan
Newburgh _____ de la Mare

John   Alice
FitzJames _____ Newburgh

John   Elizabeth
FitzJames _____ Bluet

Thomas   Isabel
Michell _____ FitzJames

Isabel   Hugh
Michell _____ Malet

Elizabeth   Thomas
Malet _____ Ivye

Judith
Ivye

See lines 1 (1) and 2 (20)

Elene Kingston

Anthony Prater's grandmother Elene was born ca. 1493 and died 1556 or 1557. We do not know for certain that her surname was Kingston. It has been surmised that Elene was a member of the Kingston family by the fact that she mentions Sir Anthony Kingston in her will. Sir Anthony (ca. 1519–1556) was the son of Sir William Kingston of Gloucester, Constable of the Tower of London, and his second wife, Elizabeth.

It is doubtful that Elene and Anthony Kingston were siblings, as Elene was born about 17 years after the birth of Anthony's father William. Anthony had two known siblings: a full sister Bridget Kingston, married to George Baynham, and a half-sister Margaret Kingston, married to John St. Loe.

Discounting Elene as a daughter of William, there are three other possible relationships between Elene and the Kingston family. The first is that Elene and Anthony were cousins, as William Kingston mentioned a brother George (who could be Elene's father) in his will. The second is that Elene was Anthony's aunt; a younger sister of William and George Kingston. The third is that Elene was Anthony's step-sister. William Kingston's first wife was Anne Berkeley (his third wife was Mary Scrope), the widow of John Guise (died 1501). Anne and John Guise had at least four children, including a son, John, born in 1485. Elene, born around 1493 would fit chronologically as a daughter of Anne and John Guise. If so, then it would be possible that William Kingston raised Elene as his step-daughter after he married the widowed Anne.

Elene married John Prater (1492–1547), the son of William Prater, and had issue: George, married to Joan Plott, the parents of Anthony Prater, husband to Judith Ivye; Joan, and John.

Judith Ivye does descend from a family named Kingston. Her maternal grandfather, Hugh Malet, was the great-great-great-great-grandson of John Malet and Elizabeth, the daughter of John Kingston. John Malet and Elizabeth Kingston also had a daughter, Ellen Malet, who was married to Walter Bluett. Ellen and Walter Bluett's great-great grandson, Nicholas Bluett, married Joan FitzJames, the sister of Judith Ivye's great-great grandfather, John FitzJames.

Judith Ivye's
Kingston connections

John
Malet _____ Elizabeth
Kingston

Walter
Bluett _____ Ellen
Malet

Baldwin
Malet _____ Amice
Lyffe

Agnes
Beaupenny _____ John
Bluett

Hugh
Malet _____ Joyce
Roynon

Maud
Chiseldon _____ John
Bluett

Alice
Trivett _____ John
Malet

Joan
St. Maur _____ Walter
Bluett

John
FitzJames _____ Alice
Newburgh

Thomas
Malet _____ Joan
Wadham

Nicholas
Bluett _____ Joan
FitzJames

John
FitzJames _____ Elizabeth
Bluet

William
Malet _____ Alice
Young

Thomas
Michell _____ Isabel
FitzJames

Elene
(Kingston?) _____ John
Prater

Isabel
Michell _____ Hugh
Malet

George
Prater _____ Joan
Plott

Thomas
Ivye _____ Elizabeth
Malet

Anthony
Prater _____ Judith
Ivye
*See lines 1 (1)
and 2 (20)*

175

Family of Sir William Kingston

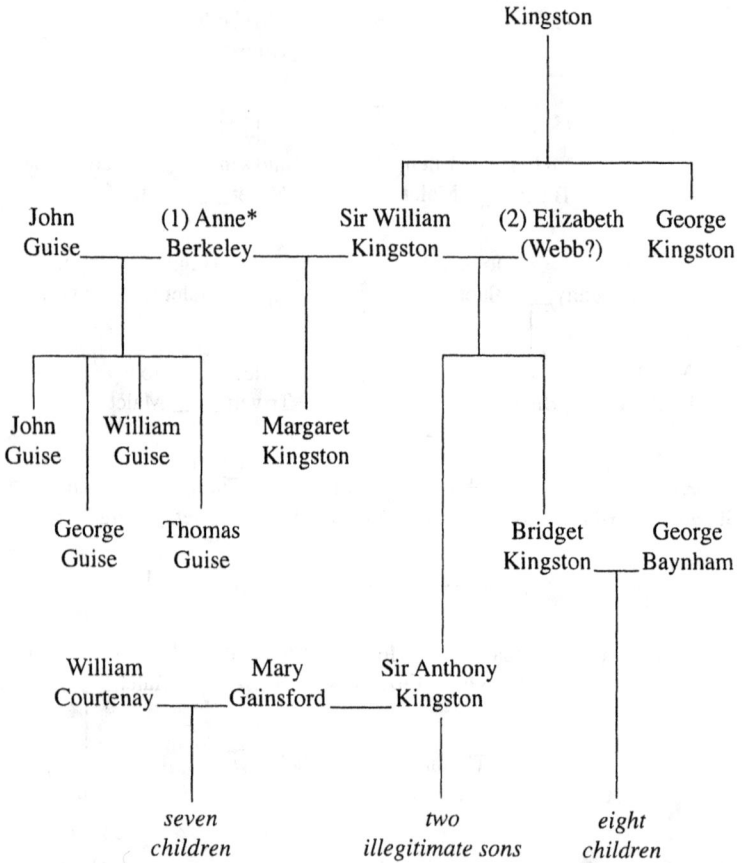

*Anne Berkeley was the sister of Richard Berkeley, who married Elizabeth Conningsby. Richard and Elizabeth Berkeley are the ancestors of the English author, Jane Austen.

176

Family of Sir William Kingston

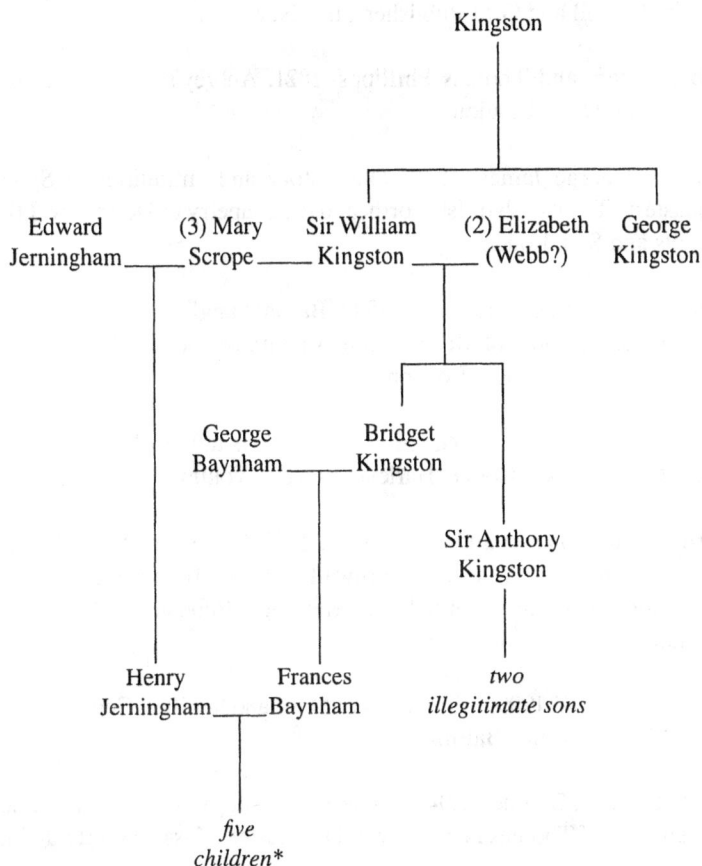

```
                                          Kingston
                                             |
        ┌──────────┬──────────────┬──────────────────┐
     Edward     (3) Mary    Sir William    (2) Elizabeth    George
   Jerningham____Scrope_____Kingston_____(Webb?)         Kingston
        |                       |
        |              ┌────────┴────────┐
        |           George           Bridget
        |           Baynham_____ Kingston
        |              |
        |              |             Sir Anthony
        |              |              Kingston
        |              |                 |
      Henry         Frances             two
   Jerningham____ Baynham        illegitimate sons
        |
       five
    children*
```

*The eldest daughter of Henry Jerningham and Frances Baynham, Jeronyma Jerningham, married Charles Waldegrave. They are ancestors of Lady Diana Spencer, Princess of Wales, first wife of Charles, Prince of Wales.

Bibliography

Ashley, Mike. 1998. The mammoth book of British kings and queens: The complete biographical encyclopedia of the kings and queens of Britain. Carroll and Graf Publishers, Inc. New York.

Aubrey, John, and Thomas Phillipps. 1821. Aubrey's collections for Wiltshire. J. Davy. London.

Aungier, George James. 1840. The history and antiquities of Syon Monastery: The parish of Isleworth, and the chapelry of Hounslow. J.B. Nichols and Son. London.

Banks, Sir Thomas Christopher. 1844. Baronia anglica concentrata; A concentrated account of all the baronies commonly called baronies in fee, two volumes. Ripon. London.

Bannerman, William Bruce, ed. 1923. The visitation of Kent: 1574. Collected by Robert Cooke. Harleian Society. Volume 74. Exeter.

Baring-Gould, Sabine and John Fisher. 2005. The lives of the British saints; the saints of Wales and Cornwall and such Irish saints as have dedications in Britain. Four volumes. Kessinger Publishing. Whitefish, Montana.

Barnes, Robert W. 1999. British roots of Maryland families. Genealogical Publishing Company. Baltimore.

Bartlett, Joseph Gardner. 1914. Newberry genealogy: The ancestors and descendants of Thomas Newberry of Dorchester, Massachusetts, 1634. Privately printed. Boston.

Baxter, Stephen. 2007. The earls of Mercia: Lordship and power in late anglo-saxon England. Oxford University Press. Oxford.

Benson, John. 1939. The Valletorts of North Tawton, *Devon & Cornwall Notes and Queries*, volume XX, no. 7, pp. 247-254

Boyan, Pearl Alexina and George Robert Lamb. 1955. Francis Tregian: Cornish recusant. Sheed and Ward. London.

Bracken, Charles William, ed. 1935. The honor of Harberton. *Report and transactions of the Devonshire Association,* volume LXVII. 254–264.

Bridgeford, Andrew. 2005. 1066: The hidden history in the Bayeux Tapestry. Walker and Company. New York.

Bridgeman, George Thomas Orlando. 1891. Collections for a history of Staffordshire, volume 12. Houghton and Hammond. Staffordshire, England.

Brown, Frederick. 2010. Abstracts of Somersetshire wills. Kessinger Publishing. Whitefish, Montana.

Burke, Sir Bernard. 1978. A genealogical history of the dormant, abeyant, forfeited and extinct peerages of the British empire. Genealogical Publishing Company. Baltimore.

Burke, John. 1999. Burke's peerage and baronetage, 106th edition. Two volumes. Morris Genealogical Books. London.

Chibnall, Marjorie. 1992. Proceedings of the Battle Conference. Boydell & Brewer. Woodbridge, Suffolk, England.

Cokayne, George Edward. 2000. The complete peerage of England, Scotland, Ireland, Great Britain and the United Kingdom. Thirteen volumes. Alan Sutton Publishing. Gloucester, England.

Collins, Arthur, and Sir Egerton Brydges. 1812. Collins's peerage of England. Nine volumes. F. C. and J. Rivington, Otridge and Son. London.

Collinson, Reverend John. 1791. The history and antiquities of the county of Somerset. Three volumes. R. Cruttwell. London.

Cosgrove, Art. 2008. A new history of Ireland, volume II: medieval Ireland 1169–1534. Oxford University Press. Oxford.

Crispin, M. Jackson and Léonce Macary. 1969. Falaise roll: Recording prominent companions of William, Duke of Normandy at the conquest of England. Genealogical Publishing Company. Baltimore.

Doliante, Sharon. 1998. Maryland and Virginia colonials: Genealogies of some colonial families. Two volumes. Genealogical Publishing Company. Baltimore.

Dormer, Ernest William. 1912. Erleigh Court and its owners. G. A. Poynder. Reading, England.

Douglas, David C. 1964. William the Conqueror. University of California Press. Berkeley and Los Angeles.

Dunning, Robert William, and William Page. 1909. Victoria County History, The Victoria history of the county of Somerset, volume 3. A. Constable and company. London.

Dwnn, Lewys. 1846. Heraldic visitations of Wales and part of the Marches, between the years 1586 and 1613. Two volumes. Samuel Rush Meyrick, ed. William Rees. London.

Engelbert, Omer. 1995. Lives of the saints. Penguin Books. London.

Faris, David. 1999. Plantagenet ancestry of seventeenth-century colonists. New England Historic Genealogical Society. Boston.

Farrer, William, ed. 2013. Early Yorkshire charters: Being a collection of documents anterior to the thirteenth century made from the public records, monastic chartularies, Roger Dodsworth's manuscripts and other available sources. 13 volumes. Cambridge University Press. Cambridge.

Forester, Thomas. 1854. The ecclesiastical history of England and Normandy. H.G. Bohn. London.

Given-Wilson, Chris, and Alice Curteis. 1984. The Royal Bastards of Medieval England. Routledge & Kegan Paul. London.

Giles, Charles Edmund. 1851. Proceedings at the general, quarterly and annual meetings, in the *Somersetshire Archaeological and Natural History Society*. London.

Gjerset, Knut. 1915. History of the Norwegian people, volume I. The MacMillan Company. New York.

Greene, Donald, and Noel Schutz. 2008. Shawnee Heritage I: Shawnee genealogy and family history. Lulu.com. Self-published.

Griffith, John Edwards. 1985. Pedigrees of Anglesey and Carnarvonshire families. Bridge Books. Wrexham, Wales.

Hughes, David. 2007. The British chronicles. Two volumes. Heritage Books. Berwyn Heights, Maryland.

Jackson, Thomas Graham. 1893. Wadham College. Oxford at the Clerendon Press. Oxford.

Jones, Arthur. 1910. The history of Gruffydd ap Cynan. Sherratt and Hughes. London.

Jourdan, Elise Greenup. 1993. Early families of southern Maryland, volume II. Family Line Publications. Westminster, Maryland.

Lloyd, John Edward. 1911. A history of Wales from the earliest times to the Edwardian conquest. Longmans, Green and Co. London.

MacKenzie, George Norbury. 1907. Colonial families of the United States, volume II. The Grafton Press. New York.

MacLean, Sir John. 1886. Historical and genealogical memoir of the family of Poyntz. William and Company. London.

MacManus, Seumas. 1990. The story of the Irish race. Random House. New York.

Malet, Arthur. 1885. Notices of an English branch of the Malet family. Harrison and Son. London.

Maund, Kari. 2006. The Welsh kings; Warriors, warlords and princes. Tempus Publishing. Stroud.

Metcalf, Walter, ed. 1878. The visitation of Essex: 1612. Collected by John Raven. Harleian Society. Volume 13. Exeter.

Metcalf, Walter, ed. 1885. The visitation of Berkshire: 1530. Collected by William Harvey. Harleian Society. Exeter.

Mickel, Emanuel J. 1999. Les enfances Godefroi and le retour de cornumarant: volume 3 of the old French crusade cycle. University of Alabama Press. Tuscaloosa, Alabama.

Moriarty, George Andrews. 1985. The Plantagenet ancestry of King Edward III and Queen Philippa. Mormon Pioneer Genealogy Society. Salt Lake City.

Mundy, Richard. 1913. The visitation of Hampshire, 1530, 1575, and 1634. Collected by Thomas Benolt. Harleian Society. Exeter.

Newman, Henry Wright. 1996. Anne Arundel gentry, volume II. Family Line Publications. Westminster, Maryland.

Nicholas, Thomas. 2000. Annals and antiquities of the counties and county families of Wales. Two volumes. Genealogical Publishing Company. Baltimore.

Norgate, Kate. 1887. England under the Angevin kings, Volume I. Macmillan and Company. London & New York.

Norwich, John Julius. 1999. A short history of Byzantium. Vintage Books (Random House). New York.

Planché, James Robinson. 1874. The conqueror and his companions. Tinsley Brothers. London.

Pole, Sir William. 2009. Collections towards a description of the county of Devon. Kessinger Publishing. Whitefish, Montana.

Prather, John William, Jr. 1987. Praters in Wiltshire, 1480–1670. Privately published. Hendersonville, North Carolina.

Prather, John William, Jr. 1999. Prater, Prather, Prator, Praytor in America, 1620–1800. Published privately. Hendersonville, North Carolina.

Prince, John. 1810. Danmonii orientales illustres, or, The worthies of Devon: A work, wherein the lives and fortunes of the most famous divines, statesmen, swordsmen, physicians, writers, and other eminent persons, natives of that most noble province, from before the Norman Conquest, down to the present age, are memorized. Longman, Hurst, Bees, and Orme. London.

von Redlich, Colonel Count Marcellus Donald Alexander Ritter. 2002. Pedigrees of some of the emperor Charlemagne's descendants. Genealogical Publishing Company. Baltimore.

Richardson, Douglas. 2004. Plantagenet ancestry. Genealogical Publishing Company. Baltimore.

Riley, Robert Shean. 1999. The colonial Riley families of the tidewater frontier, volume I. McDowell Publications. Utica, Kentucky.

Roberts, Gary Boyd. 2001. The royal descents of 500 immigrants. Genealogical Publishing Company. Baltimore.

Roberts, Gary Boyd. 2006. The royal descents of 600 immigrants. Genealogical Publishing Company. Baltimore.

Sanders, Ivor John. 2006. English baronies: A study of their origin and descent, 1086–1327. Clerendon Press. Oxford.

Schwennicke, Detlev, ed. 1978. Europäische Stammtafeln. Twenty-nine volumes. Verlag von J.A. Stargardt. Berlin.

Skaife, Robert H. 1896. Domesday book for Yorkshire. Bradbury, Agnew, and Co. London.

Smyth, Alfred P. 1977. Scandinavian kings in the British Isles. Oxford University Press. Oxford.

Stawell, Colonel George Dodsworth. 1910. A Quantock family: The Stawells of Cothelstone and their descendants, the barons Stawell of Somerton, and the Stawells of Devonshire and the County Cork, Taunton, Barnicott and Pearce. The Wessex Press. London.

Stevens, Harriet Weeks Wadhams. 1913. Wadham Genealogy. Frank Allaben Genealogical Company. New York.

Stuart, Roderick W. 1998. Royalty for commoners: The complete known lineage of John of Gaunt, son of Edward III, King of England, and Queen Philippa. Genealogical Publishing Company. Baltimore.

Sturlason, Snorre. 1990. Heimskringlas (the lives of the Norse kings). Dover Publications. New York.

Tanner, Heather. 2004. Families, friends and allies: Boulogne and politics in northern France and England, c.879–1160. Koninkijke Brill, NV. Leiden, The Netherlands.

Tanner, Mark Batt. 1875. Reginald, Count de Valletorta. *Notes and Queries,* fifth series, 3:209–211.

Taylor, Thomas. 1907. Richard, King of the Romans: His descendants. *Journal of the Royal Institution of Cornwall,* volume XVII. 413–424.

Trabue, James Duvall. 2004. The arms and ancestry of the Stocketts of Maryland. *The Augustan,* #116, Volume XXVII:4. 2–17.

Turton, Lieutenant-Colonel William Henry. 1993. The Plantagenet ancestry. Genealogical Publishing Company. Baltimore.

Turvey, Roger. 2002. The Welsh princes: The native rulers of Wales, 1063–1283. Longman and Company. London.

Urmston, William Searle Glanville-Richards. 1882. Records of the Anglo-Norman house of Glanville from A.D. 1050 to 1880. Mitchell and Hughes. London.

Vivian, John Lambrick. 1887. The visitation of Cornwall, 1530, 1573 and 1620. Harleian Society. Exeter.

Weaver, Frederic William, ed. 1885. The visitation of Somerset, 1531 and 1573. Harleian Society. Exeter.

Weaver, Frederic William, and Charles Herbert Mayo, eds. 1901. Tomb of Sir Edward Hungerford. *Devon and Cornwall notes and queries for Somerset & Dorset,* volume VII. 64–65

Wedgwood, Colonel Josiah Clement. 1936. History of parliament, 1439–1509. Her Majesty's Stationery Office. London.

Weir, Alison. 1996. Britain's royal families: The complete genealogy. Pimlico (Random House). London.

Weis, Frederick Lewis. 1997. The Magna Charta sureties. Genealogical Publishing Company. Baltimore.

Weis, Frederick Lewis. 2004. Ancestral roots of certain American colonists who came to America before 1700, 8th edition. Genealogical Publishing Company. Baltimore.

Wright, William Henry Kearley. 1889. Some account of the barony and town of Okehampton: Its antiquities and institutions. W. Masland. Tiverton.

Williams, Ann, Alfred Smyth, and D. P. Kirby, eds. 1991. A biographical dictionary of dark age Britain; England, Scotland and Wales. Routledge, Taylor and Francis Group. London.

Williams, Reverend Robert. 1852. A biographical dictionary of eminent Welshmen. Longman and Company. London.

Worsaã, Jens Jacob Asmussen. 1852. An account of the Danes and Norwegians in England, Scotland, and Ireland. J. Murray. London.

Wrottesley, George. 1903. A history of the family of Wrottesley, County Stafford. William Pollard and Company. Exeter.

Yeatman, John Pym. 1882. The early genealogical history of the house of Arundel: Being an account of the origin of the families of Montgomery, Albini, Fitzalan, and Howard, from the time of the conquest of Normandy by Rollo the Great. Mitchell and Hughes. London.

Index

Aaron Amitopolous .... **155 (8)**
Abbott, Jane, wife of John Burkett 147 (12)
Adalbert, King of Italy .... **71 (6)**, 78 (6), **83 (4)**
Adalbert I, Marquis of Ivrea in Turin 70 (6), 71 (5), 83 (2)
Adalulf, Count of Boulogne .... **32 (6)**
Adela, wife of Dreux, Seigneur de Boves 76 (8)
Adela, wife of Gui II, Count of Tonnerre 6 (10)
Adela of Bar-sur-Aube, wife of Raoul III, Seigneur de Crépy and Valois 24 (9), 37 (6)
Adela of England, wife of Etienne, Count of Champagne .... **137 (2)**
Adela of Salins 6 (9)
Adela of Savoy, wife of Louis VI, King of the Franks 150 (2)
Adela of Valois, wife of Herbert IV, Count of Vermandois .... **24 (10)**, 37 (6), 47 (6), 96 (10)
Adela of Vermandois, wife of Arnold I, Count of Flanders .... 5 (4), 31 (6), **34 (3)**, **57 (6)**
Adelaide, wife of Hildouin, Count of Roucy 152 (3)
Adelaide, wife of Osbert de Condet 43 (11)
Adelaide, wife of Richard, Duke of Burgundy 81 (4)
Adelaide of Alsace, wife of Robert "the Strong", Count of Paris 34 (1), 61 (5)
Adelaide of Anjou, wife of William I, Count of Provence 21 (9), 47 (4), 97 (13)
Adelaide of Anjou, wife of William II, Count of Arles, Count of Provence 64 (7)
Adelaide of Breteuil, wife of Raoul II, Seigneur de Crépy and Valois 24 (8)
Adelaide of Burgundy, wife of Reginar II, Count of Hainaut 81 (4)
Adelaide of Burgundy, wife of Robert, Count of Troyes 39 (3), 60 (6)
Adelaide of Hungary, wife of Vladislav II, King of Bohemia 154 (3)
Adelaide of Normandy, (Judith) wife of Renaud I, Count of Burgundy .... **45 (7)**, 79 (7), 84 (6), **106 (14)**
Adelaide of Normandy, Countess Aumale .... 7 (9), 28 (10), **42 (8)**, **119 (2)**
Adelaide of Paris, wife of Louis II, King of the Franks 4 (5), 8 (4), 17 (6), 25 (4)
Adelaide of Poitou, wife of Hugh Capet .... **21 (8)**, 47 (3), 65 (8), 81 (6), 94 (3), **97 (12)**
Adelaide of Troyes, wife of Geoffrey I, Count of Anjou .... **39 (4)**
Adelaide, Countess of Vermandois .... **24 (11)**, **37 (7)**, 47 (6), 96 (10)
Adelaide, wife of Charles, Duke of Lower Lorraine 27 (7), 82 (6), 93 (3)
Adeliz of Louvain, Queen of England 137 (5)
Adele, wife of Gautier I 24 (6)
Adele, wife of Gautier II 24 (7)
Adele, wife of Reginar III, Count of Hainaut 22 (9), 28 (8), 50 (4), 81 (5), 98 (13)
Adele of France, Countess of Contentin .... 2 (1), 5 (8), 41 (8), **49 (5)**, **67 (9)**, 114 (4), 137 (1)
Adele of Holland, wife of Baudouin II, Count of Boulogne .... **7 (7)**, 28 (9), 32 (9), 82 (7), **115 (3)**
Adelhard, Count of Paris 17 (6), 25 (4)
Adelheid of Swabia, wife of St. Ladislas I, King of Hungary 155 (13)
Adeline of Domfront, wife of Rotrou II, Vicomte of Chateaudun 52 (7)
Adelise, wife of Baldwin de Redvers, Earl of Devon 2 (5), 107 (19)
Adeliz, wife of Robert de Condet 43 (11)
Adilidis, wife of William Count of Mortain, Earl of Cornwall 120 (3)
Ædgifu of England, wife of Charles III, King of the Franks 4 (5), 8 (4), 25 (5), 92 (2), 112 (10), 134 (2)
Ældgyth (Edith) of Mercia .... 9 (18), 10 (17), **122 (3)**
Ælflaeda, wife of Edward "the Elder", King of England .... **4 (4)**, 8 (3), 25 (5)
Ælflaeda, wife of Sigurd "the Strong", Earl of Northumberland 28 (11), 42 (9), 148 (1)
Ælfgar, Earl of Mercia .... 9 (18), 10 (17), **122 (2)**
Ælfgifu, wife of Ælfgar, Earl of Mercia 9 (18), 10 (17), 122 (2)
Ælfrida of Wessex, wife of Baldwin II, Count of Flanders 5 (3), 31 (5), 34 (3), 57 (6)
Æthelhelm, Ealdorman of Wiltshire .... **4 (3)**, 8 (3)
Æthelred, King of Mercia 5 (2)
Æthelred I, King of Wessex .... **4 (2)**

Æthelswida, wife of Alfred "the Great", King of England.. 4 (4), 5 (2), 31 (5)
Æthelwulf, King of Wessex...**4 (1)**
Aelis, wife of Lambert I, Count of Mâcon 71 (6), 83 (4)
Aelis, wife of Robert I, King of the Franks 34 (1), 57 (5)
Aelis of France, Countess of Auxerre... 6 (13), **48 (5)**, **66 (9)**, 83 (7)
Agatha, wife of Edward "the Exile" 148 (2)
Agnarsson, Erik, King of Vestfold... 97 (3)
Agnes, wife of St. Leopold, Margrave of Austria.. 154 (5)
Agnes, wife of Raoul VIII, Vicomte of Maine 139 (6)
Agnes, wife of Walter Michell.. 28 (25)
Agnes of Aquitaine, wife of Ramiro II, King of Aragon 152 (4)
Agnes of Austria, wife of Vladislav II, King of Poland 154 (5)
Agnes of Evreux, wife of Simon de Montfort..**107 (15)**
Alan III, Duke of Brittany.. 36 (6), **40 (7)**, 64 (10), **108 (14)**
Alan IV, Duke of Brittany...39 (8), **40 (9)**
Alberade, wife of Reginar I, Count of Hainaut... 75 (3), 90 (2), 111 (10), 134 (2)
Alberade of Lorraine, wife of Renaud, Count of Rheims and Roucy ....**75 (5)**, 83 (5), **90 (3)**
Alberge, wife of Lancelin II, Seigneur de Beaugency 39 (7), 77 (9)
Alberic I, Count of Dammartin 51 (9), 84 (11)
Alberic II, Count of Dammartin 51 (9), 76 (11), 84 (11)
Albert I, Count of Namur.. 27 (8)
Albert I, Count of Vermandois .... **37 (3)**, **58 (6)**, 80 (5), 91 (3)
d'Alençon, Mabel, wife of Roger Montgomery 120 (2)
Alexius I, Emperor of Byzantium 155 (12)
Alexius III, Emperor of Byzantium 155 (15)
Alfhild, wife of Gudrød, King of Vestfold.. 97 (5)
Alfonso I, King of Portugal...139 (4)
Alfonso II, Count of Provence...**152 (7)**, **154 (8)**
Alfonso II, King of Aragon..**152 (6)**, 154 (7)
Alfonso VII, King of Castile and León... 151 (4), 152 (6), 154 (6)
Alfonso VIII, King of Castile...139 (3), 140 (2), 150 (5), **151 (5)**
Alfonso IX, King of Leon 139 (4)
Alfred the Great, King of England... 4 (4), **5 (2)**, 31 (5)
Alice, wife of Henry Quintyne 1 (2)
Alice, wife of Robert de Glastonia 28 (14), 52 (10)
Alice, wife of Robert White 139 (13), 141 (9)
Alice, wife of Thomas Young 2 (17)
Alice of Normandy, wife of Ranulph, Vicomte of the Bessin............................ **43 (8)**, 109 (16)
Alice of Northumberland, wife of Ralph de Toeni.. **28 (12)**, 52 (9)
Alix of Champagne, wife of Louis VII, King of the Franks 150 (3)
Altburg, wife of Walbert, Count of Threkwitigau...111 (6)
Alvaren, King of Alvheim.. 97 (5)
Alveston, Helen, wife of Hugh Hastings 137 (8)
Amicia, wife of Thomas Hastings 137 (9)
ap Anarawd, Eliseg ....**10 (14)**
Anchier, Marquis of Ivrea... 83 (2)
Andeas II, King of Hungary...**153 (2)**, 155 (17)
Andronikos ....**155 (14)**
Andronikos Doukas...155 (11)
Andronikos Doukas...155 (15)
Anna of Byzantium, wife of Louis III, Emperor of the West............................64 (4), 73 (5), 88 (6), **117 (3)**
Anna of Kiev, wife of King Henri I ....24 (11), 37 (7), 47 (5), 65 (9), **96 (9)**, 116 (6), 150 (1)

Anna Angela, wife of Theodoros I, Emperor of Byzantium.................................153 (3), **155 (16)**
Ansbertus, Gallo-Roman Senator..**118 (6)**
Anschitil, Vicomte of the Bessin..43 (8)
Ansegius ....**118 (9)**, 126 (4), 127 (1), 130 (2)
Ansfred, Vicomte d'Hiesmer...**109 (13)**
Ansfred "the Dane" Count of Hiesmer...**109 (12)**
Aoife (Eva) of Leinster..**16 (7)**, 37 (10), 50 (10)
Aremburge, wife of Ebles, Count of Poitou 21 (6), 97 (11)
Arnégonde, wife of Clotaire I, King of the Franks...124 (2)
Arnold I, Count of Flanders...**5 (4)**, **31 (6)**, 34 (3), 57 (6)
Arnold II, Count of Flanders.................................... **5 (6)**, 63 (8), 72 (6), 85 (4), 114 (3)
Arnoldus, Bishop of Metz..**118 (7)**, 126 (3), 130 (1)
St. Arnulf ....118 (8), 125 (2), **126 (3)**, 130 (2)
Arnulf, Count of Holland...**7 (6)**, 32 (9), 115 (2)
Arnulf, Emperor of Germany...74 (5), 111 (9), 133 (1)
Arnulf I, Count of Boulogne ....**32 (7)**
Arnulf II, Count of Boulogne ....7 (7), **32 (8)**, 115 (3)
Artald, Count of Lyon and Forez..6 (14), 48 (7)
ap Arthen, Dyfnwal, Prince of North Wales...**13 (1)**
ap Arthur, Noe...9 (6)
Aseda, wife of Eystein Glumra, Jarl of the Upplands......................................**97 (8)**, 113 (3)
Ashton, Elizabeth, wife of John Aylesworth ....**147 (6)**
Ashton, John...147 (5)
d'Aton, Isabel, wife of Roger Darcy 137 (12)
d'Aubigny, Alice, wife of John, Count of Eu...137 (5)
d'Aubigny, Isabel, wife of Robert de Ros...148 (8)
d'Aubigny, William..148 (8)
d'Aubigny, William, Earl of Arundel...137 (5)
Aubri, Count of Gastinois..77 (7)
Aubri II, Count of Mâcon...77 (6)
Aubri-Geoffrey, Count of Gastinois ....39 (6), **77 (8)**
Aupais, wife of Bégue, Count of Paris.. **17 (2)**, 55 (4)
Aupais, wife of Pepin II, Mayor of the Palace...54 (1), 127 (2)
d'Auvergne, Ermengarde, wife of Eudes II......................25 (9), 36 (5), 40 (7), **64 (9)**, 108 (14)
Aveline, Countess Meulan..37 (8), 47 (7), 52 (8)
Avenal, Richard...148 (5)
Avitus, Roman Emperor...118 (3)
d'Avranches, Marguerite, wife of Ranulph II...43 (9), **109 (16)**
d'Avranches, Maud, wife of William de Courcy ....48 (10), **100 (18)**
d'Avranches, Robert ....**100 (17)**
d'Avranches, William..100 (16)
Aylesworth, Frances, wife of Thomas Stockett...**147 (8)**
Aylesworth, John 147 (6)
Aylesworth, Walter...**147 (7)**
de Badlesmere, Bartholomew, Baron Badlesmere...148 (10)
de Badlesmere, Margery, wife of William de Ros, Baron Ros 148 (10)
de Badlesmere, Maud, wife of John de Vere, Earl of Oxford...........................139 (9), 143 (5)
Baldwin I, Count of Flanders 5 (3), 18 (6), 31 (4)
Baldwin II, Count of Flanders ....5 (3), **31 (5)**, 34 (3), 57 (6)
Baldwin III, Count of Flanders ....**5 (5)**, **34 (4)**, 72 (6), 85 (4)
Baldwin IV, Count of Flanders ....5 (7), 49 (5), 63 (8), 67 (9), **85 (5)**, 114 (3)
Baldwin V, Count of Flanders ....2 (1), **5 (8)**, 41 (8), 49 (5), 67 (9), **114 (4)**, 137 (1)
Baldwin V, Count of Hainaut...150 (4)
Bardolf, Hugh 43 (12)
Bardolf, Juliana, wife of Nicholas Poyntz ....**43 (13)**, 123 (2)

de Baseville, Rohese, wife of Stephen Penesherst 2 (8)
Basil I, Emperor of Byzantium ....**117 (1)**
Basilea, wife of Hugh Malet...102 (18)
Basset, Alice, wife of William Malet.. 43 (14), 101 (20), **123 (1)**
Basset, Thomas, Lord of Headington .... 101 (20), **123 (1)**
Bathilde, wife of Clovis II, King of Soissons 124 (6)
Baudouin II, Count of Boulogne.. 7 (7), 28 (9), **32 (9)**, 82 (7), 115 (3)
de Bayeux, Poppa, wife of Rollo the Viking... 21 (7), 97 (10)
Beatrice, wife of Friedrich I, Duke of Upper Lorraine.................................... 29 (7), **53 (3)**, **95 (3)**
Beatrice of Montdidier, wife of Geoffrey II, Count of Perche...**52 (7)**, 138 (2)
Beatrice of Provence, wife of Charles I, King of Sicily.. 153 (5)
Beatrice of Savoy, wife of Raymond V, Count of Provence 143 (1), 152 (8)
Beatrice of Vermandois, wife of Robert I, King of the Franks........................47 (1), **61 (5)**, 94 (2), 133 (2)
Beatrix of Hainaut, wife of Ebles I, Count of Rheims .... 50 (5), 75 (7), **81 (7)**
Beatrix of Mâcon, wife of Geoffrey III, Count of Gastinois.......................................39 (6), **77 (7)**
Beauchamp, Isabella, wife of Patrick de Chaworth.. 140 (6), 143 (3), 151 (9)
Beaufort, Joan, wife of Ralph Neville, Earl of Westmoreland.. 144 (9), **146 (3)**
de Beaumont, Agnes, wife of Louie de Brienne 139 (6)
de Beaumont, Elizabeth, wife of William Botreaux ....**139 (11)**, 141 (8)
de Beaumont, Henry, Baron Beaumont ....**139 (9)**, **143 (5)**
de Beaumont, Henry, Baron Beaumont, Earl of Buchan ....**139 (7)**, 143 (4)
de Beaumont, Isabel, wife of Gilbert de Clare, Earl of Pembroke .... 16 (7), **37 (9)**, 50 (9), 99 (17)
de Beaumont, John, Baron Beaumont ....**139 (8)**, 143 (4)
de Beaumont, John, Baron Beaumont ....**139 (10)**
de Beaumont, Maud (Mabel), wife of William Vernon, Earl of Devon.......**2 (5)**, 48 (11), 100 (20), **107 (19)**
de Beaumont, Robert, Count of Meulan...2 (4), **38 (10)**, **107 (18)**, 120 (5)
de Beaumont, Robert, Earl of Leicester 37 (8), 47 (7), 50 (9), 99 (17), 107 (17)
de Beaumont, Roger..37 (8), 47 (7), 52 (8)
de Beaumont, Waleran, Earl of Worcester..2 (4), **38 (9)**, 107 (17), 120 (5)
St. Begga .... 118 (9), 126 (4), **127 (1)**, **130 (2)**
Bégue, Count of Paris... 17 (2), **55 (4)**
Bela III, King of Hungary..**153 (1)**
Bela IV, King of Hungary.. **153 (3)**, 155 (17)
ap Beli, Gwallawg 9 (6)
de Belmeis, Alice, wife of Alan la Zouche .... 39 (10), **44 (12)**
de Belmeis, Philip 39 (10), 44 (11)
de Belmeis, Walter...44 (11)
Berengar I, King of Italy .... 23 (4), **83 (1)**
Berengar II, King of Italy ....5 (6), 70 (6), 71 (5), **83 (3)**
Berengaria of Barcelona, Queen of Castile and León 151 (4)
Berengaria of Castile, Queen of Leon .... **139 (4)**
Berengaria of Leon, Queen of Jerusalem, wife of Jean de Brienne.. **139 (5)**
Berenger, Count of Bayeux...97 (10)
Bernard (Duke Bernard) .... **56 (2)**
Bernard, King of Italy .... **56 (4)**, **57 (2)**
Bernard Roger, Count of Couserans 152 (2)
Berta, wife of Suppo, Marquis of Spoleto... 23 (4), **83 (1)**
Bertha, wife of Walter FitzRoger 9 (21)
Bertha of Blois, wife of Alan III, Duke of Brittany .... **36 (6)**, 40 (7), **64 (10)**, 108 (14)
Bertha of Burgundy, wife of Eudes I, Count of Blois .... **25 (8)**, 33 (7), 36 (4), 64 (9), **68 (7)**
Bertha of Gloucester, wife of William de Braose.. **9 (22)**, 46 (13)
Bertha of Holland, wife of Philip I, King of the Franks...150 (1)
Bertha of Lorraine, wife of Thebaud, Count of Arles.. 70 (5), **71 (3)**
Bertha of Morvois, wife of Herbert I, Count of Vermandois 34 (2), 47 (1), 57 (4)
Bertha of Swabia, wife of Rudolph II, King of Burgundy 25 (7), 68 (5), 92 (3)

189

Berthe, mother of Charibert, Count of Laon..**124 (8)**
Berthold VI, Duke of Croatia...153 (2)
Bertila of Spoleto, wife of Berengar I, King of Italy 23 (4), 83 (1)
Bertrada, wife of Amauri de Montfort...107 (15)
Bertrada, wife of Clotaire II, King of the Franks..124 (4)
Bertrada of Laon, wife of Pepin "the Short" ....17 (1), 54 (2), **124 (10)**
Bethoc, wife of Crinan "the Thane"..148 (1)
Bigger, Elizabeth, wife of Jonathan Prater 1 (4–b)
Biggs, Elizabeth, wife of George Tattershall 137 (23)
Biggs, Joanna, wife of Thomas Stockett..147 (8)
Billung, Hermann, Duke of Saxony...5 (5), 34 (4)
Bjørn I, King of Uppsala...**96 (1)**
Bjørn III, King of Uppsala..**96 (5)**
Blanca of Castile, Queen of France.......................................**140 (3)**, 150 (5), **151 (6)**
Blanca of Navarre, Queen of Castile.......................................139 (3), 140 (2), **151 (4)**
Blanche of Artois, wife of Edmund, Earl of Lancaster......................**140 (5)**, 143 (2), **151 (8)**, 152 (10)
Bledri, father of Hyfaidd ap Bledri, King of South Wales 12 (1)
ap Bledri, Hyfaidd, King of South Wales..**12 (1)**
Blichilde, wife of Ansbertus, Gallo-Roman Senator...118 (6)
Blichilde, wife of Ranulph I, Count of Poitou 21 (4)
Blichilde, wife of Rorick, Count of Maine..21 (4)
Bluet, Elizabeth, wife of John FitzJames..28 (24)
Bluet, William 28 (24)
Bodegeisel II ....118 (8), **125 (2)**
Bodo, Seigneur de Maers..78 (7), 83 (6)
Boleslav I, King of Poland..154 (1)
Boleslav III, Grand Prince of Poland...**154 (4)**
Boris-Michael, Tsar of the Bulgars...**155 (5)**
Boru, Brian, High King of Ireland...**16 (1)**
Boso, Count of Arles, Marquis of Tuscany ....70 (5), **71 (4)**, 83 (3)
Boso, King of Burgundy and Provence...64 (3), **88 (5)**, 117 (3)
Boso I, Count of Arles...**87 (1)**
Boso I, Viscount Turenne..138 (3)
Boso II, Comtes de Provence...64 (6), 73 (6)
Boso II, Count of Arles..**87 (2)**
Boso III, Count of Arles...**87 (3)**
Botreaux, Emma, wife of Joel Valletort 3 (5)
Botreaux, Margaret, Baroness Botreaux..**139 (12)**, 141 (8)
Botreaux, William...3 (5)
Botreaux, William...139 (11), 141 (8)
Bouvin, Count of Metz..33 (3), 64 (3), 87 (4)
de Braose, Eve, wife of William de Cantelou................................**9 (26)**, **16 (10)**, 44 (14), 76 (13)
de Braose, Philip...9 (22)
de Braose, Reginald ....9 (24), 16 (9), **46 (14)**
de Braose, William, Baron Braose ....**9 (25)**, 16 (9), 76 (13)
de Braose, William, Baron Braose and Bramber 9 (22), 46 (13)
de Braose, William, Baron Braose, Bramber, and Brecon.................................**9 (23)**, 46 (13)
Brashears, William..137 (25c)
Braut-Onundsson, Ingjald, King of Uppsala..97 (1)
de Brienne, Jean, Emperor of Constantinople 139 (5)
de Brienne, Louis, Viscount Beaumont-au-Maine ....**139 (6)**
de Brionne, Elisée, wife of Robert Malet..102 (16)
de Briwere, Grace, wife of Reginald de Braose 9 (24), 16 (9), 46 (14)
de Briwere, William 9 (24), 46 (14)
ap Brochwel, Cadell, King of Powys..**9 (9)**

ap Brochwel, Cynan Garwyn, King of Powys..**9 (2)**, **136 (3)**
de Brus, Agnes, wife of Walter Fauconberg.. 149 (9)
de Builly, Beatrice, wife of William, Count of Eu..137 (4)
Bulmer, Eve, wife of John de Fauconberg..149 (10)
Bulmer, Ralph..149 (10)
Burchard, Duke of Swabia.. 68 (5)
de Burgh, Elizabeth, Countess of Ulster ....**144 (5)**, 145 (3)
de Burgh, John.. 144 (3)
de Burgh, Richard, Earl of Ulster.. 144 (3)
de Burgh, William, Earl of Ulster..**144 (4)**, 145 (3)
Burkett, Elizabeth, possible wife of Eliphaz Riley 147 (12)
Burkett, John...147 (12)
ap Cadell Deyrnllwg, Cynan .... **9 (1)**, 136 (2)
ap Cadell, Hywel Dda, King of South Wales..**9 (14)**, 11 (15), 12 (3)
verch Cadel, Nesta, wife of Gwriad ap Elidwr... **9 (10)**
Cagniart, Alain, Count of Cornouaille... 40 (8), 64 (11)
Canning, Isabel, wife of Richard Ivye.. 2 (19), 28 (27)
de Cantelou, Milicent, wife of Eudes la Zouche ....**9 (27)**, 43 (17), 44 (14), **76 (14)**
de Cantelou, William.. 51 (11), 76 (12)
de Cantelou, William..**9 (26)**, 16 (10), 51 (11), 76 (12)
de Cantelou, William, Baron Abergavenny.......................**9 (26)**, 16 (10), 44 (14), **76 (13)**
Capet, Hedwig (Edith)..**22 (9)**, **50 (4)**, 75 (7), 81 (6), **98 (13)**
Capet, Hugh, King of the Franks ....21 (8), **47 (3)**, 65 (8), 81 (6), **94 (3)**, 97 (12)
Carloman, Mayor of the Palace .... **55 (2)**
Charibert, Count of Laon .... **124 (9)**
Charlemagne, King of the Franks.....................**17 (1)**, **19 (1)**, **54 (3)**, 55 (4), 56 (3), 57 (1), **124 (11)**
Charles, Duke of Lower Lorraine.. **27 (7)**, 82 (6), **93 (3)**
Charles Constantine, Count of Vienne..**64 (5)**, 73 (5), **117 (4)**
Charles I, King of Sicily.. 153 (5)
Charles II, King of the Franks .... 5 (3), 17 (5), **25 (3)**, **33 (3)**, 87 (5), 129 (11)
Charles II, King of Naples.. 153 (5)
Charles III, King of the Franks .... 4 (5), 8 (4), **25 (5)**, 92 (2), 112 (10), 134 (2)
Charles of Valois, Count of Valois... 153 (6)
de Chatellerault, Eleanor, wife of William, Duc d'Aquitaine 139 (2), 140 (1)
de Chatillon, Agnes, wife of Bela III, King of Hungary 153 (1)
de Chatillon, Renaud, Prince of Antioch 153 (1)
de Chaworth, Maud, wife of Henry, Earl of Lancaster 139 (8), 140 (6), 143 (3), 144 (4), 151 (9)
de Chaworth, Patrick 140 (6), 143 (3), 151 (9)
Chilperic, King of Burgundy 124 (1)
Chilperic, King of Soissons... 124 (1)
Chiselden, Margaret, wife of William Wadham 2 (16)
de Clare, Elizabeth, wife of John de Burgh .... **144 (3)**
de Clare, Gilbert, Earl of Gloucester and Hertford 144 (2)
de Clare, Gilbert, Earl of Pembroke .... 16 (7), 37 (9), **50 (9)**, **99 (17)**
de Clare, Gilbert FitzRichard, Earl of Clare..37 (9), 50 (8), **99 (16)**
de Clare, Isabel, Countess of Pembroke...**9 (25)**, **16 (8)**, **50 (11)**
de Clare, Margaret, wife of Bartholomew de Badelsmere 148 (10)
de Clare, Richard, Earl of Hertford.. 144 (2)
de Clare, Richard "Strongbow", Earl of Pembroke.......................................16 (7), **37 (10)**, **50 (10)**
de Clare, Richard FitzGilbert ....50 (8), **99 (15)**
Clemence of Bar-le-Duc, Countess Dammartin...................................**27 (12)**, 51 (8), **84 (10)**
de Clermont, Adelaide, wife of Gilbert de Clare.......................................37 (9), **50 (8)**, 99 (16)
de Clermont, Maud, wife of Alberic II ....**51 (9)**, 76 (11), **84 (11)**
St. Clodoule .... **128 (4)**
Clotaire I, King of the Franks 124 (2)

Clotaire II, King of the Franks .... **124 (4)**
Clotilde, wife of Thierry III, King of Soissons 124 (7)
Clotilde (Dode), wife of St. Arnulf .... **118 (8)**, 126 (3), 130 (2)
St. Clotildus .... **124 (1)**
Clovis I, King of Soissons 124 (1)
Clovis II, King of Soissons .... **124 (6)**
Cobham, John 141 (5)
Cobham, Margaret, wife of Hugh Peverell 141 (5)
de Columbiers, Joan, wife of Geoffrey Stawell .... **2 (9)**
de Columbiers, John .... **2 (8)**
de Columbiers, Philip 2 (7), 3 (7), 48 (12)
Colville, Isabel, wife of John Wandesford .... **137 (15)**, **149 (13)**
Colville, John .... 137 (14), 148 (13), **149 (12)**
Colville, William 137 (14), 148 (13), 149 (11)
Comyn, Alexander 139 (7)
Comyn, Alice, wife of Henry de Beaumont 139 (7), 143 (4)
verch Conan, Essylt Vodrwyog 9 (11), 13 (3)
Conan I, Duke of Brittany. Count of Rhennes 40 (5), 103 (13), 108 (13)
de Condet, Isabel, wife of Hugh Bardolf .... **43 (12)**
de Condet, Osbert 43 (11)
de Condet, Robert 43 (11)
Conrad I, King of Burgundy .... 25 (7), 33 (7), 36 (4), 62 (7), **68 (6)**, 92 (3)
Conrad II, Duke of Burgundy 68 (4), 89 (6)
Constance of Antioch, wife of Renaud de Chatillon, Prince of Antioch 153 (1)
Constance of Provence, wife of Boso II .... **64 (6)**, **73 (6)**
Constance of Provence, wife of Robert II .... 5 (8), 21 (9), 47 (4), **65 (8)**, 83 (7), 96 (9), 97 (13), 114 (4), 116 (6), 132 (5)
Constanza, wife of Sancho Ramirez 151 (2)
de Conteville, Herluin 120 (1)
Corbet, Robert 2 (2), 5 (10)
Corbet, Sybilla, mistress of Henry I, King of England 2 (2), 5 (10), 120 (4)
de Couci, Enguerrand 76 (8)
de Couci, Margaret, wife of Richard de Burgh, Earl of Ulster 144 (3)
de Couci, Melesinde, wife of Hugh de Gournay .... **76 (10)**
de Couci, Thomas .... **76 (9)**
de Courcy, Hawise, wife of Renaud de Courtenay .... 2 (6), 48 (10), **100 (19)**
de Courcy, William 48 (10), 100 (18)
de Courtenay, Alice, wife of Aymer de Valence 138 (5), 141 (1)
de Courtenay, Egeline, wife of Phillip de Columbiers .... **2 (7)**, 3 (7), **48 (12)**
de Courtenay, Elizabeth, wife of Pierre de Courtenay 138 (5)
de Courtenay, Joceline 48 (8)
de Courtenay, Margaret, wife of Thomas Peverell 141 (6)
de Courtenay, Miles 48 (8)
de Courtenay, Pierre 138 (5)
de Courtenay, Renaud .... **48 (9)**, 100 (19)
de Courtenay, Renaud .... 2 (6), **48 (10)**, 100 (19)
de Courtenay, Robert, Baron Oakhampton .... 2 (6), **48 (11)**, **100 (20)**
de Courtenay, Thomas 141 (6)
Cowdray, Margery, wife of William Rythe 137 (20), 141 (12)
Crawford, Nancy Cooper, wife of Bazel Prater 147 (15–f)
de Creci, Melesinde, wife of Thomas de Couci 76 (9)
de Crepi, Alix, wife of Thebaud III, Count of Blois 137 (2)
de Crepon, Gunnora, wife of Richard I, Duke of Normandy 41 (6)
Crinan "the Thane" 148 (1)
Crispin, Gilbert, Count of Brionne .... **99 (14)**
Crispin, Hesilia, wife of William Malet .... **101 (15)**

Cristina, wife of Ramiro, Count of Monçon..**151 (2)**
Cunigunde, wife of Bernard, King of Italy...56 (4), 57 (2)
ap Cynan, Selyf...**9 (3)**
Dag, King of Vestmar...97 (4)
Dagobert I, King of the Franks..**124 (5)**
Dammartin, Joanna, Countess of Ponthieu 144 (1)
Dammartin, Juliana, wife of Hugh de Gournay ....**51 (10)**, 76 (11)
Darbforgaill, wife of Diarmait MacMael nam Bo, King of Leinster ....**16 (3)**
Darcy, Alice, wife of John Colville... **137 (14)**, **148 (13)**, 149 (12)
Darcy, John, Baron Darcy.. 137 (12), 148 (12)
Darcy, John, Baron Darcy...**137 (13)**, 148 (12), 149 (12)
Darcy, Roger... 137 (12)
David "the Saint", King of Scots... **148 (3)**
de Deandon, Hamelyn.. 102 (22)
de Deandon, Mabel, wife of Baldwin Malet... 102 (22)
de la Marche, Poncia, wife of Wulgrim II, Count of Angoulême..138 (4)
Devereaux, Sibyl, wife of John Marshall 16 (8), 50 (11)
Diaz de Vivar, Rodrigo "El Cid", Count of Valencia...**151 (1)**
Diego, Count of Orviedo 141 (1)
Dietrich, Count of Ringelheim..74 (4), 90 (1), **111 (8)**, 133 (1)
Dietrich I, Count of Bar, Duke of Upper Lorraine........................ 26 (9), **29 (8)**, **53 (4)**, 62 (8)
Dietrich I (Dirk I), Count of Holland... 7 (5), 35 (4)
Dietrich II (Dirk II), Count of Holland... 7 (5), 35 (4), 115 (2)
Dode, wife of Ferreolus, Roman Senator 118 (5)
de Dol, Gelduin 100 (17)
du Donjon, (Helvis), possible wife of Renaud de Courtenay...48 (9)
Donnchad, King of Muster ....**16 (2)**
Dreux, Seigneur de Boves 76 (8)
Duncan I, King of Scots ....**148 (1)**
Dyall, Elizabeth, wife of Nicholas Poyntz 43 (15), 123 (3)
Dyall, Timothy 43 (15), 123 (3)
ap Dyfnwal, Meyric, King of Greater Ceredigion... 9 (12), **13 (2)**
Eberhard, Count in the Nordgau... 30 (7), 114 (1)
Eberhard, Marquis of Friuli 23 (3), 83 (1)
Ebles, Count of Poitou ....**21 (6)**, 97 (11)
Ebles I, Count of Rheims and Roucy... 50 (5), **75 (7)**, 81 (7)
Edburga, wife of Æthelred, King of Mercia.. 5 (2)
Eldegarde, wife of Raoul I, Count of Ostrevant.. 24 (5)
Edith, mistress of Henry I, King of England...138 (1)
Edith of Warenne, wife of Gerard de Gournay 76 (10)
Edmund I, King of Uppsala ....**96 (3)**
Edmund of Langley, Duke of York 144 (8)
ap Ednywain, Seisyll..9 (17), 10 (15)
Edward I, King of England ....**144 (1)**, 145 (1)
Edward II, King of England .... **145 (1)**, 146 (1), 153 (8)
Edward III, King of England .... 144 (5), 144 (8), **145 (2)**, 146 (1), 153 (8)
Edward IV, King of England..**144 (10)**, 146 (5), **147 (1)**
Edward "the Elder", King of England .... 4 (4), **8 (3)**, 25 (5)
Edward "the Exile" 148 (2)
Egbert, King of Wessex 4 (1)
Egbert of Saxony 111 (7)
Eldeburge of Bourges, wife of Giles de Sully 137 (3)
Eleanor of Aquitaine.. 138 (6), 139 (2), 140 (1), 141 (1), 151 (5)
Eleanor of England, Queen of Castile ....**139 (3)**, **140 (2)**, 150 (5), 151 (5)
Eleanor of Provence, Queen of England .... 140 (5), 143 (1), 144 (1), 151 (8), **152 (9)**

193

Elenora of Castile, wife of Edward I, King of England...144 (1), 145 (1)
ap Elidwr, Gwriad, King of the Isle of Man...9 (10)
ap Eliseg, Brochwel, King of Powys ....**9 (8)**
verch Eliseg, Trawst, wife of Seisyll, Prince of Wales ....9 (17), **10 (15)**
Elizabeth, wife of Eliphaz Riley...147 (12)
Emeline, wife of Hildouin, Count of Chartres 24 (8)
Emma, wife of Baldwin FitzGilbert, Seigneur de Meules... 100 (15)
Emma, wife of Richard le Goz, Vicomte d'Avranches...43 (9), 109 (15)
Emma of Alemania, wife of Gerold, Count of Anglachau..19 (1)
(Emma), wife of William d'Avranches..**100 (16)**
Emmilda of Silesia, wife of Boleslaw I, King of Poland 154 (1)
Engelberge, wife of Louis II, Emperor of the West..64 (2), 88 (5)
Engelbert, Count of Brienne ....**6 (8)**
Engeltrude, wife of Eudes, Count of Orleans ....**17 (4)**, 25 (3), 129 (10)
Engeltrude, wife of Hunroch 23 (3)
Engeltrude of Brienne, wife of Milo III, Count of Tonnerre...**6 (9)**
Erard II, Count of Brienne 139 (5)
Erembourg, Countess of Maine, wife of Fulk V, Count of Anjou 139 (1)
Eric III, King of Uppsala ....**96 (2)**
Eric V, King of Uppsala ....**96 (4)**
Eric VI, King of Sweden ....**96 (6)**
Erleigh, Eleanor, wife of Nicholas Poyntz, Baron Poyntz... 28 (21), 43 (19)
Erleigh, John...43 (19)
Ermenfroi, Count of Amiens 24 (5)
Ermengarde (Ada), mistress of Ranulph II, Count of Poitou...21 (5)
Ermengarde, wife of Boso, King of Burgundy and Provence......................................**64 (3)**, 88 (5), 117 (3)
Ermengarde, wife of Giselbert, Count of Burgundy 39 (3), 60 (6)
Ermengarde, wife of Lietaud, Count of Mâcon...71 (6), 77 (6), 83 (4)
Ermengarde, wife of Lothair I, King of Italy 20 (3), 64 (1)
Ermengarde, wife of Louis I, King of the Franks 20 (2), 64 (1)
Ermengarde, wife of Robert I, Count of Lomme...27 (8)
Ermengarde, Countess of Tonnerre...**6 (13)**, 48 (6), 83 (8)
Ermengarde of Anjou, wife of Alan IV, Duke of Brittany..**39 (8)**, 40 (9)
Ermengarde of Anjou, wife of Aubri-Geoffrey, Count of Gastinois ....**39 (6)**, 77 (8)
Ermengarde of Anjou, wife of Conan I, Duke of Brittany ....**40 (5)**, 103 (13), 108 (13)
Ermengarde of Bar, wife of Herbert III, Count of Vermandois 37 (4), 91 (4)
Ermengarde of Bar-sur-Seine, wife of Milo IV, Count of Tonnerre..6 (11)
Ermengarde of Lorraine, wife of Giselbert, Count of Darnau ....**75 (2)**
Ermengarde of Nevers, wife of Miles de Courtenay ....**48 (8)**
Ermengarde of Provence, wife of Robert I, Count d'Auvergne....................................25 (9), 36 (5), **64 (8)**
Ermentrude, wife of Herbert, Count of Gleiburg 63 (6), 114 (2)
Ermentrude of Burgundy, wife of Thierry I ....27 (11), 53 (7), **84 (8)**
Ermentrude of France..**29 (5)**
Ermentrude of Gleiberg, wife of Frederick I, Count of Luxembourg .... 5 (7), **63 (7)**, 85 (5), 114 (2)
Ermentrude (Adelaide) of Lorraine, wife of Albert I, Count of Namur..**27 (8)**
Ermentrude of Orleans, wife of Charles II, King of the Franks ....**17 (5)**, 25 (3), **129 (11)**
Erzsebet of Cumania wife of Istvan V, King of Hungary 153 (4), 155 (18)
Estrid, wife of Olav II, King of Sweden...96 (7), 116 (5), 132 (4)
Etienne (Stephanie), wife of William I, Count of Burgundy ....**45 (8)**, 53 (7), 84 (7)
Etienne (Stephen), Count of Champagne...137 (2)
Eudes, Count of Cambrai...**6 (7)**, 86 (5)
Eudes, Count of Orleans ....17 (4), 25 (3), **129 (10)**
Eudes, Count of Vermandois..24 (10), **37 (5)**
Eudes I, Count of Blois .... 25 (8), **33 (7)**, 36 (4), 64 (9), 68 (7)
Eudes I, Vicomte Porhoët...39 (9), 40 (10)

Eudes II, Count of Blois ....**25 (9)**, **36 (5)**, 40 (7), 64 (9), 108 (14)
Eudocia Ingerina, wife of Basil I, Emperor of Byzantium....................................117 (1), 117 (1A)
Euphrosyne, wife of Alexius III, Emperor of Byzantium .... **155 (15)**
Euphrosyne, wife of Andronikos Doukas...155 (15)
Euphrosyne of Kiev, wife of Geza II, King of Hungary 153 (1)
Eustace I, Count of Boulogne........................**7 (8)**, 28 (9), **32 (10)**, 42 (8), 82 (7), 119 (2)
Everingham, Catherine, wife of John de Beaumont...139 (10)
Everingham, Thomas...139 (10)
Eystein. King of the Upplands.. 97 (2)
Eystein, King of Vestfold.. **97 (3)**
Eystein Glumra, Jarl of the Upplands.. 97 (8), **113 (3)**
Eysteinsdotter, Asa, wife of Halfdan "White Leg", King of the Upplands...................... 97 (2)
Ezzo, Count of Palatine...154 (1)
Fauconberg, Joan, wife of William Colville.........................137 (14), 148 (13), **149 (11)**
Fauconberg, John, Baron Fauconberg... **149 (10)**
Fauconberg, Walter, Baron Fauconberg 149 (9)
Fauconberg, Walter, Baron Fauconberg 149 (9)
St. Fernando, King of Castile and Leon 144 (1)
Fernando II, King of Leon 139 (4)
Ferreolus, son-in-law to Flavius Afranius Syagrius 118 (2)
Ferreolus, Roman Senator..**118 (5)**
FitzAlan, Alice, wife of Thomas Holand, Earl of Kent 144 (7)
FitzGilbert, Baldwin, Seigneur de Meules.. **100 (15)**
FitzJames, Isabel (Mary), wife of Hugh Malet.. 2 (18), **28 (25)**
FitzJames, John...28 (23), **28 (24)**
FitzPiers, Reginald.. 148 (7)
FitzRichard, Osborn...9 (19), 122 (4)
FitzRoger, Walter..9 (21)
FitzRoy, Reginald, Earl of Cornwall.............................**2 (3)**, 38 (10), 107 (18), 120 (4)
FitzScrob, Richard 9 (19), 122 (4)
FitzSimon, Pons...43 (13)
de Flamville, Erneburga, wife of William Hastings 137 (6)
Flavius Afranius Syagrius ....**118 (1)**
Florence I, Count of Holland..150 (1)
Folmer I, Count of Metz 29 (8), 53 (4)
Frédégonde, wife of Chilperic, King of Soissons 124 (3)
Frederick I, Count of Luxembourg ....5 (7), 63 (7), 85 (5), **114 (2)**
Friedrich I, Duke of Upper Lorraine, Count of Bar.......................................**29 (7)**, 53 (3), 95 (3)
Friedrich II, Duke of Upper Lorraine, Count of Bar....................................26 (9), **53 (5)**, 62 (8)
Fulbert the Tanner, father of Mathilda of Flanders 41 (7), 103 (14), 119 (1)
Fulk II, Count of Anjou...24 (6), 39 (4), 64 (7)
Fulk III, Count of Anjou ....**39 (5)**, 77 (8)
Fulk IV, Count of Anjou ....**39 (7)**, 40 (9), **77 (9)**
Fulk V, Count of Anjou 139 (1)
Gainsford, Margaret, wife of Robert White..137 (19), 141 (10)
Gainsford, Nicholas 141 (10)
Garcia VII, King of Navarre..**151 (3)**
Garcia Sanchez, King of Navarre...152 (1)
de Garlande, Agnes, wife of Amauri de Montfort...38 (9), 107 (16)
de Garlande, Anseau...107 (16)
Garnier, Count of Troyes...64 (5), 73 (4), 117 (4)
Gastelin, Juliana, wife of Geoffrey Stawell..2 (10)
Gastelin, Walter..2 (10)
Gautier I. Count of Valois, the Vexin, and Amiens .... **24 (6)**
Gautier II. Count of Valois, the Vexin, and Amiens .... **24 (7)**

Gebhard, Count in the Wetterau, Duke of Lorraine...62 (5)
Geoffrey, Duke of Brittany ....36 (6), **40 (6)**, 64 (10), 108 (13)
Geoffrey I, Count of Anjou 39 (4)
Geoffrey II, Count of Perche...52 (7), 138 (2)
Geoffrey III, Count of Gastinois...39 (6), 77 (7)
Gerald I, Count of Alemania 129 (9)
Gerberge, wife of Dietrich I..7 (5), 35 (4)
Gerberge, wife of Fulk II, Count of Anjou 24 (6), 39 (4)
Gerberge, wife of Jubel Berenger, Count of Rennes 40 (5)
Gerberge of Alsace...63 (6)
Gerberge of Burgundy...**26 (8)**, 53 (5), 62 (7), **69 (7)**
Gerberge of Lorraine, wife of Albert I ....37 (3), 58 (6), **80 (5), 91 (3)**
Gerberge of Lorraine, wife of Lambert I ....7 (8), **28 (8)**, 32 (10), 82 (6)
Gerberge of Mâcon, wife of Adalbert, King of Italy.............................71 (6), 78 (6), 83 (4)
Gerberge of Saxony, wife of (1) Giselbert, Duke of Lorraine ....37 (3), 58 (6), 75 (4), **90 (2), 111 (10), 134 (2)**
Gerberge of Saxony, wife of (2) Louis IV, King of the Franks..... 8 (5), 25 (6), 68 (6), **92 (2), 112 (10), 134 (2)**
Gerhard, Count of Vaudemont..**27 (10)**, 53 (8), 84 (9)
Gerhard I, Count of Auvergne 21 (3)
Gerhard III, Count of Alsace..27 (9)
Gerhard III, Count of Egisheim..27 (10)
Gerhard IV, Duke of Upper Lorraine, Count of Alsace..27 (9)
Gerloc (Adele) of Normandy, wife of William I, Count of Poitou ....21 (7), 47 (3), 94 (3), **97 (11)**
Gerlotte of Blois, wife of Hrolf Turstan..109 (11)
Gerold, Count of Anglachau 19 (1)
Gersinda, wife of Rainier, Count of Forcalqueir.......................................152 (7), 154 (8)
Gersinda of Bigorre, wife of Bernard Roger, Count of Couserans 152 (2)
Gertrude of Saxony, wife of Florence I, Count of Holland 150 (1)
Geva of Vestfold, wife of Widukind..**111 (4)**
de Gevaudan, Dulce, wife of Ramón Berenger III, Count of Barcelona 152 (5)
Geza II, King of Hungary 153 (1)
de Giffard, Rohese, wife of Richard FitzGilbert de Clare 50 (8), 99 (15)
de Giffard, Walter...99 (15)
Gilberge of Couserans...152 (2)
Gilbert, Seigneur de l'Aigle..151 (3)
Girard, Count of Paris 17 (2), 55 (3)
Giselbert, Count in the Massgau..75 (2)
Giselbert, Count of Burgundy 39 (3), 60 (6)
Giselbert, Count of Darnau...75 (2)
Giselbert, Count of Roucy..50 (5), **75 (6)**, 81 (7)
Giselbert, Duke of Lorraine.............................37 (3), 58 (6), **75 (4)**, 90 (2), 111 (10), 134 (2)
Gisele, wife of Adalbert I, Marquis of Ivrea ....70 (6), 71 (5), **83 (2)**
Gisele, wife of Charibert, Count of Laon 124 (9)
Gisele, wife of Eberhard, Marquis of Friuli ....**23 (3)**, 83 (1)
Gisele, wife of Gerhard III, Count of Alsace..27 (9)
Gisele of Burgundy, wife of Umberto II, Duke of Savoy 150 (2)
Gisele of Lorraine, wife of Godefrid, King of Haithabu............................**74 (3)**, 111 (8)
Gisele of Vaudemont ....**27 (11)**, 51 (8), 53 (8), 84 (9)
de Glastonia, Matilda, wife of Roger de Newburgh....................................28 (14), 52 (10)
de Glastonia, Robert...28 (14), 52 (10)
Godefrid, King of Haithabu...74 (3), 111 (8)
Godehut, wife of Richard, Count d'Evreux...107 (14)
Godfrey, Count of Brionne and Eu...**99 (13)**
Godiva, Lady ....**122 (1)**
St. Gondolfus ....**125 (1)**
Gormflaith of Naas, wife of Brian Boru..16 (1)

de Gournay, Gerard 76 (10)

de Gournay, Hugh 76 (10)

de Gournay, Hugh ....51 (10), **76 (11)**

de Gournay, Milicent, wife of William de Cantelou ....9 (26), 16 (10), **51 (11)**, 76 (12)

Grimhild (Grimeut), wife of Leutaud, Count of Paris 55 (5)

Gudröd, King of Vestfold ....**97 (5)**

Guerri I, Count of Morvois 57 (4)

Gui, Count of Hornbach ....**129 (7)**

Gui I, Count of Tonnerre 6 (9)

Gui I, Duke of Spoleto 64 (2)

Gui II, Count d'Rochefort 76 (9)

Gui II, Count of Tonnerre .... **6 (10)**

Guitmond 100 (16)

Gundemariz, Cristina, wife of Diego, Count of Orviedo 151 (1)

Gunza, wife of Warin, Count of Poitiers ....**128 (5)**, 129 (6)

ap Gwallawg, Eliseg ....**9 (7)**

ap Gwriad, Merfyn Frych, King of Powys and Gwynedd ....**9 (11)**, 13 (3)

Hadrian, Count of Orleans 17 (4), 129 (9)

Halfdan, King of Vestfold .... **97 (4)**

Halfdan "Gold Tooth" 97 (1)

Halfdan "the Old", King of Denmark ....**113 (1)**

Halfdan "White Leg", King of the Upplands ....**97 (2)**

Halfdansdotter, Solveig, wife of Ingjald Braut-Onundson, King of Uppsala 97 (1)

ap Handaer, Elidwr 9 (10)

Harald Klak, King of Jutland 74 (3)

Harman, Alice, wife of John Somer ....**147 (4)**

Harman, Henry 147 (2)

Harman, Henry ....**147 (3)**

Harpoole, Sarah Elizabeth, wife of Josiah Prater 147 (15–g)

Hastings, Alice, wife of Walter Heron ....**137 (11)**

Hastings, Hugh 137 (6)

Hastings, Hugh .... **137 (8)**

Hastings, Nicholas ....**137 (10)**

Hastings, Thomas 137 (7)

Hastings, Thomas .... **137 (9)**

Hastings, William 137 (6)

Hawise, wife of Thomas de Newburgh 28 (20), 43 (20)

Hawise of Brittany, wife of Geoffrey la Zouche ....**39 (9), 40 (10)**, 44 (12)

Hawise of Brittany, wife of Hoël II, Duke of Brittany ....**39 (8), 40 (8), 64 (11)**

Hawise of Normandy, wife of Geoffrey, Duke of Brittany .... 36 (6), 40 (6), 64 (10), **108 (13)**

Hedwig, wife of Otto "the Illustrious", Duke of Saxony 74 (5), 90 (1), 111 (9), 133 (1)

Hedwig, wife of Siegfried, Count of Luxembourg 7 (6), 30 (7), 63 (7), 114 (1)

Hedwig of Namur, wife of Gerhard IV, Duke of Upper Lorraine .... **27 (9)**

Hedwig of Saxony, wife of Hugh, Count of Paris ....21 (8), 29 (7), 47 (2), 61 (6), **94 (2)**, 97 (12), **133 (2)**

Heilwig of Egisheim, wife of Gerhard, Count of Vaudemont 27 (10), 53 (8), 84 (9)

Heinrich the Fowler, King of the Saxons . 8 (5), 25 (6), 47 (2), 61 (6), 74 (5), 75 (4), **90 (1)**, 111 (9), 133 (1)

Helvise, wife of Renaud, Count of Tonnerre 6 (12), 48 (5), 83 (8)

Helwise (Heiliwich) of Friuli, wife of Huchbold, Count of Ostrevant .... **24 (4)**

Henri I, King of the Franks ....24 (11), 37 (7), **47 (5), 65 (9)**, 96 (9), 116 (6), 132 (5), 150 (1)

Henry, Count of Eu 137 (4)

Henry I, King of England .... **2 (2), 5 (10)**, 38 (10), 107 (18), 120 (4), 137 (5), **138 (1)**, 139 (1)

Henry II, Duke of Brabant 140 (4), 150 (6), 151 (7)

Henry II, King of England ....138 (6), **139 (2), 140 (1)**, 141 (1), 150 (5), 151 (5)

Henry III, King of England ....140 (5), **143 (1)**, 144 (1), 151 (8), 152 (9)

Henry of Scotland , Earl of Northumberland .... **148 (4)**

Herbert, Count of Gleiburg, ...**63 (6)**, 114 (2)

Herbert, Marquis of Burgundy 71 (3)

Herbert I, Count of Vermandois..34 (2), 47 (1), **57 (4)**

Herbert II, Count of Vermandois.......................... 5 (4), 31 (6), 33 (6), 34 (2), **57 (5)**, 80 (5), 91 (3)

Herbert III, Count of Vermandois...**37 (4), 91 (4)**

Herbert IV, Count of Vermandois ....24 (10), **37 (6)**, 47 (6), 96 (10)

Heribert, father of Bertrade of Laon 54 (2)

Herleve, mother of Willia m I ....2 (1), 5 (9), 7 (9), 28 (10), 41 (7), 49 (6), 103 (14), **119 (1), 120 (1)**, 137 (1)

Herleve, wife of Robert, Count d'Evreux 107 (13)

Hermann II, Duke of Swabia...26 (8), 53 (5), **62 (7)**, 69 (7)

Heron, Emmeline, wife of John Darcy, Baron Darcy ....**137 (12)**, 148 (12)

Heron, Emmeline, wife of Nicholas Hastings 137 (10)

Heron, Walter...137 (11)

Heron, William...137 (11)

Hester, Minerva, wife of Martin Prater... 147 (15–d)

Hilda, wife of Eystein, King of Westfold.. 97 (3)

Hildebrante, wife of Herbert II.................................... 5 (4), 31 (6), 33 (6), **34 (2)**, 57 (5), 80 (5), 91 (3)

Hildegarde, wife of Charlemagne 19 (1), 56 (3), 57 (1)

Hildegarde, wife of Richwin, Count of Scarpone.. 26 (10), 53 (6)

Hildegarde of Beaugency, wife of Fulk IV, Count of Anjou.................... 39 (7), 40 (9), 77 (9)

Hildegarde of Flanders, wife of Dietrich II, Count of Holland.......................**7 (5), 35 (4)**, 115 (2)

Hildegarde of Lorraine, wife of Fulk III, Count of Anjou 39 (5), 77 (8)

Hildegarde of Westerbourg, wife of Hermann Billung, Duke of Saxony.....................5 (5), 34 (4)

Hildouin, Count of Chartres 24 (8)

Hildouin, Count of Roucy...152 (3)

Hildouin II, Count of Montdidier 50 (6), 75 (8)

Hildouin III, Count of Montdidier 50 (6), 75 (8)

Hiltrude, wife of Ragnvald, Jarl of the North and South Møre 97 (9), 113 (4)

Himiltrude, mistress of Charlemagne 17 (1), 55 (4)

Hoël II, Duke of Brittany...39 (8), 40 (8), 64 (11)

von Hohenstauffen, Marie, wife of Henry II, Duke of Brabant 140 (4), 150 (6), 151 (7)

Holand, Eleanor, wife of Roger Mortimer 144 (7)

Holand, Thomas, Earl of Kent..144 (7)

Hrolf Nefja 97 (9), 113 (4)

Hrolf Turstan...**109 (11)**

Hrollaug, mother of Hrolf Turstan ....**109 (10)**

Hucbold, Count of Ostrevant...24 (4)

de Hugleville, Ada, wife of Geoffrey de Neufmarche 9 (20)

Hugh, Count of Clermont...27 (12), 50 (7), 84 (10), 99 (16)

Hugh "the Great", Count of Paris............................21 (8), 29 (7), **47 (2), 61 (6)**, 94 (2), 97 (12), 133 (2)

Hugh II, Count of Tours 20 (3), 64 (1)

Hugh Magnus, Duke of France.....................................24 (11), 37 (7), **47 (6), 96 (10)**

Humberga, wife of William IV, Count d'Auvergne.. 64 (8)

Hungerford, Eleanor, wife of John White .... **139 (13), 141 (9)**

Hungerford, Robert, Baron Hungerford ....139 (12), **141 (8)**

Hungerford, Thomas...141 (7)

Hungerford, Walter, Baron Hungerford 139 (12), 141 (7)

Hunroch, Marquis of Friuli... 23 (3)

Hussey, Joan, wife of Thomas Hungerford 141 (7)

Hyde, Alice, wife of John Yate 137 (21), 142 (13)

ap Hyfaidd, Llywarch, King of South Wales .... 9 (14), **12 (2)**

ap Hywel Dda, Owain, King of Deheubarth...................................... **9 (15)**, 11 (15), **12 (4)**

Ida, wife of Renaud II, Count of Nevers..6 (14), 48 (7)

Ida of Eu, wife of William Hastings .... **137 (6)**

Idonea, wife of Thomas Wandesford..137 (16)

Igor, Prince of Kiev..116 (2), 131 (1)
Imma, wife of Gerald I, Count of Alemania... 129 (9)
Industria, wife of Tonantius Ferreolus, Roman Senator.....................................118 (4)
Ingegarde of Sweden, wife of Yaroslav I, Grand Prince of Kiev .... 47 (5), 65 (9), **96 (8)**, 116 (5), 132 (4)
(Ingeltrude), mistress of Pepin, King of Italy ....**56 (3)**
Ingerman, Count of Hasbaye... 20 (2)
Inglefield, Elizabeth, wife of Robert White 142 (11)
Ioannes Doukas, Caesar...155 (11)
Ioannes I, Duke of Durazzo..155 (12)
Ioannes II, Emperor of Byzantium...**155 (13)**
Irene, wife of Andronikos...155 (14)
Irene Doukas, wife of Alexius I, Emperor of Byzantium....................................**155 (12)**
Irene Pergonita, wife of Caesar Ioannes Doukas 155 (11)
Irene of Hungary, wife of Ioannes II, Emperor of Byzantium 155 (13)
Isabel, wife of John FitzJames 28 (23)
Isabel of Angoulême, wife of John, King of England................... **138 (6)**, 141 (1), 143 (1), 152 (9)
Isabella of France, wife of Edward II, King of England........................ 145 (1), 146 (1) 153 (8)
Isabel of Scotland, wife of Robert de Ros.. **148 (6)**
Isabel of Vermandois...**37 (8)**, **47 (7)**, 50 (9), 99 (17), 107 (17), 148 (4)
Isabella of Aragon, wife of Philip III, King of France 153 (6)
Isabella of Castile, wife of Edmund of Langley... 144 (8)
Isabella of Hainaut, wife of Philip Augustus, King of France 140 (3), 150 (4), 151 (6)
Istvan V (Stephen V), King of Hungary ....**153 (4)**, **155 (18)**
St. Itta, wife of Pepin, Mayor of the Palace..127 (1), **130 (1)**
Ivan Vladislav, Tsar of West Bulgaria..**155 (9)**
Ivar Oplaendinge, Jarl of the Upplands.. 97 (8), **113 (2)**
Ivye, Judith.. **1 (1)**, **2 (20)**
Ivye, Richard 2 (19), 28 (27)
Ivye, Thomas... 2 (19), 28 (27)
"Jane", wife of Samuel Wallace...147 (12)
Jean II, Count of Hainaut 153 (7)
Jeanne, Queen of Navarre, wife of Philip IV, King of France.............................145 (1)
Jeanne of Valois, wife of William III, Count of Hainaut and Holland.................... 145 (2), 146 (1), **153 (7)**
Jimena, wife of El Cid 151 (1)
Joan of Cornwall, wife of Roger (or Ralph) Valletort...................................... **3 (4)**, **121 (5)**
John, Count of Eu .... **137 (5)**
John, King of England... 138 (6), **141 (1)**, 143 (1), 152 (9)
John of Gaunt, Duke of Lancaster...**146 (2)**, **153 (9)**
Jubel Berenger, Count of Rennes 40 (5)
Judith of Bavaria, wife of Louis I, King of the Franks 17 (5), 23 (2), 87 (5), 129 (11)
Judith of Bohemia, wife of Vladislav I, King of Poland...................................... 154 (3)
Judith of Brittany, wife of Richard II, Duke of Normandy ....**41 (6)**, 79 (7), 84 (6), 103 (13), 119 (1)
Judith of France, wife of Baldwin I, Count of Flanders.......................5 (3), **18 (6)**, **31 (4)**
Judith of Lens, wife of Waltheof II, Earl of Huntingdon ....**28 (11)**, **42 (9)**, 148 (3)
Judith of Nantes, wife of Alain Cagniart, Count of Cornouaille........................... 40 (8), 64 (11)
Juliana of Mortagne and Perche, wife of Gilbert, Seigneur de l'Aigle 151 (3)
Jutta (Judith), wife of Konrad, Duke of Swabia............................... 26 (8), 62 (6), 69 (7)
Kazimierz I, King of Poland .... **154 (2)**
Kingston, Elizabeth, wife of John Malet...2 (13), 3 (11), 102 (25)
Kingston, John 102 (25)
Konrad, Duke of Swabia .... 26 (8), **62 (6)**, 69 (7)
Krum, Khan of the Bulgars ....**155 (1)**
Kunegunde, wife of (1) Wigeric, Count d'Ardennes ....**29 (6)**, 53 (3), 95 (3), 114 (1)
Kunegunde, wife of (2) Richwin, Count of Verdun..**30 (6)**
Kuthan, Khan of the Cumanians... 153 (4), 155 (18)

de Lacy, Maud, Countess of Lincoln 144 (2)
de l'Aigle, Marguerite, wife of Garcia VII, King of Navarre... 151 (3)
St. Ladislas I, King of Hungary 155 (13)
Lainez, Diego 151 (1)
Lambert, Count of Hornbach.. **129 (8)**
Lambert, Count of Lens ....**7 (9)**, **28 (10)**, 42 (8), 119 (2)
Lambert, Count of Louvain 81 (5)
Lambert I, Count of Louvain ....7 (8), 28 (8), 32 (10), **82 (6)**
Lambert I, Count of Mâcon 71 (6), 83 (4)
Lancelin II, Seigneur de Beaugency...39 (7), 77 (9)
Landry III, Count of Nevers...48 (5), 66 (9), 78 (7), 83 (6)
Latimer, Joan, wife of Alexander Comyn.. 139 (7)
Le Bret, Adam 3 (8)
Le Bret, Lucy, wife of Hugh Valletort 3 (8)
Leo VI, Emperor of Byzantium...64 (4), 88 (6), **117 (2)**
Leofric, Earl of Mercia... 122 (1)
St. Leopold, Margrave of Austria... 154 (5)
Leowine, Earl of Mercia... 122 (1)
Leutaud, Count of Paris ....**17 (3)**, **55 (5)**, 129 (10)
Lietaud, Count of Mâcon..71 (6), 77 (6), 83 (4)
Lionel of Antwerp, Duke of Clarence...144 (5), **145 (3)**
St. Liutwin ....54 (1), 128 (5), **129 (6)**
Liv, wife of Halfdan, King of Vestfold 97 (4)
verch Llewellyn, Angharad, wife of Owain ap Hywel Dda....................... 9 (15), **11 (15)**, 12 (4)
ap Llewellyn, Gruffydd, King of Gwynedd, Powys and Deheubarth....................**9 (18)**, **10 (17)**, 122 (3)
Lloyd, Elizabeth Carter, wife of Jenkins Prater..147 (15–I)
verch Llywarch, Elen, wife of Hywel Dda ap Cadell, King of South Wales...............9 (14), 11 (15), **12 (3)**
Longland, Joan, wife of John Roynon 2 (14), 102 (27)
Lothair I, King of Italy...**20 (3)**, **64 (1)**
Lothair II, King of Lorraine .... **71 (2)**
Louis, Count of Montbéliard..26 (10), 53 (6), 84 (8)
Louis I, King of the Franks .... 17 (5), **20 (2)**, **23 (2)**, 64 (1), 83 (1), 87 (5), 129 (11)
Louis II, Emperor of the West ....**64 (2)**, 88 (5)
Louis II, King of the Franks ....4 (5), 8 (4), **17 (6)**, **25 (4)**, 114 (1)
Louis III, Emperor of the West ....**64 (4)**, 73 (5), **88 (6)**, 117 (3)
Louis IV, King of the Franks ....**8 (5)**, **25 (6)**, 68 (6), 92 (2), 112 (10), 134 (2)
Louis VI, King of the Franks.. **150 (2)**
Louis VII, King of the Franks... **150 (3)**
Louis VIII, King of the Franks.....................................140 (3), 143 (2), **150 (5)**, 151 (6), 152 (10)
Lucy, wife of Ranulph le Meschin, Earl of Chester.. 43 (10), 109 (17)
Lucy, wife of Robert de Newburgh..28 (16)
Lucy, wife of William de Ros 148 (7)
Liutgarde of Luxembourg, wife of Arnulf, Count of Holland .... 7 (6), 32 (9), **115 (2)**
Luitgarde of Vermandois, wife of Thebaud...........................25 (8), 33 (6), **36 (3)**, **59 (6)**, 68 (7)
Lyffe, Amice, wife of Baldwin Malet...**2 (13)**, **3 (11)**, 102 (26)
Lyffe, Godfrey 2 (12), 3 (9)
Lyffe, Richard..2 (12), **3 (10)**, 102 (26)
MacBricc, father of Sadb 16 (4)
(MacKay), Jane, wife of Jonathan Prather 1 (4–b), 137 (25)
MacKay, Robert 1 (4–b)
MacMael, Diarmait, King of Hy Kinsale and Leinster.. 16 (3)
Mac Murchada, Diarmait, King of Leinster.................................**16 (6)**, 37 (10), 50 (10)
Mac Murchada, Donnchad, King of Dublin.. **16 (5)**
Mahan, James 147 (14)
Mahan, Sarah, wife of Eliphaz Riley...147 (14)

Malbank, Philippa, wife of Thomas Basset.. 101 (20), 123 (1)
Malcolm II, King of Scots 148 (1)
Malcolm III, King of Scots ....**148 (2)**
Malet, Baldwin.. 2 (13), 3 (11), **102 (26)**
Malet, Baldwin... **102 (19)**
Malet, Baldwin... **102 (22)**
Malet, Baldwin... **102 (24)**
Malet, Elizabeth, wife of Thomas Ivye...**2 (19), 28 (27)**
Malet, Gilbert 101 (16)
Malet, Gilbert, Baron of Curry Malet ....**101 (19)**, 123 (1)
Malet, Hawise, wife of Hugh Poyntz.. 43 (14), **123 (2)**
Malet, Hugh..**2 (14)**, 102 (27)
Malet, Hugh..**2 (18)**, 28 (26)
Malet, Hugh "Fitchet" 102 (18)
Malet, John.. 2 (13), 3 (11), **102 (25)**
Malet, John...**2 (15)**, 102 (23)
Malet, Robert .... **102 (16)**
Malet, Robert, Baron of Curry Malet 101 (17)
Malet, Thomas .... **2 (16)**
Malet, William, Seigneur de Granville 101 (15)
Malet, William..**2 (17)**, 28 (26)
Malet, William.. **102 (20)**
Malet, William.. **102 (21)**
Malet, William, Baron of Curry Malet.. 43 (14), **101 (20), 123 (1)**
Malet, William, Baron of Curry Malet...101 (18)
Malet, William, Sire de Granville ....**102 (17)**
Malfred, Prince of the Drevianes...116 (3), 131 (2)
Malusha, wife of Sviatoslav I, Prince of Kiev...116 (3), 131 (2)
ap Mar ap Cenu ap Coel, Arthwys 135 (1)
de la Mare, Joan, wife of John de Newburgh 28 (22), 43 (21)
de la Mare, John 28 (22), 43 (21)
verch Maredudd, Angharad, wife of Llewellyn ap Seisyll................................. **9 (17)**, 10 (16), 122 (3)
St. Margaret, wife of Malcolm III, King of Scots 148 (2)
Margaret, wife of Richard Merton 2 (11)
Margaret, wife of Robert de Newburgh 28 (19)
Margaret, wife of Roger la Zouche... 9 (27), 39 (11), 44 (13), 76 (14)
Margaret, wife of Thomas I, Duke of Savoy 152 (8)
Margaret of Cornwall, wife of James Peverell..**141 (4)**
Margaret of Naples, Countess of Anjou, wife of Charles of Valois, Count of Valois .... **153 (6)**
Margery, wife of John de Newburgh...28 (18)
Marguerite of Champagne, wife of Henry, Count of Eu ....**137 (4)**
Marguerite of Lorraine, wife of Baldwin V, Count of Hainaut.......................................150 (4)
Marguerite of Perche, wife of Henry de Newburgh .... 28 (13), **52 (8)**
Marguerite of Turenne, wife of William IV, Count of Angoulême .... **138 (4)**
Maria of Byzantium, wife of Bela IV, King of Hungary .... 153 (3), **155 (17)**
Maria of Byzantium, wife of Ivan Vladislav, Tsar of West Bulgaria.............................. 155 (9)
Maria of Hungary, wife of Charles II, King of Naples .... **153 (5)**
Maria Dobronega, wife of Kazimierz I, King of Poland 154 (2)
Marija, wife of Boris-Michael, Tsar of the Bulgars 155 (5)
Marija of Bulgaria, wife of Andronikos Doukas ....**155 (11)**
Marshall, Eve, wife of William de Braose .... 9 (25), **16 (9)**, 76 (13)
Marshall, John..16 (8), 50 (11)
Marshall, William, Earl of Pembroke 9 (25), 16 (8), 50 (11)
Martel, Charles .... **54 (1)**, 57 (1), 124 (10), **127 (3)**
Martin, Margaret, wife of John Tichborne 137 (18), 141 (11)

Martin, Richard 137 (18)
Mary, wife of William Malet...102 (21)
Mary Liddia, wife of Andrew Prater 147 (15–c)
St. Mathilda (Mechtilda) 8 (5), 25 (6), 47 (2), 61 (6), 74 (5), 75 (4), 90 (1), 111 (9), 133 (1)
Mathilda, wife of Reginhert, Count of Ringelheim...74 (4), 111 (7)
Mathilda of Flanders, wife of William the Conqueror 2 (1), 5 (9), 41 (8), 49 (6), 137 (1), 138 (1), 139 (1)
Mathilda of Brabant, wife of Robert I, Count of Artois...............140 (4), 143 (2), 150 (6), 151 (7), 152 (10)
Mathilda of Saxony, wife of Baldwin III.. 5 (5), 34 (4), 72 (6), 85 (4)
Mathilda of Swabia, wife of Friedrich II, Count of Bar....................................... 26 (9), 53 (5), 62 (8)
Matilda, wife of Henry de Newburgh 28 (17)
Matilda, wife of Létard de Roucy, Seigneur de Marle 76 (7)
Matilda, Countess of Perche, wife of Rotrou II, Count of Perche 138 (2)
Matilda of Burgundy, wife of Landry III..48 (5). 66 (9), 78 (7), 83 (6)
Matilda of Carinthia, wife of Thebaud IV, Count of Blois... 150 (3)
Matilda of France, wife of Conrad I...25 (7), 33 (7), 36 (4), 62 (7), 68 (6), 92 (3)
Matilda of Huntingdon, Countess of Northumberland... 148 (3)
Matilda (Routrude) of France, wife of Gerhard I, Count of Auvergne 21 (3)
Matilda of Louvain, wife of Eustace I 7 (8), 28 (9), 32 (10), 42 (8), 82 (7), 119 (2)
Matilda, Lady of the English..139 (1), 140 (1)
Maud, wife of Bernard de St. Valeri.. 9 (23), 46 (12)
Maud (Mathilda), wife of Raymond I, Viscount Turenne 138 (3)
Maud of Cornwall..2 (4), 38 (10), 107 (18), 120 (5)
Megingoz, Count of Avalgau... 63 (6)
Meinill, Elizabeth, wife of John Darcy......................................137 (13), 148 (12), 149 (12)
Meinill, Nicholas.. 137 (13), 148 (11)
Meinill, Nicholas, Baron Meinill... 148 (11)
von Meran, Gertrude, wife of Andreas II, King of Hungary.. 153 (2), 155 (17)
Merchad, King of Leinster...16 (1)
ap Merfyn, Llewellyn..9 (15), 11 (14), 12 (4)
ap Merfyn, Rhodri Mawr, King of Gwynedd 9 (12), 13 (3)
Merton, Eleanor, wife of Matthew Stawell...2 (11), 3 (10)
Merton, Richard 2 (11)
de Meschin, Maud, wife of Philip Belmeis.. 39 (10), 44 (11)
le Meschin, Ranulph, Vicomte de Bayeux, Earl of Chester 43 (10), 109 (17)
le Meschin, William, Lord of Skipton-in-Craven.. 44 (10), 110 (17)
verch Meyric, Angharad, wife of Rhodri Mawr, King of Powys 9 (12), 13 (3)
Michael II, Grand Prince of Kiev... 154 (4)
Michael III, Emperor of Byzantium 117 (1), 117 (1A)
Michell, Isabel, wife of Hugh Malet...2 (18), 28 (26)
Michell, Thomas... 2 (18), 28 (25)
Michell, Walter 28 (25)
Mieszko II, King of Poland 154 (1)
Miles of Gloucester, Earl of Hereford 9 (21)
Milo, Lord of Monthery and Bray 46 (9)
Milo III, Count of Tonnerre 6 (9)
Milo IV, Count of Tonnerre..6 (11)
Moels, Muriel, wife of Thomas de Courtenay...141 (6)
Moking, Margaret, wife of John Tichborne..137 (17)
de Montagu, Philippa, wife of Roger Mortimer... 144 (6), 145 (4)
de Monterolier, Judith, wife of Thurstan le Goz...109 (14)
de Montfauçon, Agnes, wife of Erard II, Count of Brienne.. 139 (5)
de Montfort, Agnes, wife of Waleran de Beaumont 2 (4), 38 (9), 107 (17), 120 (5)
de Montfort, Amauri 107 (15)
de Montfort, Amauri, Count of Devreux... 38 (9), 107 (16)
de Montfort, Isabel, wife of Ralph de Toeni...28 (12)

202

de Montfort, Simon, Seigneur de Montfort...107 (15)
Montgomery, Maud, wife of Robert, Count of Mortain 120 (2)
Montgomery, Roger, Earl of Shrewsbury 120 (2)
de Montlhéry, Isabel, wife of Joceline de Courtenay 48 (8)
de Mortain, Maud, wife of Reginald FitzRoy .... 2 (3), 38 (10), 107 (18), **120 (4)**
Mortimer, Anne, wife of Richard Plantagenet, Duke of York....................................**144 (8)**, 146 (4)
Mortimer, Edmund, Earl of March..144 (6), 145 (4)
Mortimer, Maud, wife of William Malet 101 (18)
Mortimer, Robert...101 (18)
Mortimer, Roger, Earl of March 144 (6), 145 (4)
Mortimer, Roger, Earl of March ....**144 (7)**
Mullikin, James 1 (4–b)
Munderic of Vitry-en-Perthois. 125 (1)
Munia, mistress of Sancho Garcia III 152 (1)
Murchad ....**16 (4)**
Musters, Elizabeth, wife of John Wandesford 137 (15), 149 (13)
ap Mynan, Beli ....**9 (5)**
Nantilde, wife of Dagobert I, King of the Franks.. 124 (5)
Nesta, wife of Bernard de Neufmarche ....**9 (20)**
Nesta of North Wales, wife of Osborn FitzRichard ....**9 (19)**, 122 (4)
de Neufmarche, Bernard, Lord of Brecon 9 (20)
de Neufmarche, Geoffrey 9 (20)
de Neufmarche, Sibyl ....**9 (21)**
Neville, Cecily, wife of Richard Plantagenet, Duke of York...................................144 (9), **146 (4)**, 147 (1)
Neville, Emma, wife of Baldwin Malet...102 (19)
Neville, Hugh...102 (19)
Neville, John... 146 (3)
Neville, Ralph, Earl of Westmoreland...144 (9), 146 (3)
de Newburgh, Alice, wife of John FitzJames ....**28 (23)**
de Newburgh, Henry, Earl of Warwick 28 (13), 52 (8)
de Newburgh, Henry...**28 (17)**
de Newburgh, John..**28 (18)**
de Newburgh, John..**28 (21)**, 43 (20)
de Newburgh, John..**28 (22)**, 43 (21)
de Newburgh, Robert.. 28 (13), **52 (9)**
de Newburgh, Robert..**28 (15)**
de Newburgh, Robert..**28 (16)**
de Newburgh, Robert..**28 (19)**
de Newburgh, Roger...**28 (14)**, 52 (10)
de Newburgh, Thomas..**28 (20)**, 43 (20)
Nicolaus, Tsar of the Bulgars..**155 (7)**
Nocher III, Count Bar-sur-Aube 25 (9)
verch Noe, Sanan, wife of Gwallawg ap Beli... 9 (6)
de Notton, Christian, wife of Sir William Heron 137 (11)
Odele of Bois Ferrand, wife of Eudes, Count of Cambrai 6 (7), 86 (5)
Oda, wife of Bodegeisel II..118 (8), 125 (2)
O'Dell, Rachel, wife of John Prather 137 (25f)
Odo (Eudes), Count in the Wetterau 62 (5)
Ogiva of Luxembourg, wife of Baldwin IV, Count of Flanders....5 (7), 49 (5), **63 (8)**, 67 (9), 85 (5), **114 (3)**
Olav, King of Jutland...113 (3)
Olav "Tree Hewer", King of Vermaland...**97 (1)**
Olav, King of Vestfold ....**97 (6)**
Olav II, King of Sweden ....**96 (7)**, 116 (5), 132 (4)
Oleg, Prince of Kiev ....**116 (1)**
St. Olga ....**116 (2)**, 131 (1)

Omurtag, Khan of the Bulgars...**155 (2)**
Ordrad, wife of Wicbert, Count of Westphalia...111 (5)
Orlaith, wife of Donnchad Mac Murchada, King of Dublin 16 (5)
Osburgis, wife of Æthelwulf, King of Wessex...4 (1)
Oslac...4 (1)
Otto "the Illustrious", Duke of Saxony...................74 (5), 90 (1), 111 (9), 133 (1)
Otto William, Count of Burgundy ....45 (7), 78 (6), **83 (5)**, 106 (14)
ap Owain, Maredudd, King of Gwynedd...........................**9 (16)**, 10 (16), **11 (16)**
verch Owain, Tangwystyl, mother of Hyfaidd ap Bledri 12 (1)
verch Pabo, St. Arddun...**9 (1)**, **136 (2)**
Papia of Normandy, wife of Gilbert de St. Valeri.........................**46 (7)**, **105 (14)**
Papianilla, wife of Tonantius Ferreolus...118 (3)
Parvie, wife of Eudes, Count of Vermandois...24 (10), 37 (5)
Paveley, Margaret, wife of Hugh Poyntz...................43 (16), 44 (15), 76 (15)
Paveley, Margaret, wife of Hugh Poyntz...................................43 (18), 44 (16)
Paveley, William...43 (16)
Paveley, William...43 (18), 44 (16)
Pedro I, King of Castile and Leon..144 (8)
Penesherst, Alice wife of John de Columbiers..2 (8)
Penesherst, Stephen 2 (8)
Pepin, Count of Senlis ....**57 (3)**
Pepin, King of Italy..**19 (2)**, 56 (3), **57 (1)**
Pepin the Short, King of the Franks.....................17 (1), **54 (2)**, 124 (10)
Pepin I, Mayor of the Palace...127 (1), 130 (1)
Pepin II, Mayor of the Palace..54 (1), **127 (2)**
de Percy, Maud, wife of John Neville...146 (3)
Petronilla of Aragon, wife of Ramón Berenger IV, Count of Barcelona...........**152 (5)**, 154 (7)
Peverell, Catherine, wife of Walter Hungerford.......................139 (12), **141 (7)**
Peverell, James...141 (4)
Peverell, Hugh...**141 (5)**
Peverell, Thomas ....**141 (6)**
Philip I, King of the Franks...**150 (1)**
Philip II, "Augustus", King of the Franks ....140 (3), **150 (4)**, 151 (6)
Philip III, King of the Franks..153 (6)
Philip IV, King of the Franks...145 (1)
Philippa of Hainaut, wife of Edward III, King of England.........144 (5), 145 (2), 146 (1), **153 (8)**
Philippa of Luxembourg, wife of Jean II, Count of Hainaut..................................153 (7)
Philippa of Toulouse, wife of William IX, Duc d'Aquitaine...................................152 (4)
Picot, Alice, wife of Gilbert Malet..101 (19), 123 (1)
Picot, Ralph..101 (19)
Plantagenet, Edmund "Crouchback", Earl of Lancaster ....140 (5), **143 (2)**, 151 (8), **152 (10)**
Plantagenet, Eleanor, wife of John Beaumont ....139 (8), **143 (4)**
Plantagenet, Geoffrey, Count of Anjou.....................................139 (1), 140 (1)
Plantagenet, Henry, Earl of Lancaster ....139 (8), **140 (6)**, 143 (3), 144 (4), **151 (9)**
Plantagenet, Joan, wife of Gilbert de Clare, Earl of Gloucester...................**144 (2)**
Plantagenet, Mary, wife of Henry Harman ....**147 (2)**
Plantagenet, Maud, wife of William de Burgh, Earl of Ulster 144 (4), 145 (3)
Plantagenet, Philippa, Countess of Ulster......................................**144 (6)**, **145 (4)**
Plantagenet, Richard, Duke of York 144 (8), 146 (4)
Plantagenet, Richard, Duke of York ....**144 (9)**, 146 (4), 147 (1)
Plantagenet, Richard, Earl of Cornwall ....**138 (7)**, **141 (2)**
Plott, Jane, wife of George Prater 1 (1), 2 (20)
Plummer, Margaret, wife of Hugh Riley...**147 (11)**
Plummer, Thomas...147 (10)
Powell, John...1 (3)

(Powell), Mary, wife of Thomas Prater.. 1 (3)
Poyntz, Hugh.. **43 (14)**, 123 (2)
Poyntz, Hugh, Baron Poyntz... **43 (16)**, 44 (15), 76 (15)
Poyntz, Hugh, Baron Poyntz... **43 (18)**, **44 (16)**
Poyntz, Margaret, wife of John de Newburgh .... 28 (21), **43 (20)**
Poyntz, Nicholas .... **43 (15)**, **123 (3)**
Poyntz, Nicholas, Baron Poyntz .... 28 (21), **43 (19)**
Poyntz, Nicholas, Baron Poyntz .... **43 (17)**, 44 (15), 76 (15)
Poyntz, Nicholas, Lord of Tockington .... 43 (13). 123 (2)
Prater, Andrew 147 (15–c)
Prater, Anthony 1 (1), 2 (20)
Prater, Bazel..147 (15)
Prater, Bazel... 147 (15–f)
Prater, Brice Bazel 147 (15)
Prater, Brison 147 (15–n)
Prater, Cassandra 147 (15–m)
Prater, Charles 147 (15–a)
Prater, Eliphaz.. 147 (15–e)
Prater, Elizabeth.. 1 (4–b)
Prater, George 1 (1), 2 (20)
Prater, George 1 (4–b)
Prater, Holloway.. 147 (15–b)
Prater, Isaac... 147 (15–h)
Prater, Jane... 1 (4–b)
Prater, Jenkins 147 (15–l)
Prater, John... **1 (4–a)**
Prater, John.. 1 (4–b)
Prater, Jonathan... **1 (4–b)**
Prater, Jonathan.. 1 (4–b)
Prater, Josiah 147 (15–g)
Prater, King 147 (15–i)
Prater, Martin 147 (15–d)
Prater, Nancy 147 (15–k)
Prater, Ninian 147 (15–o)
Prater, Richard... **1 (4–c)**
Prater, Samuel .... **1 (4–d)**
Prater, Samuel 147 (15–j)
Prater, Thomas.. **1 (2)**
Prater, Thomas... **1 (3)**
Prater, Thomas MacKay 1 (4–b)
Prater, William... 1 (4–b)
Prater, William.. **1 (4–e)**
Prather, Elizabeth... 137 (25–h)
Prather, Jane.. 137 (25–b)
Prather, John..137 (25–f)
Prather, Jonathan 137 (25)
Prather, Joseph..137 (25e)
Prather, Margaret 137 (25d)
Prather, Martha...137 (25a)
Prather, Priscilla...137 (25c)
Prather, Sarah 137 (25g)
Prather, William... 137 (25)
Prather, William.. 137 (25g)
Prather, William..137 (25a)
Presijan, Khan of the Bulgars .... **155 (4)**

Prydyn, St. Pabo Post... 9 (1), **135 (1)**, 136 (2)
de Punchardon, Aubrea, wife of Hamelyn de Deandon... 102 (22)
Quintyne, Henry... 1 (2)
Quintyne, Margaret, wife of Thomas Prater 1 (2)
Raedburga, wife of Egbert, King of England...4 (1)
Ragnar, "the Raven".. 97 (7)
Ragnvald .... **97 (7)**, 113 (3)
Ragnvald "the Wise", Jarl of the North and South Møre.....................**97 (9)**, **109 (9)**, **113 (4)**
Rainier, Count of Forcalqueir... 152 (7), 154 (8)
Raleigh, Avicia, wife of Baldwin Malet..102 (24)
Raleigh, Simon...102 (24)
Ramirez, Sancho 151 (2)
Ramiro, Count of Monçon...151 (2)
Ramiro I, King of Aragon .... **152 (2)**
Ramiro II, King of Aragon .... **152 (4)**
Ramón Berenger III, Count of Barcelona.. 152 (5)
Ramón Berenger IV, Count of Barcelona...152 (5), 154 (7)
Ranulph I, Count of Poitou.. **21 (4)**
Ranulph II, Count of Poitou... **21 (5)**
Ranulph I, Vicomte of the Bessin 43 (8), 109 (16)
Ranulph II, Vicomte de Bayeux .... **43 (9)**, 109 (16)
Raoul I, Count of Ostrevant and Amiens... **24 (5)**
Raoul II, Seigneur de Crépy and Valois .... **24 (8)**
Raoul III, Seigneur de Crépy and Valois ....**24 (9)**, 37 (6)
Raoul VIII, Vicomte of Maine 139 (6)
Raymond, Count of Burgundy 154 (6)
Raymond I, Viscount of Turenn 138 (3)
Raymond V, Count of Provence .... 143 (1), **152 (8)**
de Redvers, Baldwin, Earl of Devon... 2 (5), 107 (19)
Reginar I, Count of Hainaut ....**75 (3)**, 90 (2), 111 (10), 134 (2)
Reginar II, Count of Hainaut .... **81 (4)**
Reginar III, Count of Hainaut...............................22 (9), 28 (8), 50 (4), **81 (5)**, 98 (13)
Reginar IV, Count of Hainaut ....22 (9), 50 (4), 75 (7), **81 (6)**, 98 (13)
Reginhert, Count of Ringelheim...74 (4), **111 (7)**
Reginhilde of Friesland, wife of Dietrich, Count of Ringelheim...............**74 (4)**, 90 (1), 111 (8), 133 (1)
Reginlinde of Nullenburg, wife of Burchard, Duke of Swabia 68 (5)
Reinald, Count of Bar-sur-Seine...6 (11), 37 (4), 91 (4)
Renaud, father of Hugh, Count of Clermont in Beauvaisis 50 (7)
Renaud, Count of Rheims and Roucy 75 (5), 83 (5), 90 (3)
Renaud, Count of Tonnerre ....**6 (12)**, 48 (6), 83 (8)
Renaud I, Count of Bar and Mousson ....27 (11), 51 (8), **53 (8)**, **84 (9)**
Renaud I, Count of Burgundy ....45 (7), **79 (7)**, **84 (6)**, 106 (14)
Renaud I, Count of Nevers .... 6 (13), 48 (5), 66 (9), **83 (7)**
Renaud II, Count of Clermont.. 27 (12), **51 (8)**, 84 (10)
Renaud II, Count of Nevers ....**6 (14)**, 48 (7)
ap Rhodri, Anarawd, King of North Wales 10 (13), 14 (4)
ap Rhodri, Cadell, King of Gwynedd ....**9 (13)**, 12 (3), 13 (4)
ap Rhodri, Conan Tindaethwy, King of North Wales 9 (11)
ap Rhodri, Merfyn, King of Powys...**11 (13)**, 15 (4)
Ribemont, Agnes, wife of Walter Giffard, Earl of Buckingham 99 (15)
Richard, Count d'Evreux...**107 (14)**
Richard, Count of Amiens...87 (4)
Richard, Duke of Burgundy..81 (4)
Richard I, Duke of Normandy .... 40 (6), 41 (6), **99 (12)**
Richard II, Duke of Normandy ....41 (6), 79 (7), 84 (6), **103 (13)**, 119 (1)

Richard III, Duke of Normandy ....5 (8), **43 (7)**, **104 (14)**, 114 (4)
Richard le Goz, Vicomte d'Avranches ....43 (9), **109 (15)**
Richarde, wife of Gerhard III, Count of Egisheim 27 (10)
Richeza of Lorraine, wife of Mieszko II, King of Poland 154 (1)
Richilde, wife of Dietrich I, Duke of Upper Lorraine 26 (9), 29 (8), 53 (4), 62 (8)
Richilde, wife of Thebaud, Count of Chartres ....**33 (5)**, 36 (3), 59 (6), 109 (11)
Richilde of Arles, wife of Bouvin, Count of Metz ....64 (3), **87 (4)**
Richilde of France, wife of Roger, Count of Maine ....**33 (4)**, **87 (6)**
Richilde of Metz, wife of Charles II, King of the Franks ....33 (3), **87 (5)**
Richilde of Poland, wife of Alfonso VII, King of Aragon ....152 (6), **154 (6)**
Richwin, Count of Scarpone 26 (10), 53 (6)
Richwin, Count of Verdun 30 (6)
Riley, Elizabeth Rebecca, wife of Samuel Prater 147 (15-j)
Riley, Eliphaz ....**147 (12)**
Riley, Eliphaz ....**147 (14)**
Riley, Hugh 147 (11)
Riley, Martha, wife of Brice Bazel Prater ....**147 (15)**
Riley, Miles 147 (11)
Riley, Nancy, wife of King Prater 147 (15-i)
Riley, Samuel ....**147 (13)**
Robert, Count d'Evreux ....**107 (13)**
Robert, Count of Mortain, Earl of Cornwall ....**120 (2)**
Robert "the Strong", Count of Paris 34 (1), 61 (5)
Robert I, Count d'Auvergne 25 (9), 36 (5), 64 (8)
Robert I, Count of Artois ....**140 (4)**, 143 (2), **150 (6)**, **151 (7)**, 152 (10)
Robert I, Count of Lomme 27 (8)
Robert I, Count of Troyes and Meaux ....**39 (3)**, **60 (6)**
Robert I, Duke of Normandy .... 2 (1), 5 (9), 7 (9), 28 (10), **41 (7)**, **47 (1)**, 49 (6), **103 (14)**, 119 (1), 137 (1)
Robert I, King of the Franks ....5 (4), 31 (6), **34 (1)**, 57 (5), 61 (5), 94 (2), 133 (2)
Robert II, King of the Franks ....5 (8), **21 (9)**, **47 (4)**, 65 (8), 83 (7), 96 (9), **97 (13)**, 114 (4), 116 (6), 132 (5)
von Rochlitz, Agnes, wife of Berthold VI, Duke of Croatia 153 (2)
de Roelt, Katherine, wife of John of Gaunt, Duke of Lancaster 146 (2), 153 (9)
de Roelt, Payne 146 (2), 153 (9)
Roger, Count of Maine ....**33 (4)**, **87 (6)**
Rogneda, wife of St. Vladimir, Grand Prince of Kiev 96 (8), 116 (4), 132 (3), 154 (2)
Rogvolod, Prince of Polotsk 116 (4), 132 (3)
Rollo the Viking, Duke of Normandy ....21 (7), **97 (10)**
de Romilly, Cecily, wife of William le Meschin 44 (10), 110 (17)
de Romilly, Robert 44 (10), 110 (17)
Rorick, Count of Maine 21 (4)
de Ros, Alice, wife of Nicholas Meinill ....137 (13), **148 (11)**
de Ros, Everard 148 (6)
de Ros, Isabel, wife of Walter de Fauconberg ....**149 (9)**
de Ros, Robert 148 (6)
de Ros, Robert 148 (8)
de Ros, William ....**148 (7)**
de Ros, William, Baron Ros ....**148 (9)**
de Ros, William, Baron Ros ....**148 (10)**
Rosala (Susanna) of Ivrea, wife of Arnold II, Count of Flanders .... 5 (6), 63 (8), **72 (6)**, **85 (4)**, 114 (3)
Rotbald I, Comtes de Provence 64 (6), 73 (6)
Rotrou, wife of Charles Martel 54 (1), 124 (10), 127 (3)
Rotrou II, Count of Perche 138 (2)
Rotrou II, Vicomte of Chateaudun 52 (7)
Rotrude, wife of Girard, Count of Paris ....17 (2), **55 (3)**
de Roucy, Ada, wife of Enguerrand de Couci .... **76 (8)**

de Roucy, Adele (Alix), wife of Hildouin III, Count of Roucy ....**50 (6), 75 (8)**

de Roucy, Ermentrude. wife of Otto William, Count of Burgundy ...... 45 (7), **77 (6), 78 (6)**, 83 (5), 106 (14)

de Roucy, Felicia, wife of Sancho Ramirez I, King of Aragon 152 (3)

de Roucy, Létard, Seigneur de Marle ....**76 (7)**

de Roucy, Marguerite, wife of Hugh, Count of Clermont ....27 (12), **50 (7)**, 84 (10), 99 (16)

de Roussillon, Eve, wife of Guerri I, Count of Morvois 57 (4)

Roynon, Joan, wife of Hugh Malet 2 (14), 102 (27)

Roynon, John 2 (14), 102 (27)

Rudolph I, King of Burgundy 68 (4), 71 (4), 89 (6)

Rudolph II, King of Burgundy .... 25 (7), **68 (5)**, 92 (3)

Rurik the Viking 116 (2), 131 (1)

Rythe, Elizabeth, wife of Nicholas Tichborne 137 (20), 141 (12), 142 (14)

Rythe, William 137 (20), 141 (12)

de Sabran, Gersinda, wife of Alfonso, Count of Provence 152 (7), 154 (8)

Sadb, wife of Murchad 16 (4)

de St. Cleere, Robert (or John) 102 (23)

de St. Cleere, Sibylla, wife of John Malet 102 (23)

de St. Lo, Elizabeth, wife of William Botreaux 139 (11)

de St. Pol, Jaquetta, wife of Richard Wydville, Earl Rivers 144 (10), 146 (5)

de St. Valeri, Bernard ....9 (23), **46 (12)**

de St. Valeri, Bernard, son of Gilbert ....**46 (8)**

de St. Valeri, Bernard, son of Walter ....**46 (10)**

de St. Valeri, Gilbert 46 (7), 105 (14)

de St. Valeri, Maud, wife of William de Braose ....9 (23), **46 (13)**

de St. Valeri, Renaud ....**46 (11)**

de St. Valeri, Walter ....**46 (9)**

Sancha of León, wife of Alfonso II, King of Aragon ....152 (6), **154 (7)**

Sancho III, King of Castile 139 (3), 140 (2), 151 (4)

Sancho Garcia, Count of Castile 152 (1)

Sancho Garcia III, King of Aragon, Castile and Navarre ....**152 (1)**

Sancho Ramierez I, King of Aragon ....**152 (3)**

Sarah, wife of James Mahan 147 (14)

ap Seisyll, Llewellyn, King of Gwynedd and Deheubarth ....9 (17), **10 (16)**, 122 (3)

ap Selyf, Mael Mynan ....**9 (4)**

Sibyl, wife of William de Cantelou I 51 (11), 76 (12)

Sidney, Margaret, wife of Nicholas Gainsford 141 (10)

Siegfried, Count of Luxembourg ....7 (6), **30 (7)**, 63 (7), **114 (1)**

Sigurd "the Strong", Earl of Northumberland 28 (11), 42 (9), 148 (1)

Sigurdsdattor, Aslag, wife of Ragnar Sigurdsson 96 (1)

Sigurdsson, Ragnar 96 (1)

Simon, Tsar of the Bulgars ....**155 (6)**

Skelly, Kesiah, wife of Eliphaz Prater .... 147 (15~e)

Somer, Elizabeth, wife of John Ashton ....**147 (5)**

Somer, John 147 (4)

Sophia, Countess Bar-le-Duc ....**26 (10), 53 (6)**, 84 (8)

Sprigg, Martha, wife of Thomas MacKay Prater .... 1 (4~b)

Sprota, wife of William Longsword, Duke of Normandy 99 (11)

Stawell, Geoffrey 2 (9)

Stawell, Geoffrey ....**2 (10)**

Stawell, Margery, wife of Richard Lyffe .... 2 (12), 3 (10). 102 (26)

Stawell, Matthew 2 (9), 3 (10)

Stawell, Matthew ....**2 (11)**

Stephens, Dorothy, wife of Thomas Yate 137 (22), 142 (15)

Stephens, Nicholas 137 (22), 142 (15)

Stockett, Elizabeth, wife of Thomas Plummer ....**147 (10)**

Stockett, Jane, wife of Walter Aylesworth 147 (7)
Stockett, Lewis 147 (7)
Stockett, Thomas 147 (8)
Stockett, Thomas (Captain) .... 137 (24), **147 (9)**
Storrada, Sigrid, wife of Eric VI, King of Sweden 96 (6)
de Sully, Agnes, wife of William of Champagne 137 (3)
de Sully, Giles 137 (3)
de Sully, Raymond 102 (20)
de Sully, Sara, wife of William Malet 102 (20)
Suppo, Marquis of Spoleto, Count of Turin 23 (4), 83 (1)
Sviatoslav I, Prince of Kiev .... **116 (3), 131 (2)**
Swearingen, Katherine, wife of John Prater 1 (4–b)
(Swearingen) Priscilla, wife of Bazel Prater 147 (15)
Sybilla, wife of Duncan I, King of Scots 148 (1)
Tattershall, Elizabeth, wife of John Yate 137 (23)
Tattershall, George 137 (23)
Teutberga of Arles, wife of Garnier, Count of Troyes .... 64 (5), **73 (4)**, 117 (4)
Teutberga of Troyes, wife of Charles Constantine, Count of Vienne .... 64 (5), **73 (5)**, 117 (4)
Thebaud, Count of Arles 70 (5), 71 (3)
Thebaud, Count of Chartres 33 (5), 36 (3), 59 (6), 109 (11)
Thebaud, Seigneur de Bois Ferrand 6 (7), 86 (5)
Thebaud I, Count of Blois .... 25 (8), **33 (6)**, 36 (3), 59 (6), 68 (7)
Thebaud III, Count of Blois 137 (2)
Thebaud IV, Count of Blois 150 (3)
Theodora, wife of Theophilus, Emperor of Byzantium 117 (1A)
Theodoros I, Emperor of Byzantium 153 (3), 155 (16)
Theophilus, Emperor of Byzantium 117 (1A)
Thierry I (Dietrich), Count of Montbéliard .... 27 (11), **53 (7)**, 84 (8)
Thierry III, King of Soissons .... **124 (7)**
Thomas I, Duke of Savoy 152 (8)
Thora, wife of Ragnvald 97 (7), 113 (3)
Thurstan "le Goz", Vicomte d'Avranches 109 (14)
Thweng, Lucy, wife of Nicholas Meinill, Baron Meinill 148 (11)
Tichborne, Jane, wife of Francis Yate .... **137 (21)**, 142 (14)
Tichborne, John 137 (17)
Tichborne, John .... **137 (18)**, 141 (11)
Tichborne, Nicholas .... **137 (19)**, 141 (11)
Tichborne, Nicholas .... **137 (20)**, **141 (12)**, 142 (14)
de Toeni, Godelbreda, wife of Robert de Newburgh .... **28 (13)**, 52 (9)
de Toeni, Ralph 28 (12), 52 (9)
de Toeni, Roger 107 (14)
Tonantius Ferreolus, Praetorian Prefect .... **118 (3)**
Tonantius Ferreolus, Roman Senator .... **118 (4)**
Toste, Skoglar 96 (6)
de Toteneis, Aenor, wife of Philip de Braose 9 (22)
Trivett, Alice, wife of John Malet 2 (15)
Trivett, Thomas 2 (15)
Trojan, Tsar of West Bulgaria .... **155 (10)**
Trussebut, Roese, wife of Everard de Ros 148 (6)
Ní Tuathail, Mor, wife of Diarmait, King of Leinster, ... 16 (6), 37 (10), 50 (10)
Ua Tuathail, Muirchertach 16 (6)
Turnbough, Isom 147 (15–m)
Turner, Solomon 137 (25b)
Tzautzina, Zoe, wife of Leo VI, Emperor of Byzantium 64 (4), 88 (6), 117 (2)
Umberto II, Duke of Savoy 150 (2)

Urraca, Queen of Castile 154 (6)
Urraca of Portugal, Queen of Leon, wife of Fernando II, King of Leon 139 (4)
de Valence, Aymer, Count of Angoulême..**138 (5)**, 141 (1)
Valletort, Hugh ....**3 (8)**
Valletort, Joan, mistress of Richard Plantagenet, Earl of Cornwall................................141 (2)
Valletort, Joel ....**3 (5)**
Valletort, John ....**3 (7)**
Valletort, Juliana, wife of Godfrey Lyffe... 2 (12), **3 (9)**
Valletort, Phillip ....**3 (6)**
Valletort, Reginald 141 (2)
Valletort, Robert (Reginald)..3 (4), 121 (5)
Valletort, Roger (Ralph) 3 (4), 121 (5)
de Vaux, Beatrice, wife of William de Briwere... 9 (24), 46 (14)
de Vaux, John 148 (9)
de Vaux, Maud, wife of William de Ros, Baron Ros.. 148 (9)
de Vere, John, Earl of Oxford 139 (9), 143 (5)
de Vere, Margaret, wife of Henry de Beaumont.. 139 (9), 143 (5)
Vernon, Mary, wife of Robert de Courtenay, Baron Oakhampton ....**2 (6)**, 49 (11), 100 (20)
Vernon, William.. 2 (5), 49 (11), 100 (20), 107 (19)
St. Vladimir, Grand Prince of Kiev.......................................96 (8), **116 (4)**, **132 (3)**, 154 (2)
Vladislav I, King of Poland...**154 (3)**
Vladislav II, King of Bohemia.. 154 (3)
Vladislav II, King of Poland..**154 (5)**
Wadham, Joan, wife of Thomas Malet 2 (16)
Wadham, William 2 (16)
Waite, Elizabeth, mistress of Edward IV, King of England 147 (1)
Walbert, Count of Threkwitigau..**111 (6)**
Waldrada, wife of Conrad II, Duke of Burgundy 68 (4), 89 (6)
Waldrada, wife of Hadrian, Count of Orleans.. 17 (4), **129 (9)**
Waldrada, wife of Lothair II, King of Lorraine...71 (2)
Walker, Nancy Permelia Ann Battles, wife of Ninian Prater.. 147 (15–o)
Wallace, Eleanor, wife of Samuel Riley..147 (13)
Wallace, Samuel 147 (13)
Wallis, Margaret, wife of Richard Martin 137 (18)
Walter of Cornwall...**141 (3)**
Waltheof II, Earl of Huntingdon, Northampton and Northumberland 28 (11), 42 (9), 148 (3)
Wandesford, Joan, wife of John Tichborne...**137 (17)**
Wandesford, John...137 (15), 149 (13)
Wandesford, John...149 (13)
Wandesford, Thomas..**137 (16)**
Ward, William...137 (25b)
de Warenne, Ada, wife of Henry, Earl of Northumberland..148 (4)
Warin, Count of Poitiers and Paris 128 (5), 129 (6)
Warnechin, Duke of Engern..111 (4)
Welf I, Duke of Bavaria 23 (2)
Wells, Mary, wife of George Yates and Thomas Stockett..............................137 (24), 147 (9)
Wells, Richard..137 (24), 147 (9)
White, Agnes, wife of Thomas White...142 (12)
White, Anne, wife of Nicholas Tichborne .... 137 (19), **141 (11)**
White, Frances, wife of Thomas Yate ....**142 (13)**
White, John 139 (13), 141 (9)
White, Robert..137 (19), **141 (10)**
White, Robert..139 (13), 141 (9)
White, Robert..**142 (11)**
White, Robert..142 (12)

White, Thomas ....**142 (12)**
Wicbert, Count of Westphalia ....**111 (5)**
Widukind (Wittekind) 111 (4)
Wigeric , Count d'Ardennes 29 (6), 30 (6), 53 (3), 95 (3), 114 (1)
Willa of Tuscany, wife of Berengar II, King of Italy .... 5 (6), **70 (6)**, **71 (5)**, 83 (3)
Willa of Tuscany, wife of Boso, Count of Arles 70 (5), 71 (4), 83 (3)
Willa of Vienna, wife of Rudolph I, King of Burgundy ....**68 (4)**, 71 (4), **89 (6)**
William, Count of Eu 137 (4)
William, Count of Mortain, Earl of Cornwall .... 2 (3), **120 (3)**
William, Duc d'Aquitaine 139 (2), 140 (1)
William the Conqueror ...**2 (1)**, 5 (9), 7 (9), 28 (10), **41 (8)**, 42 (8), 49 (6), 100 (15), 119 (1), 119 (2), **137 (1)**, 138 (1)
William "the Lion", King of Scots ....**148 (5)**
William I, Count of Arles, Count of Provence ....**64 (7)**
William I, Count of Burgundy ....**45 (8)**, 53 (7), **84 (7)**
William I, Count of Nevers ....6 (13), **48 (6)**, **83 (8)**
William I, Count of Poitou, Duc d'Aquitaine ....**21 (7)**, 47 (3), 94 (3), 97 (11)
William I, Count of Provence 21 (9), 47 (4), 97 (13)
William II, Earl of Surrey 148 (4)
William III, Count of Hainaut and Holland 145 (2), 146 (1), 153 (7)
William IV, Count of Angoulême 138 (4)
William IV, Count d'Auvergne 64 (8)
William IX, Duc d'Aquitaine 152 (4)
William "Longsword", Duke of Normandy .... 33 (6), **99 (11)**
William of Champagne, Sire de Sully ....**137 (3)**
Wulgrim II, Count of Angoulême 138 (4)
Wydville, Elizabeth, wife of Edward IV, King of England 144 (10), 146 (5)
Wydville, Richard, Earl Rivers 144 (10), 146 (5)
Ximena, wife of Garcia Sanchez, King of Navarre 152 (1)
Yaroslav I, Grand Prince of Kiev .... 47 (5), 65 (9), 96 (8), **116 (5)**, **132 (4)**
Yate, Francis ....137 (21), **142 (14)**
Yate, John .... **137 (23)**, 142 (13)
Yate, John 137 (21)
Yate, Thomas .... **137 (22)**, **142 (15)**
Yate, Thomas 142 (13)
Yates, Anne, wife of William Prather .... 1 (4–b), **137 (25)**
Yates, George ....**137 (24)**
Young, Alice, wife of William Malet 2 (17), 28 (26)
Young, Thomas 2 (17)
Ysgythrog, Brochwel, King of Powys .... **9 (1)**, 136 (2)
Zautes, Stylian 117 (2)
Zbyslava of Kiev, wife of Boleslav III, Grand Prince of Poland 154 (4)
la Zouche, Alan, Duke of Brittany ....**39 (10)**, 44 (12)
la Zouche, Elizabeth, wife of Nicholas Poyntz ....43 (17), **44 (15)**, **76 (15)**
la Zouche, Eudes ....9 (27), 43 (17), **44 (14)**, 76 (14)
la Zouche, Geoffrey, Vicomte Porhoët 39 (9), 40 (10), 44 (12)
la Zouche, Roger ....9 (27), **39 (11)**, **44 (13)**, 76 (14)
Zvinitsa (father of Presijan, Khan of the Bulgars) .... **155 (3)**